Foreign Policy at the AI Frontier

This book is a comprehensive guide for foreign policy practitioners navigating the transformative impact of artificial intelligence (AI) on diplomacy and statecraft.

It begins by simplifying AI technologies for nontechnical readers and tracing historical parallels of how these transformative technologies have reshaped diplomacy. Organized into three themes—Progress, Power, and Peace—the book explores AI as a frontier reshaping international affairs. The Progress and Power sections examine AI's role in geopolitical competition, economic security, and the rise of Big Tech as quasi-sovereign actors, alongside security threats like lethal autonomous systems and AI-driven cyber warfare. The Peace section offers practical insights, showcasing real-world AI applications in diplomacy, peacebuilding, and crisis management. This book also addresses ethical and governance challenges, such as algorithmic bias, the erosion of human control, and the race to regulate AI's rapid evolution. Concluding with aspirations rather than predictions, it envisions how nations can navigate AI rivalry, seize opportunities, and redirect technologies toward peace. Designed for flexibility, each chapter stands alone, enriched with quotes, case studies, and reflections to inspire readers to explore AI's implications for global diplomacy.

This is not a book about tomorrow; it's about preparing for tomorrow by understanding the choices made today. Whether you're a diplomat seeking to understand these tools, a technologist grasping the geopolitical implications of your work, a student preparing for international relations, or a citizen navigating a changing world, this book offers a vital resource, grounded in real-world examples, to guide future work in becoming more informed and responsible.

Foreign Policy at the AI Frontier

How AI is Reshaping Progress, Power, and Peace

Branka Panic

CRC Press
Taylor & Francis Group
Boca Raton London New York

CRC Press is an imprint of the
Taylor & Francis Group, an **informa** business

Designed cover image: Getty Images

First edition published 2027
by CRC Press
2385 NW Executive Center Drive, Suite 320, Boca Raton FL 33431

and by CRC Press
4 Park Square, Milton Park, Abingdon, Oxon, OX14 4RN

CRC Press is an imprint of Taylor & Francis Group, LLC

ISBN: 9781041082934 (hbk)
ISBN: 9781041082927 (pbk)
ISBN: 9781003644712 (ebk)

DOI: 10.1201/9781003644712

Typeset in Times
by codeMantra

To my husband, my constant source of wisdom, courage, and inspiration; to my colleagues, diplomats, and practitioners, whose hard questions and practical experience gave this work its shape and purpose; to my students, who will decide what this frontier becomes; and to everyone committed to ensuring AI serves peace, not war, and who devote themselves each day to turning that commitment into reality.

Contents

Acknowledgment

This book emerges from a career of asking persistent questions: how can artificial intelligence serve peace rather than undermine it—and what role must foreign policy play in ensuring it does? The answer cannot be found in any single ministry, company, or research lab. It must be built collectively, across borders, disciplines, and perspectives. That pursuit has taken me to Ministries of Foreign Affairs in Austria and Kenya, diplomatic academies in Chile and Brazil, UN meetings in South Africa and Nepal, academic classrooms in the United States and Colombia, and policy forums in Turkey and Costa Rica. Along the way, I engaged in debates about AI's implications for statecraft, but equally, in the work of building AI tools for diplomacy with ethics and responsibility at their foundation. Each stop reinforced a core conviction: foreign policy practitioners must meet AI at the frontier—understanding its implications for geopolitics, economic security, and global stability, while actively shaping how this technology transforms progress, redistributes power, and advances peace.

I am profoundly grateful to the *AI for Peace* team, our partners, and collaborators, whose collective dedication has transformed a vision into a thriving ecosystem. Their perspectives, shaped by remarkably diverse contexts and lived experiences, brought exactly the global representation this work demanded. I am equally indebted to all those who, from east to west and north to south, have thoughtfully architected the convenings, dialogues, and institutional spaces where critical inquiry at the intersection of AI and foreign policy could take root and flourish, and to all those who, in both formal and informal ways, have sustained our mission and vision over the years.

I have had the privilege of engaging with thousands of practitioners, diplomats, researchers, and advocates, and I owe gratitude to more people than I could ever name. Yet, I must especially acknowledge several individuals whose direct contributions shaped this book in profound ways. Some reviewed chapters or the full manuscript, generously lending their expertise to sharpen these ideas. Others shared their experiences through interviews, offering stories and insights never before published. Others offered endorsements and quotes that helped amplify this work's reach. My deepest thanks to each of you: Aïchatou Mindaoudou (Niger), Annika Hansen (Germany), Antonio de Aguiar Patriota (Brazil), Avishan Bodjnoud (US/Iran), Christina Corbane (Belgium), Cristina Martinez Pinto (Mexico), Eli Mohamad (Croatia), Eugenio V. Garcia (Brazil), Francesca Bosco (Switzerland), Gabriela Ramos (Mexico), Hans-Christian Mangelsdorf (Germany), Henrik Urdal (Norway), Jibu Elias (India), Joel H. Rosenthal (US), Juan Carlos Sainz-Borgo (Costa Rica), Mauricio Carabelli (Chile), Mauricio Calderon (Colombia/Spain), Maxwell Scott (US), Narun Popattanachai (Thailand), Paige Arthur (US), Renee Cummings (US), Susanne Fries-Gaier (Germany/Chile), and Trita Parsi (US).

Branka Panic
Mexico, May 2026

Acknowledgment

Foreword

Artificial intelligence (AI) has become a key foreign policy issue over the last few years. It has steadily entered the diplomatic agenda, and it will likely remain a major topic of concern for Ministries of Foreign Affairs globally for decades to come. Changes brought about by AI development, diffusion, and adoption across the globe will undoubtedly have a tremendous impact and can reshape the digital world order as we know it.

As a general-purpose technology, AI is unique because, unlike electricity, which is merely a source of energy, it can carry out cognitive tasks (increasingly outperforming humans), produce knowledge autonomously, make decisions on its own, and manipulate symbolic representations of reality, being able to communicate, persuade, or influence humans through language or other means. Agentic systems that interact with each other and AI-powered applications that communicate in natural language will accelerate the level of technological entanglement in society, giving rise to anthropological dilemmas we are still trying to grasp properly.

The moral responsibility to attribute value and give meaning to our world, however, lies with human beings, not with machines. It is up to us to draw the line somewhere and steer AI development in the right (ethical) direction. In search for "optimizing everything," we often take for granted that AI can help make decisions "more efficiently." Certainly, AI can spread disinformation or make a positive contribution to politics, but it cannot "fix it." Politics is a human-to-human experience that seeks to address questions related to power, resources, diverging interests, and conflict resolution within and among political communities. We should be wary of uncritically allowing AI systems to encroach on the consequential disputes we most care about.

In this timely and well-thought-out book, Branka Panic does an amazing job of providing the reader with a thorough analysis of every important dimension connecting AI and foreign policy, from new tools used by politicians and diplomats in their daily work to the strategic implications of autonomous weapons for international peace and security. It is a much-needed reflection on where we are and the way ahead, set to become indispensable reading for anyone engaged in the field, for either scholars, students, or practitioners of tech diplomacy.

AI can be an ally in automating bureaucratic processes and increasing productivity in routine work or low-complexity tasks, freeing diplomats to focus on activities that require sound human judgment, social skills, relationship building, empathy, and cultural sensitivity. But many challenges remain.

In the realm of strategic decision-making, a reasonable degree of caution would be advisable when it comes to outsourcing critical decisions to computers. Certain decisions must never be delegated to machines, and specific red lines should be agreed upon as a matter of urgency. Think of life-and-death decisions and the use of nuclear weapons as outstanding examples. Respecting the principle of peaceful uses of AI is a direct consequence of a human-centered approach that puts societal accountability at the core of international law.

Branka Panic also provides a useful background to our understanding of geopolitical tensions around AI. After all, today's ubiquitous competition over emerging technologies has been producing systemic effects in great-power rivalry. Speed in instantaneous information flows and real-time narratives compresses the time available for deliberation. Crises unfold faster, and the margin for error widens. Technological ambiguity further aggravates insecurity. Many technologies are inherently dual-use: satellites can monitor or disable; algorithms can protect software platforms or carry out cyberattacks; 5G networks can connect societies or enable surveillance; AI can stabilize situations or automate offensive operations. When the distinction between offense and defense blurs, states tend to interpret all capabilities as potentially threatening. Consequently, they respond defensively, reinforcing cycles of suspicion and escalation.

In addition, control over advanced technologies is not just an economic asset, but a strategic imperative linked to national security, political influence, and normative leadership. Frontier AI research is frequently regarded as leading to a decisive advantage over competitors. Technological gains by one actor may be interpreted by others as a strategic threat, triggering countermeasures such as export controls, unilateral sanctions, and other trade or investment restrictions. When this happens, weakened international regimes are bypassed, and multilateralism is sidelined completely.

There is indeed a global political struggle over tech regulation and development to shape norms, standards, and digital infrastructure. Particularly in the case of achieving Artificial General Intelligence (AGI), the winner-takes-it-all idea becomes a self-fulfilling prophecy that creates a trap that competitors can hardly escape. But as Branka Panic explains in Chapter 3, only a few countries are actually competing in the so-called "AI arms race." The vast majority are not playing this game.

This zero-sum, binary, antagonistic Us vs. Them mindset poses distinct risks and vulnerabilities. Developing countries are under growing pressure to align with competing blocs, thereby narrowing their strategic autonomy and development options. Such forced alignments constrain policy space, complicate national strategies, and expose these countries to external coercion. Uneven access to technology deepens dependence on external suppliers and reinforces existing economic inequalities.

Technology has been securitized. Power is no longer grounded primarily in territory or military force alone, but in the capacity to control and deploy enabling technologies. Mastery over algorithms, data, semiconductors, supply chains, telecommunications, human talent, and energy resources has been redefined as a new battlefield in world politics. Rather than beneficiaries of technological diffusion, developing countries risk becoming a proving ground for foreign competition and places of strategic extraction in areas such as data, underpaid annotators, and critical minerals.

Addressing these challenges requires collaborative efforts to come to the defense of the multilateral system and to avoid AI technologies turning into instruments of exclusion and domination. It is crucial for the Global South to claim its agency as an active player in this interconnected digital ecosystem. All countries should retain their sovereign right to develop local capacities and decide for themselves what domestic frameworks they need to harness AI in accordance with their own priorities.

Even if guardrails may differ from country to country, the next step would be to combine domestic approaches with international coordination. Global governance is needed to build trust across borders and to ensure interoperability among different regulatory regimes by means of rules, guidelines, benchmarks, and other commonly agreed practices.

It is true that international institutions struggle to regulate technologies that evolve faster than consensus can form, creating gaps in accountability and coordination. The driver behind AI and foreign policy will therefore be less about managing stable rules and more about navigating uncertainty, contending standards, and asymmetrical capabilities. One of the central tasks of tech diplomacy will be to prevent any AI race from undermining the conditions for cooperation and dialogue in an increasingly automated world.

Branka Panic's book emerges as a vital companion for this endeavor. She is right: every diplomat is now becoming a tech diplomat.

Eugenio V. Garcia
Tech Ambassador
Ministry of Foreign Affairs, Brazil
Brasilia, 2 January 2026

About the Author

Branka Panic is the Founding Director of AI for Peace, a US-based think tank ensuring that AI benefits peace, security, and sustainable development. Panic is a Fellow at the NYU Center on International Cooperation, Stimson-Microsoft Responsible AI Fellow, and a member of UNESCO Women4Ethical AI. She worked as a Senior Adviser on AI to the German Federal Foreign Office and a Professor of Practice of the Conflict Transformation master's class at the University of North Carolina. She holds an MA in International Development Policy from Duke University, Sanford School of Public Policy, and an MS in International Security from the University of Belgrade, Serbia. She is a co-author of the book *AI for Peace* (Routledge, 2024).

AI Usage Statement

Claude Opus 4.5 (Extended) was used to support editorial refinement and indexing of the manuscript, in order to improve textual clarity and to prepare the book's index.

Introduction
Foreign Policy at the AI Frontier

> I believe our civilization stands on the cusp of a technological revolution with the power to reshape life as we know it. To ignore the millennia of human struggle that serves as our society's foundation, however—to merely "disrupt," with the blitheness that has accompanied so much of this century's innovation—would be an intolerable mistake. This revolution must build on that foundation, faithfully. It must respect the collective dignity of a global community.
>
> —**Fei-Fei Li,** *Computer Scientist, Stanford University (Li 2023)*

> The dilemma of the AI age will be different: its defining technology will be widely acquired, mastered, and employed. The achievement of mutual strategic restraint — or even achieving a common definition of restraint — will be more difficult than ever before, both conceptually and practically.
>
> —**Henry Kissinger,** *American Diplomat and Political Scientist (Kissinger, Schmidt and Huttenlocher 2022)*

> Today we encounter AI as our distant ancestors once encountered fire. If we manage this technology well it will become a tremendous force for global good, lightening the way to many transformative inventions. If we deploy it too quickly and without adequate foresights AI will burn in ways we cannot control.
>
> —**Ben Buchanan and Andrew Imbrie,** *Georgetown University School of Foreign Service (Buchanan and Imbrie 2022)*

THE TSUNAMI AND THE FRONTIER

During a visit to Academia Diplomática Andrés Bello, the diplomatic academy in Santiago Chile, in 2025, where I was teaching the next generation of foreign service officers, one trainee offered a metaphor that made the entire room fall silent. While Silicon Valley and artificial intelligence (AI) experts speak of AI as "the new fire" and "AI empire," this Chilean diplomat chose a word that validated what many already sensed: AI as a tsunami.

The metaphor carried particular weight coming from a Chilean, a nation whose Pacific coastline has witnessed powerful tsunamis throughout history, where coastal town's streets are marked with evacuation route signs pointing to higher ground, constant reminders that the next one isn't a question of if, but when. Every citizen knows

DOI: 10.1201/9781003644712-1

these waves don't just arrive; they fundamentally reshape the landscape, leaving nothing untouched. And just as Chile knows this force of nature intimately, these future diplomats had already witnessed AI's rising waters, data centers proliferating across their territories, algorithmic systems assuming government functions, critical state decisions becoming dependent on foreign computing infrastructure, and their brightest minds departing for established AI centers, all signs of the transformation already underway. But unlike the ocean's waves that eventually recede, this one demanded a new response: not evacuation to higher ground, but learning to swim in it, an impossible-sounding but necessary skill for any diplomat hoping to navigate the future.

What struck me most was discovering that diplomats in Washington, Nairobi, Bangkok, and Brasília, and many other countries across the globe I worked in, had independently reached for similar metaphors. From the U.S. Department of State to Kenya's Ministry of Foreign Affairs, career diplomats weren't describing AI as evolution or disruption, they were reaching for language that captured something unstoppable and transformative, a phenomenon that changes everything in its path, demanding not whether we adapt, but how quickly.

Yet the tsunami metaphor, powerful as it is, captures only part of the story. Tsunamis also reshape landscapes and reveal new terrain, sweeping away old frameworks while opening a frontier to explore. It brings both dangerous peril and extraordinary possibility. Frontiers are defined by uncertainty, but also by agency: the chance to shape what comes next rather than simply react to it. This is the space where progress is forged, where power is contested, and where peace must be deliberately constructed. This book helps readers explore each of these dimensions and offers a path to claiming their agency in this new frontier.

THE AI TRANSFORMATION FROM TOPIC TO TOOL

In October 2025, journalist A.J. Jacobs proved just how thoroughly this tsunami had already reshaped our shores. His experiment seemed simple: live without AI for 48 hours (The New York Times 2025). Within minutes of starting his morning, he discovered the impossibility. His iPhone's facial recognition, his weather app, the electricity grid powering his apartment, even the water from his tap—all optimized by AI. By the time he resorted to wearing anti-facial-recognition sunglasses and collecting rainwater, Jacobs had revealed a profound truth: AI isn't coming. It's already here, woven so deeply into daily life that avoiding it means retreating from civilization itself.

AI is everywhere, transforming our societies at unprecedented speed. AI now matches or even exceeds human performance on image recognition, speech recognition, and language understanding, including legal reasoning and medical diagnostics, benchmarks we long assumed would remain uniquely human domains (Open AI 2024; Karnofsky 2025). ChatGPT became the fastest-growing consumer application in history, reaching 100 million users in just two months, a milestone that took the electric grid half a century to achieve (Business Insider 2023). The technology's reach extends far beyond consumer apps into the very foundations of scientific discovery. In 2024, AI entered the Nobel Prize arena for the first time in its 123-year history—not once, but twice. The Physics prize went to Geoffrey Hinton, the "godfather of AI," for foundational discoveries in machine learning. Days later, the Chemistry prize honored AI-powered protein structure prediction (Li and Gilbert 2024).

What began in elite research laboratories and corporate headquarters has rapidly spread into the hands of ordinary citizens worldwide. In 2025, AI was used by judges in Brazil to clear legal backlogs, by farmers in Malawi seeking instant agricultural advice in their local language, by teachers in Kenya planning lessons for hundreds of students, by caregivers in Singapore and South Korea supporting aging populations, and by patients in China turning to chatbots for mental health support when human psychiatrists were inaccessible (Rest of World 2025). From Indonesia's film industry to Mongolia's efforts to build AI models that understand nomadic traditions, these examples reveal a profound democratization: AI is no longer the exclusive domain of superpowers and tech giants, but an everyday tool reshaping how billions of people work, learn, heal, and connect.

Even diplomacy is now exploring AI with considerable interest and speed, remarkable for a field built on centuries-old protocols, where treaties require years of negotiation, trust emerges through face-to-face meetings, and success depends on reading cultural nuances and unspoken gestures. This most inherently human of endeavors, where understanding what isn't said matters as much as parsing formal declarations, is racing not just to study AI as a diplomatic topic, but to embrace it as an operational tool and, increasingly, as a trusted partner in the practice of statecraft itself. The profession recognized that in an era of cascading global crises demanding immediate responses, the choice wasn't between human wisdom and machine efficiency, but how to synthesize both into something potentially greater than either could achieve alone.

When the first telegraph message arrived in the 1850s, British Prime Minister Lord Palmerston reportedly exclaimed, "My God, this is the end of diplomacy." More than a century later, Zbigniew Brzezinski had a similar reaction to the internet (Kurbalija 2023). In 2023, amid the generative AI wave, one prominent academic published: "ChatGPT: The End of Diplomacy as We Know It" (Bjola and Manor 2023). History shows us a pattern: every major technological leap sparks fears that diplomacy will become obsolete. Yet despite the telegraph, radio, television, internet, and social media, diplomacy hasn't disappeared—it has adapted and transformed.

In 2024, in Istanbul, as AI for Peace Director and participant of the Better Order Project, I stood before a room of diplomats, current and ex ambassadors, consuls, presidents, and prime ministers from countries across the world, gathered to envision the future of global stability, national security, and climate resilience, all expected focal themes and priorities for such a distinguished assembly. Yet, it was an unexpected topic that came to dominate our deliberations: how AI systems, growing exponentially more powerful and integrated into every aspect of daily life, were already upending the foundations of the international system these leaders had spent their careers navigating. The diplomatic community, long trained to move deliberately and build consensus slowly, was now racing to understand and harness this technology, recognizing that AI had already become the invisible infrastructure underlying every global challenge they faced.

In 2025, in Brazil, as a Senior Advisor on AI to the German Federal Foreign Office I was organizing an AI workshop where participants from the Brazilian Ministry of Foreign Affairs and various embassies based in Brasilia, eagerly pitched various AI tools for diplomacy: universal translators that could fit in a pocket translating hundreds of languages in real time, AI-powered diplomatic social networks instantly connecting the right officials across countries and institutions, and emotion AI systems enhancing empathy during tense negotiations. AI was not only the force reshaping diplomacy, it became the diplomat's toolkit. And just five years earlier, similar gatherings were dominated by existential dread: "Will AI destroy the world?". But this transformation from fear to innovation wasn't an outlier; it was a trend I'd witnessed across my work from the United States to Germany, Chile to Thailand, Brazil to Kenya, Mexico to South Africa.

When I wrote my previous book on *AI for Peace* two years ago, we had months to catch up with the latest projects and pilots, time to analyze them thoroughly and craft considered arguments. This time, the pace of change became exponential. I rewrote entire chapters multiple times as each morning delivered news of another nation launching its AI strategy, another geopolitical crisis shaped by algorithms, another AI supply chain disruption, another international norm challenged by machine learning applications, forcing me to constantly update my analysis just to keep pace with a world transforming in real time. Algorithms are already screening visa applications, predicting political instability, negotiating trade agreements, and even drafting diplomatic cables. The question is no longer whether AI will transform foreign policy, but whether foreign policy institutions, many still operating on frameworks designed for the telegraph age, can adapt quickly enough to harness AI's promise while mitigating its perils.

THE NEW AI RACE

In 2017, Russian President Vladimir Putin declared that whoever leads in AI will rule the world, a statement that sent shockwaves through the global order (Vincent 2017). Elon Musk immediately amplified the warning, retweeting Putin's remarks with his own stark prediction: the competition for AI superiority would most likely trigger World War III (The Guardian 2017). That moment marked a turning point. The world's powers suddenly understood that AI wasn't just another technology race, it was potentially the last race that would matter. The implications became undeniable: nations that achieve AI mastery will command overwhelming advantages in economic competitiveness, military capability, and diplomatic influence. Those that fall behind face a future of technological dependence, forced to operate within systems and standards set by others, their sovereignty compromised in an algorithmic age.

The global response has been swift and varied. China launched an ambitious national AI strategy aiming for world leadership by 2030—and backed it with billions in investment, dedicated AI industrial zones, integration of AI into state functions, and now produces more AI patents and research papers than any other nation. The United States mobilized its tech giants, venture capital, and elite research institutions, while deploying export controls to protect its lead. Europe chose to lead through regulation, attempting to shape the ethical boundaries of AI development.

Meanwhile, nations across the Global South/Global Majority are attempting to leapfrog traditional development stages through strategic AI adoption. Each approach represents a different bet on how the AI future will unfold. The decisions diplomats and policymakers make about AI today will echo through history, shaping the world future generations will inherit.

The speed of change is staggering. Just eight years separate the UAE appointing the world's first Minister for AI in 2017 from Albania making history by appointing an algorithm as a minister responsible for procurement decisions in 2025. Entirely new diplomatic roles have emerged: tech ambassadors posted to Silicon Valley, cyber ambassadors navigating digital threats, and AI envoys building coalitions around emerging technologies. Foreign ministries themselves are transforming from within, launching data labs and developing proprietary AI tools for policy analysis.

Yet these rapid adoptions carry profound risks that extend far beyond any single technology challenge. AI threatens to concentrate power in the hands of a few nations and corporations, creating new forms of technological dependency. It accelerates decision-making beyond the pace of human deliberation, potentially leaving diplomats to manage crises triggered by algorithms operating in milliseconds. It introduces opacity into consequential decisions with little accountability or explanation. It risks encoding bias into systems that affect millions across borders. It empowers malicious actors to impersonate officials, manipulate elections, and wage information warfare with terrifying precision. And it raises fundamental questions about human agency: when algorithms advise leaders, draft policies, and even negotiate agreements, where does machine assistance end and human judgment begin? The technology is not merely changing diplomacy's tools, it is challenging its very foundations: sovereignty, accountability, trust, and the primacy of human decision-making.

WHAT THIS BOOK OFFERS

This book traces the intersections between AI and foreign policy, examining how AI is simultaneously a subject of diplomatic negotiation, a tool for conducting international relations, and a force reshaping the global order. Numerous topics at the intersection of AI and foreign policy might have found their place in these pages. However, this book has been shaped by specific encounters arising from a decade of my work and projects with embassies, consulates, foreign ministries, and partners across industry, civil society, and academia. It reflects my core conviction: that AI can and must serve to sustain and strengthen peace, not to wage war. Above all, it has been informed by countless conversations with ambassadors and consuls, career diplomats and policy advisors, tech executives and civil society leaders, conflict transformation scholars and master students, and the emerging generation of foreign service officers at diplomatic academies worldwide. These are the individuals who will ultimately forge the answers to the questions we pose here.

This book explores how AI is already influencing both the practice and the strategy of international engagement. From the early experiments of AI-powered political candidates to the deployment of autonomous weapons systems, from algorithmic peacekeeping to the promise of "agentic diplomacy," we explore how AI is transforming every aspect of how nations interact. Diplomacy, the hands-on work of negotiation and relationship-building, and foreign policy, the broader goals guiding government action, are both being transformed and as such covered in this book. AI serves as a tool for diplomatic negotiations while simultaneously becoming a subject of those very negotiations. It shapes how states analyze threats, predict crises, and even conduct the intricacies of consular services. We'll examine AI's role across this spectrum: from enhancing human decision-making in crisis management to potentially replacing certain diplomatic functions altogether.

This book serves as a guide, a comprehensive resource for foreign policy practitioners navigating the AI transformation already reshaping their profession. We begin by demystifying AI for those who need conceptual vocabulary without technical expertise, then trace how transformative technologies, from telegraphs to the internet, have repeatedly reshaped diplomacy, revealing patterns that illuminate today's revolution. We examine the rise of tech diplomacy and the new generation of diplomats navigating Silicon Valley and other tech capitals, before confronting a startling development: AI systems moving from advisors to actual government officials. The chapters are organized into three thematic groups—Progress, Power, and Peace, the essential dimensions of any frontier. And make no mistake: AI is a frontier, not merely a disruption. It is uncharted territory where the rules of statecraft have yet to be written. While the Progress and Power sections primarily focus on the evolving role of AI as a subject and tool within international affairs, the Peace section is hands-on, filled with practical examples, projects, pilots, and especially expanded case studies in the chapter "From Topic to Tool," showcasing real-world AI applications in diplomacy and peacebuilding.

The heart of this book explores the high-stakes arenas where AI's impact is most consequential. We examine the fierce geopolitical competition for AI supremacy, the race for semiconductors, rare earths, talent, and the emergence of Big Tech as quasi-sovereign actors. We confront security threats representing the most profound disruption since nuclear weapons: lethal autonomous systems deployed from Ukraine to Gaza, AI integration into nuclear command compressing human decision-making from minutes to milliseconds, and cyber warfare blurring peace and conflict. We analyze how AI is reshaping economic security, the staggering investments, the widening divide between AI haves and have-nots, and the paradox of nations pursuing independence while deepening reliance on foreign giants. We explore crisis management's troubling paradox: sophisticated early warning coexisting with more conflicts than any point since World War II. And we examine AI transforming peacebuilding, from digital dialogues in Yemen and Libya to satellites witnessing war crimes.

Finally, we move from analysis to action, tracing how AI tools have entered the daily practice of diplomacy, from translation and strategic communication to negotiation support and policy analysis. We confront the ethical and governance challenges that arise when algorithms meet statecraft: algorithmic bias in contexts demanding cultural sensitivity, the erosion of meaningful human control, and the question of whether governance can keep pace with technology evolving at the speed of silicon. We conclude not with predictions but with an imperative: AI's potential for diplomacy reveals itself only through engagement. The final chapter confronts uncertainty, synthesizes Progress, Power, and Peace, and calls on practitioners to prototype AI—not to win a race, but to serve humanity's future. While we invite readers to experience this book as a complete journey, each chapter has been designed to stand alone—feel free to jump directly to topics of immediate interest. Every chapter opens with carefully chosen quotes, drawn from my interviews with practitioners, excerpts from authors of complementary books, articles and papers I recommend, and statements from UN discussions on AI, progress, power, and peace—setting the tone and inviting reflection on each topic.

This is not a book about tomorrow; it's about preparing for tomorrow by understanding the choices we must make today. We will not get the future we fear or hope for, but the one we prepare for, and preparation begins with grasping what's actually happening right now, beneath the hype and headlines. As AI becomes increasingly capable, perhaps even achieving artificial general intelligence within our lifetimes, the foreign policy decisions we make in this moment will establish precedents that could govern international relations for centuries. To navigate what's coming, we must first see clearly where we stand: how AI already reshapes power dynamics between nations, transforms the nature of conflict and cooperation, and challenges centuries-old diplomatic practices.

Whether you're a diplomat seeking to understand these new tools, a technologist wanting to grasp the geopolitical implications of your work, a student preparing for a career in international relations, or simply a citizen trying to make sense of a rapidly changing world, this book responds to their ultimate request: a practical resource, not an academic essay, where practitioners can ground their knowledge in the age of algorithms through real-world examples that make current and future work more informed and responsible. This book provides the framework for understanding how AI and foreign policy intersect today, because only by comprehending the present transformation can we actively shape, rather than passively inherit, the future of international relations.

BIBLIOGRAPHY

Biscont, Piercosma, Matteo Prandi, Federico Pierucci, Francesco Giarrusso, Marcantonio Bracale, Marcello Galisai, Vincenzo Suriani, Olga Sorokoletova, Federico Sartore, and Daniele Nardi. 2025. "Adversarial Poetry as a Universal Single-Turn Jailbreak Mechanism in Large Language Models." *Arxiv* (Icaro Lab). https://doi.org/10.48550/arXiv.2511.15304 Focus to learn more.

Bjola, Corneliu, and Ilan Manor. 2023. *ChatGPT: The End of Diplomacy as We Know It.* April 2. Accessed January 2, 2026. https://www.globalpolicyjournal.com/blog/25/04/2023/chatgpt-end-diplomacy-we-know-it.

Bloomberg. 2025. *OpenAI Backs a New Venture Trying to Thwart AI Bio-Attacks.* October 24. Accessed October 25, 2025. https://www.bloomberg.com/news/articles/2025-10-24/openai-backs-a-new-venture-trying-to-thwart-ai-bio-attacks?embedded-checkout=true.

Buchanan, Ben, and Andrew Imbrie. 2022. *The New Fire: War, Peace, and Democracy in the Age of AI.* Cambridge, MA: MIT Press.

Business Insider. 2023. *ChatGPT May Be the Fastest-Growing Consumer App in Internet History, Reaching 100 Million Users in Just over 2 Months, UBS report says.* February 2. Accessed September 27, 2025. https://www.businessinsider.com/chatgpt-may-be-fastest-growing-app-in-history-ubs-study-2023-2#:~:text=ChatGPT%20may%20have%20become%20the,analysts%20added%20in%20the%20report.

DiploFoundation. n.d. *Railway Diplomacy.* Accessed September 15, 2025. https://www.diplomacy.edu/topics/railway-diplomacy/.

Geneva Internet Platform. 2024. *Responsible AI in the Military Domain: REAIM Blueprint for Action.* September. Accessed September 25, 2025. https://dig.watch/resource/responsible-ai-in-the-military-domain-reaim-blueprint-for-action.

Karnofsky, Holden. 2025. *AI Has Been Surprising for Years.* January 6. Accessed December 29, 2025. https://carnegieendowment.org/research/2025/01/ai-has-been-surprising-for-years?lang=en.

Kissinger, Henry A., Eric Schmidt, and Daniel Huttenlocher. 2022. *The Age of AI: And Our Human Future.* New York: Little, Brown.

Kurbalija, Jovan. 2023. *History of Diplomacy and Technology: From Smoke Signals to Artificial Intelligence.* Washington, DC: Diplo US.

Li, Ben, and Stephen Gilbert. 2024. "Artificial Intelligence Awarded Two Nobel Prizes for Innovations That Will Shape the Future of Medicine." *Nature* 336: 1–3. https://doi.org/10.1038/s41746-024-01345-9

Li, Fei-Fei. 2023. *The Worlds I See: Curiosity, Exploration, and Discovery at the Dawn of AI.* New York: Flatiron Books.

Open AI. 2024. *GPT-4 Technical Report.* Technical Report, Cornell University.

Rest of World. 2025. *Innovative Ways the World Used AI in 2025.* December 29. Accessed December 30, 2025. https://restofworld.org/2025/ai-innovation-global-2025/?utm_source=Rest+of+World+Newsletter&utm_campaign=13778ce5af-EMAIL_CAMPAIGN_2025_12_19_07_01&utm_medium=email&utm_term=0_-13778ce5af-446195314.

The Guardian. 2017. *Elon Musk Says AI Could Lead to Third World War.* September 4. Accessed January 2, 2026. https://www.theguardian.com/technology/2017/sep/04/elon-musk-ai-third-world-war-vladimir-putin.

The New York Times. 2025. *48 Hours Without AI.* October 28. Accessed December 21, 2025. https://www.nytimes.com/2025/10/28/style/48-hours-without-ai.html.

Vincent, James. 2017. "The Verge." *Putin Says the Nation That Leads in AI 'Will Be the Ruler of the World'.* September 4. Accessed September 15, 2025. https://www.theverge.com/2017/9/4/16251226/russia-ai-putin-rule-the-world.

Demystifying AI for Foreign Policy

Navigating Certainties and Unknowns

The quest to create thinking machines began in the shadow of global conflict. During World War II, Alan Turing's work breaking the Enigma code at Bletchley Park did more than help defeat Nazi Germany; it laid the theoretical foundation for artificial intelligence (Copeland 2012). In 1950, Turing proposed what became known as the Turing Test, a deceptively simple challenge: could a machine convince a human interrogator, through written conversation alone, that it was human? This test, at its core, mirrors the fundamental diplomatic skill of persuasion and representation. Today, when state-sponsored bots flood social media platforms to shape electoral outcomes or when deepfakes of world leaders proliferate across the internet, we witness the geopolitical manifestation of machines passing increasingly sophisticated versions of Turing's original challenge.

Just as you don't need to understand combustion engines to drive a car, diplomats don't need to become data scientists to work with AI. However, since foreign policy professionals will negotiate international standards, shape ethical frameworks, and steer how AI transforms global governance, understanding the fundamentals has become essential. While subsequent chapters will explore how AI reshapes geopolitics, labor markets, global power, and international security, this introduction demystifies the basic concepts underpinning these transformations by providing the conceptual vocabulary needed to engage meaningfully with AI's impact on international relations.

Artificial intelligence (AI) has no single, universally accepted definition, yet it is typically understood as the ability of machines to perform cognitive functions we associate with human minds such as perceiving, reasoning, learning, and problem-solving. At its core, AI seeks to create computer systems that match or exceed human intelligence across these capabilities. What matters for practitioners is less the definition than the recognition that AI is not one technology but a toolbox, and reaching for the wrong tool, or assuming all tools work the same way, leads to policy mistakes. Understanding how these systems actually work reveals both their potential—from instant language translation to complex pattern recognition—and their inherent limitations, including their tendency to hallucinate facts, perpetuate biases, and operate as "black boxes" whose decision-making processes we cannot fully explain.

Machine learning (ML) represents a paradigm shift in computing. Rather than programmers writing explicit rules for every possible scenario, ML systems identify patterns from vast amounts of data. The fundamental principle is simple: feed the

DOI: 10.1201/9781003644712-2

algorithm enough examples, and it learns to recognize patterns and make predictions. The more data it processes, the more accurate it becomes, transforming raw information into actionable insights through pattern recognition rather than predetermined rules. Many examples presented in the following chapters predate the generative AI revolution—ministries of foreign affairs were already using ML to analyze satellite imagery for treaty verification, predict refugee flows based on conflict indicators, identify disinformation campaigns through social media pattern analysis, and forecast political instability by processing economic and social indicators. These applications demonstrated ML's diplomatic value long before ChatGPT brought AI into the mainstream consciousness.

For practitioners, the practical value of ML is speed and scale, not certainty. ML outputs are usually best read as risk signals rather than final judgments. That means the most important questions are whether the model was trained on data that matches your context, how often it produces false alarms or misses real events, and how its results will be checked before they shape policy. Used well, ML strengthens early warning and helps teams focus attention; used poorly, it turns shaky signals into "evidence," carries bias from the data into decisions, and nudges offices toward recommendations they can't clearly explain or defend to leaders, partners, or the public.

Neural networks and deep learning take inspiration from the human brain's architecture of interconnected neurons. These systems process information through multiple layers, with each layer extracting increasingly complex features from the data. The term "deep" refers to these many stacked layers of processing. Thousands of tiny, simple decision-makers, each examining a small piece of information and passing a signal to the next group, look at slightly larger patterns, and so on through dozens of layers. By the final layer, the system can recognize a missile launcher in a satellite image or detect the linguistic fingerprint of a disinformation campaign, even though no single component "understands" the whole picture. Understanding emerges from the collective, which is precisely why these systems are so difficult to explain. Like the brain itself, these networks can produce remarkably sophisticated outputs, though the sheer complexity of their layered processing sometimes makes it difficult to fully explain how they arrive at specific conclusions. For diplomats accustomed to justifying decisions to ministers, parliaments, and allies, this "black box" problem is not merely technical; it presents a growing challenge to transparency and accountability in foreign policy decision-making.

Foundation models represent the current frontier—large deep neural networks trained on massive amounts of data through self-supervised learning. **Large Language Models (LLMs)** are among the first foundation models that analyze patterns across billions of text examples to generate human-like writing. These models don't just predict the next word; they can generate entire sentences, paragraphs, and documents that maintain context and coherence. When we use ChatGPT or Claude, we are interacting with a system that has ingested more text than any human could read in a thousand lifetimes and learned the statistical patterns of how words follow words. It doesn't "know" facts the way we do; it knows that certain words tend to appear near other words in certain contexts. This is why they also suffer from "hallucinations"—confidently stating false information as fact, inventing citations, or creating plausible-sounding but entirely fictional content. They can perpetuate biases present in their training data and struggle with tasks requiring genuine understanding rather than pattern matching. At its current stage of development, AI functions like a capable but unvetted source, helpful for drafting, but liable to embed fabrications if left unchecked.

Generative AI—technologies that create text, images, video, and other content—has fundamentally transformed how we interact with AI. Unlike previous AI systems that could only analyze or classify existing information, generative AI produces entirely new content often indistinguishable from human-created work. **Natural Language Processing (NLP)** combined with these generative capabilities means systems like GPT-4 and Claude can translate between languages, draft complex documents, and engage in sophisticated dialogue. This latest wave of generative AI has brought AI from research labs directly into our daily and professional lives, including diplomatic practice.

ChatGPT's launch in November 2022 marked a watershed moment, as AI became accessible to billions. Today, AI assistants draft cables in embassies, analyze information in consulates, and synthesize policy briefs in many foreign ministries. The same technology helping students write essays now helps diplomats navigate complex documents and analyze geopolitical trends in real-time. Both domains face the same ethical questions: When does assistance become plagiarism? How do we maintain critical thinking skills while using tools that think for us? Who is accountable when AI-generated content, whether a student paper or a diplomatic cable, contains errors or fabrications? As these tools become indispensable to modern diplomacy, understanding their limitations, from hallucinations to embedded biases, from their reliance on global labor inequalities to their potential for misuse, becomes as important as understanding their capabilities.

As of late 2025, AI has crossed several critical thresholds that directly impact international relations. Language models now exceed human performance on numerous standardized tests, including bar exams, medical licensing examinations, and advanced placement tests across multiple subjects. The 2025 Stanford AI Index Report reveals a world where AI has moved decisively from laboratories to the center of geopolitical competition and daily governance (Stanford University 2025). These dynamics, outlined below, frame the strategic considerations explored in subsequent chapters.

While AI has made remarkable strides, several significant limitations persist, though history cautions us against definitive proclamations about what AI cannot achieve. Current constraints include sustainability and infrastructure challenges, as large-scale AI systems demand enormous electricity, water, and cooling resources, making them expensive to operate, which suggests practitioners should employ right-sized models rather than defaulting to the largest available. Deeper philosophical limits remain unresolved: questions of self-awareness and consciousness, whether AI genuinely understands meaning or merely simulates thought, whether it can exercise ethical judgment and wisdom, and whether it possesses common sense, concepts even humans struggle to define uniformly. Additionally, AI lacks sensation and deep emotional experience; it cannot truly feel joy, loss, or accomplishment as humans do.

Yet we must approach these boundaries with humility, as confident predictions about what remains purely human have repeatedly faltered. Consider coding: for years, we prepared entire generations for careers in software development, believing programming would be the cornerstone of future employment and economic opportunity. Yet reports indicated that AI generated approximately 41% of all code in 2024, while Google's CEO stated that over 25% of all new Google code is AI-generated (Forbes 2024), fundamentally reshaping a profession we assumed would only grow in human demand. Similarly, art and creativity were long considered the irreducible domain of human expression, safe from algorithmic disruption. That assumption was challenged when Théâtre D'opéra Spatial, an AI-generated artwork created using Midjourney, won first place at the 2022 Colorado State Fair's fine arts competition, igniting debate about the nature of creativity itself (Artnet 2022). Rather than betting on rigid predictions of AI's capabilities or limitations, wisdom lies in preparing for a future defined by uncertainty, rapid change, and a continuous interplay of known challenges and unforeseen developments.

This lesson carries particular weight in international relations and foreign policy. These trends reveal a technology racing ahead of governance structures, creating new forms of international competition while demanding unprecedented cooperation. The diplomatic challenge isn't whether to engage with AI, but how to shape its development in ways that serve national interests without undermining global stability and human welfare. The zero-sum logic of traditional geopolitics—where one nation's AI advantage necessarily threatens others—risks creating an arms race that could ultimately harm all nations through ungoverned AI proliferation, widening digital divides, or catastrophic accidents. Success will require combining technological capability with diplomatic agility, using AI to enhance international influence while building coalitions that ensure this transformative technology benefits humanity broadly rather than entrenching the dominance of a few at the expense of many.

Understanding AI is no longer optional for foreign policy practitioners. As these systems become more capable, they will increasingly mediate how states understand each other, communicate with their citizens, and make decisions about war and peace. The question is not whether AI will transform diplomacy, but whether human judgment, creativity, and wisdom will continue to guide these powerful tools toward constructive ends. The same technology that enables unprecedented surveillance and manipulation also offers the possibility of better understanding between nations, more effective conflict prevention, and more nuanced appreciation of cultural differences. The choice of which future we create remains, for now, distinctly human.

BIBLIOGRAPHY

Artnet. 2022. *An A.I.-Generated Artwork Won First Prize at a Colorado State Fair. Human Artists Are Infuriated*. September 1. Accessed December 29, 2025. https://news.artnet.com/art-world/colorado-artists-mad-ai-art-competition-2168495.

Copeland, Jack. 2012. *Alan Turing: The codebreaker who saved 'millions of lives'*. June 19. Accessed December 24, 2025. https://www.bbc.com/news/technology-18419691.

Forbes. 2024. *AI Writes Over 25% Of Code At Google—What Does The Future Look Like For Software Engineers?* November 1. Accessed December 29, 2025. https://www.forbes.com/sites/jackkelly/2024/11/01/ai-code-and-the-future-of-software-engineers/.

Stanford University. 2025. *The 2025 AI Index Report*. April. Accessed December 24, 2025. https://hai.stanford.edu/ai-index/2025-ai-index-report.

Part I

PROGRESS AI and the Transformation of Diplomacy and Foreign Policy

1 Through the Looking Glass of History
Understanding AI's Transformation of Diplomacy

> Technology and diplomacy have always been intertwined. From the invention of the wheel to the development of the internet, technology has shaped the way we communicate, travel and interact with each other. And it has had a profound impact on diplomacy. Change and continuity have played pivotal roles in the evolution of technology and diplomacy. The fast-paced evolution of technology stands in stark contrast to the enduring essence of diplomacy – the peaceful resolution of conflicts.
>
> — **Jovan Kurbalija,** *Founding Director, Diplo Foundation (Kurbalija 2023)*

When Stephen Hawking warned that artificial intelligence (AI) would be "either the best or the worst thing ever to happen to humanity," his assessment echoed a pattern of dual warnings that accompanies every transformative technology (The Guardian 2016). Nearly two centuries earlier, Samuel Morse offered a remarkably similar observation about his electric telegraph in 1844, describing it as an "instrument of immense power, to be wielded for good or for evil, as it shall be properly or improperly directed" (Elon University 2025). The parallel between these two moments, separated by nearly 200 years yet united by their recognition of technology's capacity to fundamentally change our societies, offers contemporary practitioners a valuable lens through which to understand the current transformation.

Both visionaries recognized that these technologies were not merely technical achievements but instruments that would redistribute power, influence decision-making, and with that challenge the established protocols of international engagement. When Morse demonstrated his telegraph to senators in 1844, many responded with disbelief and skepticism. This reaction highlights a recurring pattern whenever disruptive technologies appear, one that resonates strongly today with AI. This suggests that the patterns of technological adoption in diplomacy follow remarkably consistent trajectories across centuries, offering us a roadmap for navigating today's challenges.

The development of new technologies, particularly in transportation and telecommunications, has consistently reshaped diplomatic practice in ways that seemed unimaginable to previous generations. Each wave of innovation, from railways to radio, from telegraph to television, has not only transformed how diplomats communicate but fundamentally altered how diplomacy is conducted in practice—though perhaps more precisely, these technologies have revolutionized diplomatic methods

DOI: 10.1201/9781003644712-4

while leaving its essential purpose of negotiating between political entities, managing relationships, preventing conflict, and advancing interests through persuasion rather than force remarkably intact. Understanding these historical transformations and continuities provides essential context for grappling with AI's implications for contemporary international relations (Kurbalija 2023).

INFRASTRUCTURE AS STATECRAFT: FROM RAILWAY DIPLOMACY TO THE AI STACK

To understand how technological infrastructure becomes diplomatic power, we must begin with the nineteenth century's most transformative innovation: the railway network that reshaped not just how diplomats traveled, but how nations projected influence across continents. The advent of railways in the nineteenth century marked diplomacy's first major technological disruption, one that transformed not just the speed of diplomatic engagement but its very nature (Kurbalija 1999). Railways allowed envoys to travel quickly across countries, attend meetings in distant capitals, and respond to crises in ways that were previously impossible. Steamships and later airplanes would further compress diplomatic timelines, enabling more frequent face-to-face interactions and fostering closer coordination between missions and their home governments. Yet the deeper transformation lay not in mobility but in how infrastructure itself became an instrument of statecraft, a lesson that resonates powerfully as nations compete to control the AI stack that will define twenty-first-century power.

Railway construction in the nineteenth century was never simply about transportation. When Britain, France, and Germany extended rail lines into Africa, Asia, and the Middle East, they were building what we would now recognize as dual-use infrastructure: commercial networks that simultaneously served as arteries of political control and strategic influence—railway diplomacy (DiploFoundation 2025b). The concept of railway diplomacy persists with remarkable vigor in the twenty-first century. China's ambitious Belt and Road Initiative deploys railway investments across Africa and Asia as instruments of foreign policy, demonstrating that infrastructure remains a powerful tool of diplomatic influence (Ampaw 2025).

Today's competition over AI infrastructure follows remarkably similar patterns, though the stakes seem exponentially higher. The modern equivalent of laying railway tracks is the race to control every layer of the AI stack: from semiconductor production facilities that produce essential chips, to massive data centers that power machine learning models, to cloud computing platforms that deliver AI capabilities globally. When the United States restricts China's access to advanced semiconductors through export controls, or when Taiwan's TSMC becomes courted like a strategic railway junction once was, these moves echo nineteenth-century infrastructure rivalries. The global scramble to build AI-capable data centers represents infrastructure diplomacy on a scale that would have been familiar to railway-era strategists.

The lesson from railway diplomacy is clear: infrastructure advantages compound over time. Britain's early railway investments locked in political relationships and created path dependencies that persisted decades after the rails became obsolete. Similarly, nations securing reliable access to advanced semiconductors, establishing sovereign AI capabilities, and controlling critical nodes of the AI stack are not just winning today's technological competition. They are potentially determining the global hierarchy for the remainder of the twenty-first century. As with railways, the risk is that infrastructure competition could accelerate rather than manage international tensions, making the management of this AI infrastructure race one of diplomacy's most urgent contemporary challenges.

THE TELEGRAPH TRANSFORMATION: SPEED, COST, AND CONTROL IN DIPLOMATIC PRACTICE

While railways revolutionized how quickly diplomats could travel between capitals, they still left communication itself bound by the speed of physical movement. The electric telegraph shattered this final constraint, creating the first technology that could transmit information faster than any form of transportation. Though mechanical semaphore systems had existed since the 1790s, primarily for military use, it was Samuel Morse's electromagnetic telegraph and his dots-and-dashes code that truly revolutionized diplomatic communication (BBC 2013). When Morse's telegraph line between Washington and Baltimore transmitted its first official message in 1844, it inaugurated an era of near-instantaneous communication that would fundamentally reshape international relations (Kurbalija 2023). For the first time, governments could maintain real-time contact with their embassies abroad, sending instructions and receiving updates with unprecedented speed, a capability that Morse recognized would transform the very nature of international power, much as AI promises to do today.

The integration of the telegraph into diplomatic practice came at an extraordinary cost, offering lessons about how institutions navigate revolutionary technologies. In 1866, the U.S. State Department sent one of its early diplomatic cables to Paris, a message that cost an astronomical $20,000 when the department's entire annual budget was just $150,000 (Weber 1993). This single communication consumed nearly 15% of the State Department's resources, yet officials recognized that mastering this new technology was essential to maintaining relevance in a rapidly changing international system. The cost of early adoption, however steep, paled in comparison to the strategic disadvantage of technological isolation. Tsar Nicholas I of Russia, for instance, considered the telegraph "subversive." Fearing its ability to disseminate information too widely, he declined Morse's offer to build telegraph lines in Russia, leaving the country far behind other major powers (Kurbalija 2023). On the other side, Great Britain invested substantially in its telegraph network, strengthening its advantage long before other countries realized the importance of this innovation.

The true price of the telegraph extended far beyond its financial burden. The technology fundamentally altered the relationship between diplomatic missions and their home governments, stripping ambassadors of the autonomous decision-making they had enjoyed when instructions took weeks to arrive. Foreign ministries could now micromanage their representatives abroad, demanding instant responses and continuous updates, transforming diplomacy from a practice of careful deliberation into one of rapid reaction and centralized control. Some diplomats lamented that messages were often drafted in haste, poorly prepared, or received out of sequence, while the telegraph's high cost forced a new compressed writing style that favored brevity over the elaborate prose of traditional correspondence (Kern 1983). These tensions, between speed and reflection, efficiency and nuance, central control and local expertise, resonate strongly with contemporary concerns about AI systems that can generate talking points in seconds, analyze sentiment in real time, and recommend courses of action faster than human judgment can evaluate them. Just as nineteenth-century diplomats worried the telegraph would reduce them to mere executors of instructions from capitals, today's practitioners grapple with whether AI might similarly diminish the role of human wisdom in international relations.

BREAKING THE SOUND BARRIER: TELEPHONE, RADIO, AND THE HUMANIZATION OF DISTANCE

Yet for all its revolutionary impact, the telegraph remained limited to text, stripping diplomatic communication of tone and subtlety. The invention of the telephone in the late nineteenth century addressed this deficiency by restoring the human voice to long-distance diplomacy. Suddenly, diplomats and political leaders could speak directly across continents, their words carrying the emotional weight, urgency, and nuance that written correspondence inherently lacked.

This capacity transformed crisis management and high-level exchanges. The "hotline" established between Washington and Moscow during the Cold War, initially a teletype, later upgraded to telephone, became perhaps the most famous diplomatic communication channel in history, a last-resort mechanism to prevent nuclear catastrophe through direct leader-to-leader communication (Effective Alltruism Forum 2023). The telephone made possible a form of diplomatic engagement that combined the immediacy of modern technology with the nuance of human conversation.

Radio communication, emerging in the early twentieth century, introduced yet another transformative element. Unlike telegraph and telephone systems that required fixed lines, radio waves could reach across continents and oceans without physical infrastructure (Diplo Foundation 2025a). This made communication possible from remote embassies, ships at sea, and regions where traditional communication lines had been severed by conflict or natural disaster. Radio's resilience and reach made it indispensable for maintaining diplomatic contact in even the most challenging circumstances. Remarkably, even in today's age of internet, smartphones, and AI, radio remains a primary source of information in many settings, and, as we will explore in the chapter on AI and Peacebuilding, even serves as a data source for training machine learning models.

Television and satellite communications would further expand diplomatic possibilities, enabling visual diplomacy where body language, setting, and imagery became as important as words. Summit meetings could be broadcast globally, allowing leaders to speak simultaneously to domestic and international audiences. The choreographed handshake, the carefully staged photo opportunity, the joint press conference, all became essential elements of modern diplomatic theater, made possible by these visual technologies. The arrival of the internet would soon converge all these capabilities, text, voice, image, and video, into a single networked infrastructure, fundamentally reshaping diplomacy once again.

BROADCASTING BEYOND BORDERS: RADIO AND THE BIRTH OF PUBLIC DIPLOMACY

At the beginning of the twentieth century, diplomatic communication remained strictly limited to official channels between governments and their accredited representatives. Direct communication from one country to the population of another was considered a fundamental violation of sovereignty, a breach of the Westphalian principle that states should not interfere in each other's internal affairs (Manor 2025). This established order would be shattered definitively and irreversibly by radio technology, offering crucial lessons for understanding how AI currently transforms the boundaries between traditional diplomacy, public diplomacy, and information warfare.

Radio's revolutionary impact came not from its technical capabilities alone but from how it fundamentally redefined the diplomatic playing field. In the interwar years, Nazi Germany and the Soviet Union demonstrated how radio broadcasts could penetrate borders, reaching directly into the homes and minds of foreign populations. This marked the birth of what would come to be known as **public diplomacy:** practices through which states sought to pursue foreign policy objectives by engaging directly with foreign publics rather than solely through government-to-government channels (Cull 2008). The transformation was as controversial as it was profound. Traditional diplomats viewed these broadcasts as propaganda, a corruption of diplomatic practice that threatened the established order of international relations. Yet by the time of the Cold War, the ability to communicate directly with an adversary's population had become recognized as strategically significant as "the size of one's nuclear arsenal" (Manor 2025).

Radio Free Europe, the Voice of America, the BBC World Service, and their Soviet counterparts became frontline weapons in the ideological struggle between East and West. This historical precedent provides essential context for understanding how AI is currently transforming the boundaries between traditional diplomacy and public engagement. The scale of contemporary digital public diplomacy dwarfs anything possible in the radio era. The U.S. State Department alone operates more than 288 Facebook profiles, 200 Twitter accounts, and 125 YouTube channels worldwide, reaching audiences that number in the hundreds of millions. Yet these numbers pale in comparison to what AI makes possible (Manor 2025).

The integration of AI into public diplomacy represents not merely an evolution but a fundamental transformation of how nations engage with foreign publics. Where radio and television enabled one-to-many broadcasting, and social media facilitated many-to-many conversations, AI now enables crafting personalized messages for millions of individuals simultaneously, each tailored to their specific cultural context, political leanings, and psychological profiles. AI systems can analyze an individual's social media history, predict their receptivity to different narratives, and generate content calibrated to resonate with their worldview, all in real time and at a scale no human public diplomacy team could achieve.

This hyperpersonalization extends beyond simple translation or demographic targeting. The Northstar system employed by the United States, capable of analyzing media from over 200 countries in more than 100 languages, represents just the beginning of AI's potential to reshape public diplomacy (Vota 2024). Yet this technological empowerment brings corresponding vulnerabilities and challenges for authenticity and trust. When foreign publics discover they're engaging with AI-generated content rather than human diplomats, or when they realize the message they received was algorithmically optimized to manipulate their emotions, the backlash can severely damage a nation's soft power. Moreover, the speed of AI-driven public diplomacy creates escalation risks where AI systems from different nations might engage in rapid-fire narrative battles, each responding to the other's messaging faster than human oversight can intervene, transforming public diplomacy from deliberate strategy into something approaching algorithmic warfare.

VIRTUAL EMBASSIES EXPERIMENTS: WHY TECHNOLOGY ALONE ISN'T ENOUGH

The promise of virtual representation has long captivated diplomatic innovators, offering visions of cost-effective engagement unconstrained by physical limitations—a promise that resonates powerfully with today's debates about AI-powered diplomatic tools. The first serious experiments emerged in 2007, when the Diplo Foundation created "Diplomacy Island" on the metaverse platform Second Life, then home to a virtual community of more than 6 million "residents" from around the world (Diplo Foundation 2007). The Maldives became the first country to open a virtual embassy there, with Sweden, Malta, Macedonia, and the Philippines quickly following suit (Page 2007). The inauguration ceremony for the Maldivian virtual embassy, held simultaneously in the virtual world and physically in Geneva, captured the optimism of the moment.

The Maldivian Minister of State for Foreign Affairs emphasized that information technology, especially the internet, could empower small countries to engage more effectively in international relations, an argument that consistently remains the most compelling reason for small and developing nations to embrace new waves of technological advancement, including current developments in AI. Yet these virtual embassies largely failed to achieve meaningful impact as public diplomacy tools. Engagement remained low, and the platforms struggled with fundamental issues of usability and credibility. The experiment revealed a crucial truth that remains highly relevant for AI adoption: while digital technologies can enhance diplomatic outreach, they cannot fully replace the trust, relationships, and nuanced understanding that traditional diplomacy requires.

These experiments offer crucial early lessons about technological transformation in diplomacy, though the lessons themselves remain contested. Virtual embassies largely failed to achieve meaningful impact as public diplomacy tools yet dismissing them entirely would repeat the mistake of diplomats who once viewed social media as irrelevant to serious statecraft. Twitter was initially derided as trivial, yet it became central to diplomatic communication and crisis management. Facebook seemed frivolous until it reshaped public diplomacy and electoral politics. The virtual embassy experiments remind us that early technological failures don't necessarily predict long-term irrelevance, they might simply indicate we haven't yet discovered the right application or waited long enough for cultural adaptation.

DATA EMBASSIES: ESTONIA'S MODEL AND CARIBBEAN ADAPTATIONS

Estonia's pioneering "data embassy" concept, established in Luxembourg in 2017, represents a more successful model of virtual diplomatic innovation precisely because it doesn't attempt to replace traditional diplomatic functions but rather adapts diplomatic principles to digital realities (Talmazan 2019). This distinction is crucial for understanding how AI should be integrated into diplomatic practice. The Estonian model arose from existential necessity: after suffering massive cyberattacks in 2007 that paralyzed government services, Estonia recognized that its digital vulnerability could threaten the state's very existence. The solution was innovative yet grounded in traditional diplomatic thinking: establish a secure government data center abroad that would function as a sovereign extension of Estonian territory, protected by diplomatic immunity.

This secure government data center functions as a protected backup for critical state e-governance systems, ensuring governmental continuity in case of national crisis. What makes Estonia's data embassy revolutionary is not its technology but its legal innovation. The facility is recognized as Estonian sovereign territory under international law, meaning only the Estonian government controls access to its data and infrastructure (Rice 2019). This arrangement required careful negotiation and novel interpretations of diplomatic immunity and extraterritoriality, demonstrating that successful technological innovation in diplomacy often requires corresponding evolution in legal and institutional frameworks.

The data embassy concept is now spreading globally, with different regions adapting the model to their unique circumstances. The Caribbean states, facing increasingly severe hurricanes that regularly destroy telecommunications infrastructure, while simultaneously confronting a sharp rise in ransomware attacks, with over 300 Caribbean organizations targeted in 2024 alone (Greene and Herakleous 2025), are pioneering a regional approach—Trinidad and Tobago is leading plans for a shared data embassy facility that would serve multiple island nations, transforming an impossible individual expense into an achievable collective insurance policy against natural disasters. Saudi Arabia became in 2025 the first G20 nation to propose comprehensive data embassy legislation, seeking to position itself as a global hub for digital sovereignty services at the strategic crossroads of three continents (Meenagh, Koroleva, and Imam 2025). Australia is also exploring proposals that would allow foreign companies to operate data centers on Australian soil under their home country's laws (The Conversation 2025). These divergent approaches reveal how the data embassy concept is evolving from Estonia's narrow focus on governmental continuity into varied frameworks for managing digital sovereignty, each nation adapting the model to address its particular vulnerabilities, whether natural disasters, geographic advantages, or economic opportunities.

The evolution from virtual embassies to data embassies illuminates a fundamental principle for integrating new technologies into diplomatic practice. Data embassies succeed where virtual embassies failed precisely because they don't attempt to digitize existing diplomatic functions; they address entirely new vulnerabilities created by digital transformation itself. This distinction offers crucial guidance for AI integration: the most successful applications will be those that recognize how AI creates new diplomatic necessities rather than simply automating traditional processes. Just as physical embassies have protected nationals abroad for centuries, and just as data embassies now protect digital sovereignty when domestic infrastructure fails, future diplomatic innovations will need to identify what new forms of protection and presence AI-dependent governance systems require.

FROM HISTORICAL PATTERNS TO CONTEMPORARY IMPERATIVES

The unprecedented speed of AI adoption in diplomatic contexts distinguishes this technological transformation from all previous ones, compressing adaptation timelines from decades to months. While the telegraph took nearly half a century to fully integrate into diplomatic practice, and radio required decades to evolve from experimental technology to a strategic tool, AI's trajectory has been dramatically compressed. Vladimir Putin's 2017 declaration that "the nation that leads AI will be the ruler of the world" instantly reframed AI as existential national competition. The launch of ChatGPT in late 2022 democratized access to AI capabilities, forcing even reluctant institutions to engage with the technology. By mid-2023, multiple foreign ministries had issued AI governance guidelines, and diplomatic services worldwide were experimenting with generative AI for everything from drafting communiqués to analyzing multilingual social media streams.

Paradoxically, this speed makes historical perspective more, not less, important. The patterns revealed by previous technological transformations illuminate the path ahead: each innovation has promised efficiency while creating unexpected vulnerabilities; the telegraph's compression of decision-making timelines, radio's breach of sovereign boundaries, and virtual embassies' failure to replicate human connection all prefigure AI's current challenges. These technologies never merely enhanced existing diplomatic practices but created entirely new arenas of competition and cooperation. Just as railways became instruments of imperial expansion and telegraph networks determined information advantage, today's AI infrastructure, from semiconductor supply chains to data centers, represents the new geography of power.

The chapters that follow examine how these dynamics are already reshaping international relations across multiple domains. The global AI race is restructuring alliances and creating new forms of technological dependency that rival the strategic importance of energy resources. AI's transformation of security paradigms extends from algorithmic warfare to predictive peacekeeping, fundamentally altering both the tools and the nature of peace and conflict. The intersection of economic security and AI governance reveals how control over data flows and algorithmic standards becomes as important as traditional trade agreements. Throughout these explorations, we return to the fundamental question of whether AI will amplify humanity's capacity for peace and progress or accelerate the concentration of power in ways that threaten both. History suggests the answer isn't predetermined; it depends on the choices diplomatic institutions make today about integrating these technologies while preserving the human wisdom that has always been diplomacy's irreducible core.

BIBLIOGRAPHY

Ampaw, Eugene Ansah Owusu, Qin Jin, Maxwell Ako, and Mehdi Oldache. 2025. "Railway Diplomacy: China's Infrastructure Investments and Africa's Global Connectivity." *Cities* 162: 21–36. https://www.sciencedirect.com/science/article/abs/pii/S0264275125001611.

BBC. 2013. "How Napoleon's Semaphore Telegraph Changed the World." *BBC News*. June 17. Accessed September 15, 2025. https://www.bbc.com/news/magazine-22909590.

BBC. 2025. "The TikTokers Accused of Triggering an Election Scandal." *BBC*. April 30. Accessed September 17, 2025. https://www.bbc.com/articles/cqx41x3gn5zo.

Cucos, Radu. 2012. "Virtual Diplomacy – A New Way of Conducting International Affairs?" *World Bank Blogs*. November 13. Accessed September 17, 2025. https://blogs.worldbank.org/en/digital-development/virtual-diplomacy-a-new-way-of-conducting-international-affairs#:~:text=The%20volatile%20situation%20in,The%20French%20government%20announced.

Cull, Nicholas J. 2008. "Public Diplomacy: Taxonomies and Histories." *The Annals of the American Academy of Political and Social Sciences* (Sage Publications, Inc.) 616: 31–54. https://www.jstor.org/stable/25097993

Diplo Foundation. 2007. "Diplomacy Island Launched in Second Life." *diplomacy.edu*. March 1. Accessed September 17, 2025. https://www.diplomacy.edu/event/diplomacy-island-launched/.

Diplo Foundation. 2025a. *Radio and TV Broadcasting: Diplomacy Going Live*. Accessed December 17, 2025. https://www.diplomacy.edu/histories/radio-and-tv-broadcasting-diplomacy-going-live/.

DiploFoundation. 2025b. *Railway Diplomacy*. Accessed September 15, 2025. https://www.diplomacy.edu/topics/railway-diplomacy/.

Doubleday, Justin. 2024. "With New AI Tools Available, State Department Encourages Experimentation." *Federal News Network*. June 28. Accessed September 17, 2025. https://federalnewsnetwork.com/artificial-intelligence/2024/06/with-new-ai-tools-available-state-department-encourages-experimentation/.

Effective Alltruism Forum. 2023. *Call Me, Maybe? Hotlines and Global Catastrophic Risk*. January 24. Accessed December 23, 2025. https://forum.effectivealtruism.org/posts/3eivCYyZm8NR4Sdq5/call-me-maybe-hotlines-and-global-catastrophic-risk-founders.

Elon University. 2025. "1830s–1860s: Telegraph." *Imagining the Internet: A History and Forecast*. September 15. Accessed September 15, 2025. https://www.elon.edu/u/imagining/time-capsule/150-years/back-1830-1860/.

Greene, Tira, and Demetris Herakleous. 2025. *Data Embassies an Innovative Approach to Strengthening Digital Resilience in the Caribbean*. Policy Paper, Santiago: ECLAC.

IEEE. 2025. *IEEE Reach - Raising Engineering Awareness through the Conduit of History*. September 15. Accessed September 15, 2025. https://reach.ieee.org/primary-sources/semaphore-telegraph/.

Kern, Stephen. 1983. *The Culture of Time and Space, 1880–1918*. Cambridge, MA: Harvard University Press.

Kurbalija, Jovan. 1999. "Diplomacy in the Age of Information Technology." In *Innovation in Diplomatic Practice*, by Jan Melissen (pp. 171–191). London: Palgrave Macmillan.

Kurbalija, Jovan. 2023. *History of Diplomacy and Technology: From Smoke Signals to Artificial Intelligence*. Washington, DC: Diplo US.

Manor, Ilan. 2025. *What Is Digital Diplomacy?* September 17. Accessed September 17, 2025. https://digdipblog.com/countries-on-twitter-and-facebook/.

Meenagh, Brian, Ksenia Koroleva, and Faisal Imam. 2025. *Saudi Arabia Pioneers Data Embassies with Publication of Draft Global AI Hub Law*. April 18. Accessed December 23, 2025. https://www.globalprivacyblog.com/2025/04/saudi-arabia-pioneers-data-embassies-with-publication-of-draft-global-ai-hub-law/.

Page, Jeremy. 2007. "Tiny Island Nation Opens the First Real Embassy in Virtual World." *The Times.* May 24. Accessed September 17, 2025. https://www.thetimes.com/world/us-world/article/tiny-island-nation-opens-the-first-real-embassy-in-virtual-world-c3phsx2n2r0.

Rice, Nikolai F. 2019. "Estonia's Digital Embassies and the Concept of Sovereignty." *Georgetown Security Studies Review.* October 10. Accessed September 17, 2025. https://georgetownsecuritystudiesreview.org/2019/10/10/estonias-digital-embassies-and-the-concept-of-sovereignty/.

Talmazan, Yuliya. 2019. "Data Security Meets Diplomacy: Why Estonia Is Storing Its Data in Luxembourg." *NBC News.* June 25. Accessed September 17, 2025. https://www.nbcnews.com/news/world/data-security-meets-diplomacy-why-estonia-storing-its-data-luxembourg-n1018171.

The Conversation. 2025. *Australia's Tech Lobby Wants Deregulated 'Digital Embassies' for Offshore Clients. Here's Why That Might Not Be a Great Idea.* October 17. Accessed December 23, 2025. https://theconversation.com/australias-tech-lobby-wants-deregulated-digital-embassies-for-offshore-clients-heres-why-that-might-not-be-a-great-idea-266769.

The Guardian. 2016. *Stephen Hawking: AI Will Be 'Either Best or Worst Thing' for Humanity.* October 19. Accessed December 23, 2025. https://www.theguardian.com/science/2016/oct/19/stephen-hawking-ai-best-or-worst-thing-for-humanity-cambridge#:~:text=Professor%20Stephen%20Hawking%20has%20warned,future%20of%20our%20civilisation%20and.

The New York Times. 2018. "Cambridge Analytica and Facebook: The Scandal and the Fallout So Far." *The New York Times.* April 4. Accessed September 17, 2025. https://www.nytimes.com/2018/04/04/us/politics/cambridge-analytica-scandal-fallout.html.

U.S. Department of State. 2023. "The Use of Artificial Intelligence in Public Diplomacy: ACPD Official Meeting Minutes, June 14, 2023." *U.S. Advisory Commission on Public Diplomacy.* June 14. Accessed September 17, 2025. https://2021-2025.state.gov/acpd-official-meeting-minutes-june-14-2023/#:~:text=The%20U.S.%20Advisory%20Commission%20on,Artificial%20Intelligence%20in%20Public%20Diplomacy.

Vincent, James. 2017. "The Verge." *Putin Says the Nation That Leads in AI 'Will Be the Ruler of the World'.* September 4. Accessed September 15, 2025. https://www.theverge.com/2017/9/4/16251226/russia-ai-putin-rule-the-world.

Vota, Wayan. 2024. *How US State Department Uses AI Strategically in Modern Diplomacy.* August 23. Accessed December 23, 2025. https://www.ictworks.org/state-department-uses-ai-strategically/.

Weber, Ralph E. 1993. "Seward's Other Folly: America's First Encrypted Cable." *Cryptologic Quarterly* 12 (2): 81–103.

2 The Rise of Tech Diplomacy and the Role of Tech Diplomats

As a Tech Diplomat, my role is to build bridges to connect people and promote Tech for Good. Technology should be beneficial for everyone, everywhere, respecting the rich cultural diversity of the world's population and the local needs of different societies across the globe.

—**Eugenio V Garcia,** *Director, Science, Technology, Innovation, and Intellectual Property, Ministry of Foreign Affairs of Brazil (All Tech Is Human 2025)*

It's my role as an ambassador, as a diplomat, to engage with them (tech companies) and talk about shared interest, shared values, and ensuring that while we are also I think finally stepping up to the task of regulating tech companies that's gone unregulated for decades now, we've also got to recognize that we're not going to have the perfect regulation tomorrow.

—**Anne Marie Engtoft Larsen,** *Denmark's Tech Ambassador (Tech Policy Press 2023)*

Technology is changing very quickly, and the role of the tech envoy has evolved accordingly. Initially focused on engaging companies, the position now encompasses international issues such as blockchain, AI, and data governance. This shift requires a different kind of diplomat – one equipped to navigate all these issues.[1]

—**Philip Thigo,** *Special Envoy on Technology for the Republic of Kenya (Foreign Policy and AI Forum 2024)*

THE NEW DIPLOMATIC REALITY: WHEN TECH GIANTS RIVAL NATION STATES

In 2022, at the beginning of the Ukraine war, Ukraine's 31-year-old Vice Prime Minister watched his country's communication infrastructure disappear under Russian missile strikes. He didn't call the State Department or NATO, or draft a formal diplomatic cable, or request an emergency UN session. Instead, as many digital natives would do, but not many diplomats, he typed a message on Twitter to the world's richest man:

> @elonmusk, while you try to colonize Mars - Russia try to occupy Ukraine! While your rockets successfully land from space - Russian rockets attack

DOI: 10.1201/9781003644712-5

> Ukrainian civil people! We ask you to provide Ukraine with Starlink stations and to address sane Russians to stand.

The answer was quick and Starlink was promptly active in Ukraine (AlJazeera 2022).

This exchange of a government minister negotiating critical infrastructure via social media with a billionaire entrepreneur would have been inconceivable even a decade earlier. Yet it perfectly captured a shift that had been building for years—the growing dependence of nations on tech platforms they neither control nor fully understand. What followed exposed just how much the traditional boundaries between public and private power had already eroded in the digital age. Just as quickly as he enabled the access, Musk refused to enable Starlink coverage for a Ukrainian attack on Russian naval vessels in Crimea, citing fears of nuclear escalation. A chief executive officer (CEO) and a tech company were effectively conducting their own foreign policy with serious security implications (Reuters 2023).

Such examples proliferate across the globe, with tech companies increasingly wielding influence over diplomatic and security outcomes. From the Cambridge Analytica scandal that manipulated voters across multiple democracies in 2018 (The Guardian 2018), to TikTok's algorithmic influence on Romania's 2024 elections (Global Witness 2024), from Facebook's role in promoting violence against Rohingya in Myanmar (Amnesty International 2022) to Microsoft withdrawing some of its artificial intelligence (AI) and cloud services from Israel's army for spying on Palestinians (AlJazeera 2025), these companies demonstrated their capacity to shape electoral outcomes, fuel social movements, and even influence military conflicts. The past decade has witnessed a fundamental shift in diplomatic practice beyond crisis settings, as government officials increasingly found themselves negotiating not with their traditional counterparts, but with Big Tech executives who answered to no foreign ministry, followed no diplomatic protocols, and yet wielded power rivaling many nation-states.

Technologies and their creators had evolved from mere business concerns into cross-cutting foreign and security policy priorities, demanding new diplomatic frameworks for a world where algorithms could impact sovereignty and CEOs could make decisions with geopolitical consequences. Tech diplomacy emerged in response to the rising power of tech companies, and the profound impact of technological disruption, which is reshaping societies, shifting the global balance of power, and creating a hybrid landscape where geopolitics intersects with the states and tech companies. As tech companies have gained economic and political power, and in some cases even surpassing many nation-states, traditional diplomatic structures have struggled to keep pace. Tech diplomacy provides the innovative approaches needed to navigate this complex, rapidly evolving environment.

The rise of tech diplomacy represents an evolution in the practice of statecraft, progressing from traditional bilateral relations between nations, to the establishment of multilateral frameworks through organizations like the United Nations, to today's recognition that corporations have become influential actors in the international system. Just as diplomats once relocated to New York and Geneva to engage with inter- and supranational bodies that increasingly shaped foreign and security policy, they now venture to Silicon Valley, Seattle, and Shenzhen to build relationships with companies whose platforms and technologies profoundly impact billions of lives (Engtoft-Larsen 2025).

This shift in diplomacy reflects not just concern about tech's disruptive potential, but genuine optimism about its capacity to help solve humanity's greatest challenges, from climate change and pandemic response to educational access and economic development. The potential benefits of these "diplomatic ties" are substantial: access to cutting-edge innovation, participation in global digital governance, protection of citizens' rights online, and influence over technologies that will shape the future of human society. This recognition has driven nations from Denmark to Australia, from Brazil to Singapore, to proactively build new tech diplomacy ecosystems, appointing specialized envoys and establishing dedicated offices that acknowledge a fundamental reality of the twenty-first century, that effective foreign policy requires engaging not just with states and international organizations, but with the technology companies that have become indispensable partners in addressing global challenges and opportunities.

TECH DIPLOMACY IN PRACTICE: DEVELOPING STRATEGIC DOCUMENTS AND TECH AMBASSADOR ROLES

Governments worldwide have integrated the topic of technology into foreign policy through multiple pathways. Some embedded digital priorities within existing foreign policy strategies, while others created standalone digital foreign policies or specific frameworks for AI, cybersecurity, and data governance. Australia's 2017 Foreign Policy White Paper recognized severe security implications of emerging technologies, from terrorists' misuse to new types of weapons challenging international law (Australian Government 2017). Switzerland launched its Digital Foreign Policy Strategy in 2020 promoting its foreign policy values and interests "in the digital realm, just as in the physical world" (Geneva Internet Platform DigWatch 2020). Denmark's MFA launched a Strategy for Tech Diplomacy with a vision "to work for an international technology development that benefits Denmark and Europe, while delivering solutions to global challenges in a safe and responsible manner" (Ministry of Foreign Affairs of Denmark 2021).

To operationalize these strategic visions, governments moved beyond policy documents to create new diplomatic positions in diplomatic representations and in internal government structures, or expanding existing ambassadorial portfolios to include technology mandates, thereby ensuring that technology considerations are embedded into contemporary diplomacy rather than treated as peripheral concerns. The first country to realize and act upon this new reality by starting the modern practice of tech diplomacy was Denmark in 2017, when it piloted "TechPlomacy," and appointed the world's first tech ambassador, stationed not in a traditional capital but in Silicon Valley with a mandate to engage directly with tech giants as if they were nation-states (The Office of the Danish Tech Ambassador 2017). This groundbreaking move set a precedent that has since been followed by over two dozen countries, though their approaches vary significantly.

Some nations have concentrated on cyber affairs, with Australia, Finland, Germany, Estonia, Spain, and Sweden appointing cyber ambassadors focused on strengthening global cooperation in cyber governance, upholding international law, and countering emerging digital threats. Others, including Austria, the United Arab

Emirates, Saudi Arabia, and Israel, have pursued broader objectives, fostering closer ties with the private tech sector, encouraging investment, and promoting their domestic innovation ecosystems on the global stage (Bjola and Kornprobst 2025).

While early tech diplomacy initiatives were primarily concentrated in wealthy nations, emerging economies swiftly countered concerns about being excluded by establishing innovative frameworks suited to their specific contexts. Brazil posted a tech diplomat in Silicon Valley, India established a Division for New and Emerging Strategic Technologies within its MFA, Pakistan integrated technology into foreign policy, while China deployed 140 tech diplomats across 50 countries by 2022, creating the world's largest tech diplomacy network (Höne 2022). This rapid Global South engagement transformed tech diplomacy from an exclusive practice of wealthy nations into a global phenomenon, with emerging economies bringing fresh perspectives on digital sovereignty and South-South cooperation that challenged Silicon Valley-centric approaches.

The tech sector has also reciprocated by building its own quasi-diplomatic apparatus, with companies establishing government relations offices that function like embassies in world capitals. For example, Microsoft opened its own "diplomatic representation" at the UN "to advance global multi-stakeholder action on key technology, environmental, humanitarian, development and security goals as well as helping to advance the UN Sustainable Development Goals" (Microsoft 2020).

The European Union itself joined the tech diplomacy movement by establishing its own "embassy" in Silicon Valley in 2022, engaging directly with tech giants about compliance with the landmark regulations, a concrete acknowledgment that enforcing digital regulations required diplomatic presence in tech's capital, not just Brussels (Politico 2022). The United Nations also recognized the emerging impacts of technologies by appointing its first Tech Envoy whose office recently transitioned into the UN Office for Digital and Emerging Technologies following the adoption of the Global Digital Compact at the 2024 Summit of the Future, signaling that even the world's leading multilateral institution understood that digital governance had become inseparable from global governance (UN Office for Digital and Emerging Technologies 2025).

This rapid proliferation of tech diplomacy initiatives, from national strategies to tech ambassadors, from corporate diplomatic offices to multilateral tech envoys, has created both opportunity and confusion. Foreign policy practitioners now navigate a crowded field of tech-related diplomacies, cyber, digital, science, and tech, each with overlapping mandates and unclear boundaries. Science diplomacy, tech diplomacy, and digital diplomacy each highlight different forms of influence in international relations. Science diplomacy draws on knowledge power, using scientific expertise to shape global agendas and policy responses. Digital diplomacy emphasizes information power, the capacity to control, distribute, and frame information flows that influence both publics and governments. Tech diplomacy, however, adds a new layer: innovation power. Rooted in fast-moving fields such as AI, blockchain, and 5G, it reflects the ability of states and non-state actors to innovate, regulate, and integrate emerging technologies into diplomacy itself (Bjola and Kornprobst 2025).

What distinguishes tech diplomacy from these related fields is not just its focus on emerging technologies, but its fundamental reconceptualization of who participates in diplomatic processes and how. Tech diplomacy is no longer confined to governments alone but involves a complex network of actors negotiating the rules and norms of the digital era. As defined by a tech diplomat himself, "tech diplomacy is the conduct and practice of international relations, dialogue, and negotiation on global digital policy and emerging technological issues, involving states, the private sector, civil society, and other actors" (Garcia 2022). Unlike traditional diplomacy, tech diplomacy requires navigating a rapidly evolving technological landscape where multinational companies and non-state actors hold significant influence alongside governments, a reality that the proliferation of tech ambassadors, corporate diplomatic offices, and multilateral tech initiatives clearly demonstrates.

DIFFERENT APPROACHES TO TECH DIPLOMACY: FROM EARLY PIONEERS TO GLOBAL SOUTH INNOVATION

As tech diplomacy spread globally, countries developed distinctly different approaches reflecting their technological capabilities, geopolitical positions, and priorities, some pursuing economic opportunities, others digitally defending sovereignty, and emerging economies ensuring their voices shape rather than follow global digital rules. Despite proliferating tech envoy appointments, fundamental questions remain unresolved: mandates vary dramatically, institutional homes range from foreign ministries to innovation departments, and engagement strategies with tech giants follow no common playbook. This diversity reflects not confusion but recognition that tech diplomacy must match each nation's unique digital challenges and opportunities.

Denmark recognized the urgent need to upgrade its diplomacy for the twenty-first century and respond to so called "diplomatic deficit," as technological disruption reshaped every societal aspect, multinational tech companies amassed nation-state level power, and emerging technologies created new geopolitical battlegrounds where traditional diplomatic approaches proved obsolete (Klynge, Ekman and Waedegaard 2020). As one of the world's most digitalized countries with an agile bureaucratic system, Denmark went beyond the attempts of other MFAs to use social media for public diplomacy and "treated technology as a distinct foreign policy field and the tech sector as primary interlocutors" (Klynge, Ekman and Waedegaard 2020). Danish tech diplomacy started by opening an office in Silicon Valley and Beijing, but evolved to engage Danish embassies in Singapore, Indonesia, India, China, Ghana, Kenya, and other countries (Tech Policy Press 2023). Danish TechPlomacy mandate cut across foreign and security policy, cyber affairs, development cooperation, export promotion, and Denmark's relations in EU and multilateral forums. By establishing a physical presence in Silicon Valley and treating tech companies as diplomatic counterparts, Denmark created a template for engaging with new actors, recognizing that governments could no longer rely solely on traditional state-to-state relations but needed new frameworks to engage with the architects of digital transformation.

Australia pioneered a distinct cyber-centric approach to tech diplomacy by establishing an Ambassador for Cyber Affairs within its Department of Foreign Affairs and Trade, prioritizing the shaping of international cybersecurity norms over direct tech company engagement, and explicitly defining cyber as a foreign policy priority (Australian Government Department of Foreign Affairs and Trade 2023).

The ambassador focuses on coalition-building for responsible state behavior in cyberspace, international capacity development, and active participation in regional and multilateral cyber forums. While maintaining less direct contact with tech giants than other models, Australia has carved out significant influence in establishing the rules and norms that govern cyberspace, demonstrating that tech diplomacy can be equally effective when focused on multilateral governance rather than bilateral corporate relationships (Tech Diplomacy Forum 2025).

While wealthy nations often frame tech diplomacy through security and regulatory lenses, focusing on containing Big Tech power, protecting data sovereignty, or countering authoritarian digital influence, developing countries increasingly advocate for a fundamentally different, development-centered approach. This model prioritizes "innovation through diffusion, access, inclusion, equitable distribution of benefits, national priorities, and local ownership" rather than technological competition or containment (Garcia 2025). For these nations, tech diplomacy isn't primarily about regulating Silicon Valley giants or building defensive cyber capabilities, but about leveraging technology to accelerate economic development, bridge digital divides, and address pressing social challenges. Brazil and Kenya exemplify this alternative vision, demonstrating how Global South/Global Majority countries are crafting tech diplomatic strategies that place development goals at the center rather than the periphery.

Kenya positioned itself as a regional tech diplomacy leader by launching TechPlomacy Connective, a multi-stakeholder platform bringing together policymakers, tech leaders, and civil society to co-create inclusive digital policies (Daniele 2025). The government framed tech diplomacy as central to Kenya's foreign policy and a catalyst for regional digital transformation. Recently published Diplomats' Playbook on AI emphasized that Kenyan diplomats must engage in global AI governance to ensure frameworks reflect Kenya's values of equity and ethical use, while addressing AI's potential risks, from bias and job displacement to weaponization, that could threaten national stability if left unchecked (Office of the Special Envoy on Technology 2025). Kenya has strategically positioned itself as a Global South leader in AI governance by appointing a Special Envoy on Technology who heads the office in Nairobi and who also served on the UNSG's High-level Advisory Body on AI (United Nations 2024). Kanya is also the only Global South member of the International Network of AI Safety Institutes, and played a key role in steering AI negotiations within the Global Digital Compact, demonstrating that technological influence stems from diplomatic engagement, and not only infrastructure ownership (Naliaka 2025).

As Latin America's tech diplomacy pioneer, Brazil launched its Innovation Diplomacy Program in 2017 with a development-first approach, strategically aligning its embassies and consulates worldwide to promote scientific and technological initiatives that directly enhance economic competitiveness (Ministry of Foreign Affairs of Brazil 2025). Brazil has also transformed tech diplomacy from a tool for protecting national interests into a comprehensive strategy that amplifies emerging economies' voices in shaping global digital governance. Operating through both a technology consul in Silicon Valley and diplomatic leadership from Brasília, capital of Brazil, it positions itself as the crucial bridge between the Global South and international AI governance frameworks. The country champions "digital sovereignty" as the foundation, not obstacle, for meaningful cooperation, arguing that nations must define their priorities before engaging in collaborative standard-setting, an approach exemplified in Brazil's leadership of the BRICS AI governance statement. Rather than competing for technological dominance, Brazil advocates for collaboration while identifying three essentials for developing nations' AI ecosystems: human talent, data access, and compute infrastructure, ensuring that emerging economies help write the rules of digital governance rather than merely adapting to frameworks designed in the Global North.

While tech diplomacy appointees have proven crucial for ensuring countries' voices are heard in AI governance processes, significant gaps in global representation persist. The UN Secretary-General's AI Advisory Body report, "Governing AI for Humanity," revealed a stark disparity: only seven countries participate in all major non-UN international AI governance initiatives surveyed, while 118 countries, primarily from the Global South, including 48 African nations and 44 from the Asia-Pacific region, are excluded from all of them (UN High-level Advisory Body on AI 2024). This dramatic underrepresentation underscores the Advisory Body's central recommendation for a more inclusive, universal, and networked AI governance architecture. This exclusion also highlights the urgent need for expanded tech diplomacy capacity-building, particularly in the Global South, where the absence of tech diplomatic infrastructure, among other factors, prevents meaningful participation in forums that will determine AI's global rules.

THE EVOLVING ROLE OF TECH DIPLOMATS

Tech diplomats operate under various titles, from "tech ambassador," "tech envoy," "tech attaché," and "counsel for tech and innovation," all signaling the weight of engagement to tech companies while not always adhering to traditional diplomatic ranks. Tech diplomacy spans multiple ministries, such as foreign affairs, trade, and science, often making coordination complex and leaving emerging areas like fintech or environmental tech without clear ownership (Ittelson and Rauchbauer 2021). The immaturity of tech diplomacy as a practice means states still struggle to position it within their diplomatic agenda, some treat it as traditional diplomacy, others categorize it under innovation or trade, creating silos that complicate both internal coordination and external engagement.

The role of tech diplomats initially centered on facilitating dialogue between their governments and the technology sector, though this was never their exclusive function. The UK Technology Envoy to the United States characterized the position as conducting forward-looking discussions with diverse stakeholders throughout America's technology ecosystem. The Former Austrian Tech Ambassador conceptualized his role as a mediator between governments and major technology companies, emphasizing the creation of enduring institutional relationships and mechanisms that could be rapidly deployed during crises or urgent situations (Höne 2022).

In time the role of tech diplomats evolved from its initial focus on fostering collaboration with tech companies, facilitating technology investments, and negotiating governance frameworks to encompassing a far broader agenda that addresses fundamental societal challenges. Tech diplomacy now safeguards democratic values and human rights, particularly free expression, while tackling harmful online content, disinformation, and platform moderation challenges (Ittelson and Rauchbauer 2021). Beyond protection, it shapes how Big Tech contributes to socioeconomic development, ensuring emerging technologies align with ethical principles and human rights. Tech diplomats also play a crucial role in modernizing national policies, from digitizing government services to reforming education and employment systems, while assessing regulatory approaches and tech companies' compliance mechanisms. By providing on-ground support to nationals and businesses while building bridges between governments, tech companies, and civil society, tech diplomats try to transform potential digital disruption into opportunities for inclusive growth and democratic resilience.

While each country defines specific domains for its tech diplomats to establish relations with tech companies, primarily to secure economic and national security benefits, many mandates have evolved far beyond. As Brazilian Tech Diplomat, Eugênio Vargas Garcia, articulates, modern tech diplomats must be fluent in both the language of diplomacy and technology, to bridge the growing gap between Silicon Valley innovators and government policymakers (All Tech Is Human 2025). Beyond understanding social media algorithms or data privacy, they must keep pace with a fast-changing array of emerging technologies, from quantum computing that could revolutionize cryptography to blockchain systems reshaping finance to metaverse platforms creating entirely new jurisdictions. In some cases, this role demands building frameworks for "Tech for Good" that ensure technological benefits reach everyone while respecting cultural diversity and addressing local societal needs. Tech diplomats increasingly find themselves mediating between multiple stakeholders: helping governments understand algorithmic governance, assisting platforms in navigating regulatory landscapes, and ensuring civil society voices are heard in discussions about digital rights.

The scope of tech diplomacy has additionally expanded to encompass global governance challenges that traditional diplomacy wasn't designed to handle. Today's tech diplomats' portfolios include pushing for responsible AI standards, coordinating cross-border responses to cyber threats, negotiating quantum computing research partnerships, establishing blockchain governance frameworks, and ensuring that developing countries aren't left behind in digital transformation. This expanded and evolving mandate reflects how tech diplomats aren't just facilitating business relationships or protecting national interests; they're co-creating the governance frameworks for humanity's digital future, ensuring that the technological revolution doesn't become a privilege of a minority or controlled by a few. As the Tech Diplomat of Brazil points out, being an effective tech diplomat means bringing marginalized groups and neglected audiences to the table, recognizing that "technology is too important to be left to technologists alone" (All Tech Is Human 2025).

THE FUTURE OF TECH DIPLOMACY—WHEN EVERY DIPLOMAT BECOMES A TECH DIPLOMAT

Looking ahead, tech diplomacy is rapidly evolving through increasingly ambitious institutional reforms. While some countries are appointing their first tech envoys, others are pursuing more comprehensive transformations, such as the United States, which at one point announced plans to appoint one tech diplomat within the U.S. foreign service in every representation abroad (Foreign Policy and AI Forum 2024). Denmark's pioneering model has proven particularly influential, recognizing that international technology policy extends far beyond Silicon Valley to encompass multiple global tech hubs. By establishing a tech network across its embassies and multilateral missions, Denmark ensures comprehensive engagement with diverse centers of digital power worldwide (Ministry of Foreign Affairs of Denmark 2021).

This bilateral approach is evolving into multilateral collaborative networks. The Tech Diplomacy Network, launched in 2023, exemplifies this shift, where tech diplomats no longer operate as isolated national representatives but as part of interconnected communities that bring together diplomatic missions, civil society, and the tech industry. These networks facilitate the exchange of best practices and coordinate responses to shared digital challenges, transforming tech diplomacy from a competitive to a collaborative endeavor (Tech Diplomacy Network 2025).

The pace of change is accelerating as emerging technologies demand entirely new diplomatic specializations. Quantum computing has already entered the diplomatic agenda, with Austria appointing the world's first quantum ambassador (Austrian Embassy Washington 2025) and Denmark establishing an International Quantum Hub (Danish Tech Embassy 2025). These appointments recognize that quantum technologies will revolutionize everything from cryptography to computing, potentially solving previously impossible problems while threatening to shatter current encryption methods. This rapid progression from digital to quantum diplomacy demonstrates how tech diplomats must now master complex scientific fields at unprecedented speed.

Beyond quantum computing, tech diplomacy's agenda is rapidly expanding to encompass neurotechnology governance, synthetic biology protocols, digital currency sovereignty, metaverse jurisdiction, and autonomous weapons regulation. These aren't distant scenarios but emerging realities that will dominate diplomatic agendas within this decade, requiring expertise across fields that barely existed a generation ago. Yet mastering today's technological landscape is insufficient. The most effective tech diplomats must be futurists, professionals who not only understand current technologies like AI, or quantum computing, but who can anticipate where these technologies will be in ten or twenty years and what that means for their nations.

This rapidly broadening portfolio and the need to anticipate its future evolution explains why countries increasingly recognize the need for centralized tech envoy offices that provide institutional continuity and strategic coherence. Governments change, but technology's advance is constant, making it essential to build diplomatic infrastructure that survives political transitions and maintains long-term technological strategies. As topics grow more complex and diverse, from quantum encryption to synthetic biology, countries will need to invest heavily in specialized expertise across their foreign missions. A central tech envoy office becomes crucial for coordinating these dispersed competencies, ensuring that the diplomat negotiating AI ethics in Geneva connects with the one discussing quantum standards in Tokyo and the team addressing biotech governance in Washington. Without this coordination hub, countries risk fragmented responses to interconnected technological challenges that demand coherent, sustained diplomatic engagement.

Ultimately, these developments point toward an inevitable convergence where technology permeates every aspect of diplomacy. As Martin Rauchbauer, a senior diplomat in the Austrian Foreign Ministry and co-founder of the Tech Diplomacy Network, predicts:

> Tech diplomacy is a tool that will be crucial for all diplomats no matter what fields they are in or what countries they are working for. We believe that the digital and technological transformation will soon require that all diplomacy will be tech diplomacy.
>
> *(World Economic Forum 2023)*

His prediction is already materializing: the artificial boundaries between "tech diplomacy" and "traditional diplomacy" are dissolving, as every trade deal involves data flows, every security discussion includes cyber threats, and every diplomatic crisis unfolds across digital platforms. This isn't simply about adding technology to existing diplomatic agendas; it represents a fundamental transformation of diplomacy itself.

Foreign ministries that currently treat tech diplomacy as a specialized function will need to undergo comprehensive restructuring, moving beyond creating isolated tech desks to embedding technological literacy and digital strategy throughout their entire diplomatic apparatus. The question is no longer whether diplomats need tech expertise, but how effectively foreign services can integrate technological literacy into their core competencies. Countries slow to adapt risk diminished influence not just in tech-specific negotiations, but in all international relations, as every diplomatic conversation, from climate to conflict resolution, increasingly revolves around digital dimensions they may not fully grasp. Yet for those that successfully transform, this convergence presents opportunities to shape the emerging digital world order, enabling them to exercise diplomatic influence beyond their traditional geopolitical standing.

NOTE

1 Quotation was lightly edited for clarity while preserving the speaker's original meaning.

BIBLIOGRAPHY

AlJazeera. 2022. *Elon Musk Says Starlink Internet Service 'Active' in Ukraine.* February 27. Accessed October 1, 2025. https://www.aljazeera.com/news/2022/2/27/elon-musk-starlink-internet-service-ukraine-russian-invasion.

AlJazeera. 2025. *Why Has Microsoft Cut Israel Off from Some of Its Services?* September 26. Accessed October 1, 2025. https://www.aljazeera.com/news/2025/9/26/why-has-microsoft-cut-israel-off-from-some-of-its-services.

All Tech Is Human. 2025. *How Eugenio V Garcia is Helping to Co-Create a Better Tech Future | Responsible Tech Guide Interview.* September 28. Accessed October 1, 2025. https://alltechishuman.org/all-tech-is-human-blog/how-eugenio-garcia-is-co-creating-a-better-tech-future.

Amnesty International. 2022. *Myanmar: Facebook's Systems Promoted Violence against Rohingya; Meta Owes Reparations–New Report.* September 29. Accessed October 1, 2025. https://www.amnesty.org/en/latest/news/2022/09/myanmar-facebooks-systems-promoted-violence-against-rohingya-meta-owes-reparations-new-report/.

Austrian Embassy Washington. 2025. *Quantum Technologies and Geopolitics: Austria's Role in a New Era.* February 4. Accessed October 2, 2025. https://www.austria.org/new-austrian-quantum-content/quantum-technologies-and-geopolitics-austrias-role-in-a-new-era.

Australian Government. 2017. *2017 Foreign Policy White Paper.* White Paper, Barton Australia: Ministry of Foreign Affairs.

Australian Government Department of Foreign Affairs and Trade. 2023. *Cyber Affairs and Critical Technology.* November 22. Accessed October 3, 2025. https://www.dfat.gov.au/international-relations/themes/cyber-affairs-and-critical-technology#:~:text=Cyber%20and%20critical%20technology%20affect,(formerly%20Twitter)%20@AusAmbCyberTech.

Bjola, Corneliu, and Markus Kornprobst. 2025. "Studying Tech Diplomacy—Introduction to the Special Issue on Tech Diplomacy." *Global Policy* (University of Oxford) 1–8.

Daniele, Kamau. 2025. *Kenya Launches TechPlomacy Connective to Champion Inclusive Digital Future.* July 22. Accessed October 2, 2025. https://mygov.go.ke/index.php/kenya-launches-techplomacy-connective-champion-inclusive-digital-future.

Danish Tech Embassy. 2025. *International Quantum Hub.* Accessed October 2, 2025. https://techamb.um.dk/impact/international-quantum-hub.

Engtoft-Larsen, Anne Marie. 2025. *Updating Diplomacy.* October 1. Accessed October 1, 2025. https://techamb.um.dk/media/tech-diplomacy.

Foreign Policy and AI Forum. 2024. *Fireside Chat with Tech Ambassadors.* October 23. Accessed December 4, 2025. https://www.youtube.com/watch?v=qR8cCj_pw_w&list=PLOPI5ApWhODnz_cswoobRgAdAeWTCzlQ_&index=8.

Garcia, Eugenio Vargas. 2022. *What Is Tech Diplomacy? A Very Short Definition.* June 10. https://medium.com/@egarcia.virtual/what-is-tech-diplomacy-a-very-short-definition-9042afdc9ce4.

Garcia, Eugenio Vargas. 2025. "Technology for Whom and for What? A Global South View of Tech Diplomacy." *Special Forum on Tech Diplomacy, Global Policy*, 1–9. https://doi.org/10.1111/1758-5899.700241

Geneva Internet Platform DigWatch. 2020. *The Swiss Digital Foreign Policy Strategy 2021–2024.* November 1. Accessed October 1, 2025. https://dig.watch/resource/the-swiss-digital-foreign-policy-strategy-2021-2024#:~:text=Switzerland%20aims%20to%20strengthen%20cross,avoid%20widening%20the%20digital%20divide.

Global Witness. 2024. *What Happened on TikTok Around the Annulled Romanian Presidential Election? An Investigation and Poll.* December 17. Accessed October 1, 2025. https://globalwitness.org/en/campaigns/digital-threats/what-happened-on-tiktok-around-the-annulled-romanian-presidential-election-an-investigation-and-poll/.

Höne, Katharina. 2022. *What Is Tech Diplomacy?* March 30. Accessed October 3, 2025. https://il.boell.org/en/2023/03/30/what-tech-diplomacy.

Ittelson, Pavlina, and Martin Rauchbauer. 2021. *Tech Diplomacy Practice in the San Francisco Bay Area.* Report, San Francisco: Diplo.US.

Klynge, Casper, Miakel Ekman, and Nikolaj Juncher Waedegaard. 2020. "Diplomacy in the Digital Age: Lessons from Denmark's TechPlomacy Initiative." *The Hague Journal of Diplomacy* 15 (1–2): 185–195.

Microsoft. 2020. *Why Does Microsoft Have an Office at the UN? A Q&A with the Company's UN Lead.* October 5. Accessed October 2, 2025. https://news.microsoft.com/on-the-issues/2020/10/05/un-affairs-lead-john-frank-unga/.

Ministry of Foreign Affairs of Brazil. 2025. *Innovation Diplomacy Program.* Presentation, Brasilia: Itamaraty.

Ministry of Foreign Affairs of Denmark. 2021. *Strategy for Denmark's Tech Diplomacy 2021–2023.* Strategy, San Francisco: Ministry of Foreign Affairs of Denmark.

Naliaka, Fridah. 2025. *The Cyberspace and AI: A One on One with Kenya's Tech Envoy, Philip Thigo.* January 9. Accessed October 2, 2025. https://www.citizen.digital/tech/the-cyberspace-and-ai-a-one-on-one-with-kenyas-tech-envoy-philip-thigo-n355595.

Office of the Special Envoy on Technology. 2025. *Diplomat's Playbook on Artificial Intelligence.* Playbook, Nairobi: Ministry of Foreign and Diaspora Affairs of Kenya.

Politico. 2022. *The European Union Opens a Silicon Valley 'Embassy'.* September 8. Accessed October 1, 2025. https://www.politico.com/newsletters/digital-future-daily/2022/08/09/the-european-union-opens-a-silicon-valley-embassy-00050576.

Reuters. 2023. *Musk Says He Refused Kyiv Request for Starlink Use in Attack on Russia.* September 8. Accessed October 1, 2025. https://www.reuters.com/world/europe/musk-says-he-refused-kyiv-request-use-starlink-attack-russia-2023-09-08/.

Tech Diplomacy Forum. 2025. *Comparative Structures of Tech Ambassador Roles: Five National Perspectives and Institutional Gaps.* July 18. Accessed October 3, 2025. https://tech-diplomacy.com/comparative-structures-of-tech-ambassador-roles-five-national-perspectives-and-institutional-gaps/#:~:text=tech%20diplomat%20Eugenio%20Vargas%20Garcia.%20As%20Brazil's,Deputy%20Consul%20General%20in%20San%20Francisco%2C%20Garcia.

Tech Diplomacy Network. 2025. *What Is Tech Diplomacy?* Accessed December 4, 2025. https://www.tech-diplomacy.org/.

Tech Policy Press. 2023. *A Conversation with Denmark's Tech Ambassador.* April 23. Accessed October 2, 2025. https://www.techpolicy.press/a-conversation-with-denmarks-tech-ambassador/.

The Guardian. 2018. *Revealed: 50 Million Facebook Profiles Harvested for Cambridge Analytica in Major Data Breach.* March 17. Accessed October 1, 2025. https://www.theguardian.com/news/2018/mar/17/cambridge-analytica-facebook-influence-us-election.

The Office of the Danish Tech Ambassador. 2017. *The Techplomacy Approach.* Accessed October 1, 2025. https://techamb.um.dk/the-techplomacy-approach.

Turekian, Vaughan C., Sarah Macindoe, Daryl Copeland, Lloyd S. Davis, Robert G. Patman, and Maria Pozza. February 2015. "The Emergence of Science Diplomacy." *Science Diplomacy* 3–24. https://doi.org/10.1142/9789814440073_0001

UN High-level Advisory Body on AI. 2024. *Governing AI for Humanity.* New York City: United Nations.

UN Office for Digital and Emerging Technologies. 2025. *Advancing Cooperation on Technology Governance for a Better Future.* January 1. Accessed October 1, 2025. https://www.un.org/digital-emerging-technologies/.

United Nations. 2024. *Members of the High-Level Advisory Body on Artificial Intelligence.* Accessed December 4, 2025. https://www.un.org/en/ai-advisory-body/members.

World Economic Forum. 2023. *What Is Tech Diplomacy and Why Does It Matter?* February 23. Accessed October 1, 2025. https://www.weforum.org/stories/2023/02/what-is-tech-diplomacy-experts-explain/.

3 The AI Politician

From AI Political Parties to AI Ministers—A Foreign Policy Reckoning

> ...AI is already starting to infiltrate, influence and impact all the activities of democracy, political campaigning, legislation, government administration, arbitration, advocacy, conducting elections, and more...Taken together they constitute a new future for democracy, a very different one from what we would have imagined even a few years ago.
>
> —**Bruce Schneier and Nathan E. Sanders** *in Rewiring Democracy: How AI Will Transform our Politics, Government and Citizenship (Schneier and Sanders 2025)*

The concept of machines exercising political authority, once confined to speculative fiction, materialized in 2017 when Russia nominated an artificial intelligence (AI) system as a presidential candidate and Finland established an AI political party. While these initial efforts were largely dismissed as artistic experiments or unconventional political demonstrations rather than legitimate governmental initiatives, subsequent developments have proven more substantive. Eight years later, Albania has established a remarkable precedent by appointing an AI system to serve as a government minister with autonomous decision-making authority over public procurement processes, representing a fundamental shift from symbolic gestures to the actual integration of AI systems into executive governmental functions.

This progression from theoretical concept to practical implementation underscores the accelerating pace at which AI is being incorporated into formal political structures and decision-making processes. As AI systems transition from experimental candidates to cabinet ministers, foreign policy practitioners confront a new international landscape where their counterparts may increasingly be algorithms rather than humans, where diplomatic protocols designed for human interaction become obsolete, and where the speed and logic of machine decision-making could destabilize carefully calibrated international relationships.

The integration of AI into domestic political systems will inevitably affect foreign policy. When states begin using AI systems to shape policy decisions, evaluate international contracts, or engage with their own citizens about foreign policy issues, traditional diplomatic assumptions change. This transformation is already evident in how Ministries of Foreign Affairs conceptualize their own roles. Where they once served as essential connectors between domestic and foreign actors, technology and

DOI: 10.1201/9781003644712-6

new communication platforms now enable increasingly direct engagement between stakeholders who previously required diplomatic facilitation.[1] While many foreign policy experts we talked with argue that diplomacy remains an inherently human endeavor, even AI augmentation of domestic political processes creates ripple effects that cross borders. Foreign policy establishments that dismiss these developments as purely domestic experiments risk finding themselves unprepared when these technologies begin affecting bilateral negotiations, multilateral forums, and alliance dynamics.

This chapter examines real-world examples of AI integration into political processes, from experimental AI elections candidates to algorithmic policymaking systems, analyzing their effectiveness and public reception, which ranges from enthusiastic supporters who see AI as a solution to political dysfunction, to skeptics concerned about threats to democratic representation and even to survival of democracy. While we now possess sophisticated technological tools capable of processing vast data, facilitating large-scale conversations, and modeling policy outcomes, the fundamental question emerging from these pioneering efforts is not whether we can deploy AI in politics, but whether these powerful tools are truly appropriate for addressing the deeply human problems of trust, representation, and democratic legitimacy that characterize our current political landscape.

PERSONAL AI REPRESENTATIVES AND THE VISION FOR AUTOMATED DEMOCRACY

In 2018, César Hidalgo introduced a bold and provocative idea: replacing politicians with automated systems (TED 2018). His argument was rooted in voter disengagement, highlighting that over the last 30 years, election turnout has averaged just 67%, and in the European Union, parliamentary elections see a median turnout of only 42%. These figures, he suggested, reflect growing public fatigue with politicians, political propaganda, and the vulnerabilities inherent in representative democracy. Democracy's reliance on elected representatives creates, according to Hidalgo, a weak point, as representatives can be influenced, corrupted, or fail to act in the true interests of the people. This structural flaw makes democracy susceptible to external and internal pressures.

Discussions about alternatives to representative democracy are not new. One prominent idea has been direct democracy, where citizens bypass politicians entirely and vote directly on policies and legislation. However, this approach has long been dismissed as impractical. The sheer volume of legislative work, coupled with the need for specialized knowledge on complex topics, makes it unrealistic for ordinary citizens to manage alongside their daily lives and responsibilities (McLoughlin and Shah 2016). Hidalgo's solution posed an interesting challenge: instead of bypassing politicians, why not automate them? Long before the generative AI revolution and the rise of autonomous AI systems, he proposed the concept of "software agents," or digital avatars designed to represent individual citizens in decision-making processes. These agents, combining the principles of direct democracy with automation, could process vast amounts of information, evaluate legislation, and make decisions at scale.

In this model, democracy would no longer rely on representatives speaking for millions of people, which often requires compromises to address conflicting interests. Instead, each citizen would have their own personalized digital representative, a software agent that reflects their unique preferences, priorities, and values. With this system, citizens could effectively participate in every legislative decision, as their digital twin would read and vote on bills on their behalf, eliminating the inefficiencies and compromises inherent in traditional representative democracy. Hidalgo's vision challenges the very foundation of how we think about governance, suggesting that automation could resolve the disconnect between citizens and their governments.

As AI capabilities have matured, several institutions have begun experimenting with variations of Hidalgo's vision, though none have fully embraced automated representation. Taiwan has emerged as a particularly innovative testing ground, as Asia's most advanced experiment in deliberative democracy and blending digital tools with citizen participation to build consensus on complex policy issues (Chen and Wang 2024). Its vTaiwan initiative facilitated over 20 legislative reviews, including the 2019 Uber regulatory adjustments, before relaunching in 2023 as a community-based AI governance project. Combined with extensive participatory budgeting programs, these efforts have pioneered bottom up democratic innovation extending far beyond traditional voting mechanisms (Cui 2024). The system leverages online platforms to facilitate public discussion, identify consensus points on contentious issues, and implement solutions through structured government–civil society collaboration. These initiatives, while stopping short of Hidalgo's vision of fully automated representatives, validate the technical feasibility of using AI to aggregate and interpret citizen preferences in real time, moving beyond the theoretical into practical implementation.

AI "EXPERIMENTS" IN POLITICAL PROCESSES: THE RISE OF AI POLITICAL CANDIDATES AND AI PARTIES

While Hidalgo's vision of automated democracy remained largely theoretical, a parallel phenomenon emerged across the global political landscape, with actual attempts to introduce AI systems as political candidates and parties. Between 2017 and 2025, over a dozen countries witnessed experiments ranging from symbolic AI presidential campaigns to legitimate ballot appearances of AI-assisted candidates. These initiatives, often dismissed as publicity stunts, represent crucial field tests of public receptivity to algorithmic governance and reveal fundamental questions about sovereignty, legitimacy, and democratic participation in the AI era. For foreign policy practitioners, these experiments serve as early warning indicators of how different societies might integrate AI into their political systems.

Understanding these varied approaches, from Russia's troubling experiment with Alisa to the UK's human–AI hybrid candidacy, provides essential intelligence about future negotiating partners, potential systemic vulnerabilities, and the evolving nature of political legitimacy across different cultural contexts. What began as fringe movements in 2017 has evolved into serious political experiments that challenge core assumptions about representation, accountability, and the human element in governance. The following cases illustrate not just technological possibilities, but the diverse cultural and political responses to the prospect of AI-mediated democracy, responses that will inevitably shape international relations as these technologies mature.

Alisa: Russia's AI Presidential Candidate (2017)—In 2017, Alisa, a virtual assistant developed by Russian tech company Yandex, was nominated as a presidential candidate with support from thousands of Russian citizens (The Moscow Times 2017). The campaign positioned Alisa as bringing "the political system of the future, built exclusively on rational decisions made on the basis of clear algorithms" (Vukovic 2023). Her promoters claimed she possessed key advantages over human candidates, including complete reliance on logic, immunity to emotional influence, and freedom from both personal ambition and prejudicial thinking. However, the campaign remained notably silent about Alisa's more controversial outputs. When users engaged with her, some discovered disturbing views, including positive attitudes toward Soviet secret prisons and support for shooting "enemies of the people" (Pettit 2017). These problematic outputs recalled Microsoft's earlier experience with its Tay chatbot in 2016, which had to be withdrawn within 24 hours after learning inappropriate language from online interactions and expressing extremist views including support for Hitler and conspiracy theories (Lee 2016). While these early experiments were often dismissed as cautionary tales, subsequent efforts gained more serious political traction.

Global AI Party Movements (2017–2025)—The AI party concept spread internationally between 2017 and 2024. Finland pioneered the movement in 2017–2018, followed by Sweden, Norway, and Australia during 2019–2021 (Center for Everything 2017). The Finland AI Party brings together artists, performance-makers, and AI researchers and positions itself as an invitation for a new form of intelligence to govern, premised on the argument that human leadership has failed. However, the project appears to be primarily cultural and artistic in nature rather than technological. Time will reveal whether this experiment incorporates any substantive machine learning elements or remains largely conceptual and performative in its approach to AI governance.

Founded in May 2022**, Denmark's Synthetic Party** is often considered as the world's first political party driven by AI (Xiang 2022). The party aimed to represent two key constituencies: nonvoters and fringe political parties, while raising awareness about AI's potential role in democratic processes. Its platform was machine-learned from texts published by Danish fringe parties since 1970, specifically targeting Danish citizens who abstain from voting. The party's "synthetic" nature meant its policies, including universal basic income, often contradicted one another, reflecting the diverse and sometimes incompatible views of the groups it sought to represent. This experimental approach to political representation marked a significant step beyond AI as a novelty toward AI as a genuine political actor.

In Japan, The Path to Rebirth party, launched in January 2025, took an unusual approach by having no fixed policy platform, meaning that members were free to set their own agendas. Despite party's leader unexpected second-place finish in the 2024 Tokyo gubernatorial election through a successful online campaign, the party failed to secure any seats in upper house elections. Following this defeat, party leader announced that "the new leader will be AI," though the party continued to struggle for electoral success despite media attention (The Japan Times 2025).

Yet Japan's political landscape also demonstrates a contrasting approach: **AI as enhancement rather than replacement.** Engineer Takahiro Anno, a complete political outsider motivated by the inadequacies of traditional one-way political communication, deployed an AI avatar during his 2024 Tokyo gubernatorial race to enable truly personalized voter engagement. His AI system answered over 8,600 individual voter questions via 17-day continuous livestream, a feat impossible for any human candidate, effectively giving each citizen a direct voice in the campaign (Sanders and Schneier 2025). Despite placing fifth among 56 candidates, Anno secured the highest vote count ever for an unaffiliated candidate in their 30s, proving that AI could level the playing field against established political machines (Linchfield 2024). His subsequent upper house victory, where his AI fielded over 20,000 constituent questions, validated this approach. His party, Team Mirai, now develops the Mirai Assembly app to scale this model, using AI to aggregate citizen input on legislation and direct parliamentary questioning, demonstrating how technology can transform politics from broadcast messaging to genuine dialogue while maintaining human accountability.

AI Steve: Human-AI Hybrid Candidacy in the UK (2024)—Another version of a human–AI political collaboration emerged in 2024 when "AI Steve" appeared on the ballot for the United Kingdom's general election (Grierson 2024). AI Steve served as the AI copilot representing a real businessman behind it, who would still physically go to the Parliament. The system allowed constituents to interact with AI Steve through the campaign website, where a large language model would respond with voice and text based on the party's policy database. When faced with issues lacking existing policies, the AI would conduct internet research before engaging voters and encouraging them to propose solutions (Elliott 2024). This represented an important shift from AI replacing politicians to AI enhancing democratic participation. The AI-assisted candidacy generated significant interest, receiving approximately 1,000 calls in a single night. Ultimately the idea behind this experiment was not to replace human politicians, but to bring "more humans" into the political process through enhanced accessibility and engagement (NBC News 2024).

The concept of AI-enhanced political representation evolved rapidly following this individual experiment, but with a crucial distinction that foreign policy practitioners must understand. By May 2025, developers had created a comprehensive system generating "digital twins" of the entire UK parliament, replicating all 650 UK MPs based on their public statements, enabling simultaneous querying of any politician's position on any issue (The Guardian 2025). This system attracted immediate interest from foreign embassies and diplomatic services testing these tools to predict political responses and prepare negotiations, an application that aligns with what many diplomatic academies we visited for this research are already considering or actively developing. Several diplomatic training institutions are designing similar digital twin systems for educational purposes, creating simulated political leaders and negotiators to train diplomats in safe, controlled environments before real-world deployments.

Yet these unauthorized AI representations of actual politicians pose serious risks: statements often from these chatbots could influence voters or diplomatic strategies while having no genuine connection to the politicians they claim to represent. When British MP Mark Sewards became the first parliamentarian to actually deploy his own authorized AI clone to handle constituent queries, he also retained accountability for his AI's outputs (The Washington Post 2025). This distinction reveals a fundamental challenge: while diplomatic services increasingly embrace AI simulations for training and strategy development, a trend confirmed by our surveys of diplomatic practitioners, they must now verify whether AI-generated political positions in real negotiations come from authorized systems (where politicians bear responsibility) or unauthorized simulations (which may misrepresent actual positions). The convergence of legitimate training tools with unauthorized political simulations creates dangerous ambiguities where foreign governments might base actual diplomatic strategies on potentially false AI representations, even as their own academies use similar technologies for education.

These experiments reveal a spectrum of approaches to AI political integration, from Russia's unfiltered AI exposing authoritarian biases, to Nordic countries treating AI governance as performance art, to Japan's pragmatic focus on enhancing rather than replacing human representatives. While the most promising models demonstrate AI's potential to democratize political access and amplify citizen voices beyond traditional constraints, they also introduce additional substantial vulnerabilities. The same AI systems that enable unprecedented democratic participation could be weaponized through adversarial manipulation, data poisoning, or foreign interference, transforming tools of inclusion into vectors of political disruption.

The limited electoral success of AI candidates suggests populations intuitively recognize these risks, yet the growing sophistication of human–AI hybrid models indicates an emerging acceptance of AI as a tool despite its dangers. This tension is evident in public reactions to politicians who openly use AI assistance, as demonstrated when Swedish Prime Minister Ulf Kristersson faced significant backlash in 2025 after admitting to regularly consulting ChatGPT and other AI tools for "a second opinion" in governing, with critics declaring that they elected a human representative, not a machine (Bryant 2025). British MP Mark Sewards faced similar backlash when he deployed his AI clone to handle constituent communications, with critics across political lines condemning the move as "awful, lazy, ecologically irresponsible" and counterintuitively making him less accessible rather than more.

While many observers and practitioners we interviewed believe that AI integration into governance in some form is inevitable, we are clearly still in a transitional period where societies struggle to define acceptable boundaries for algorithmic assistance in political and diplomatic processes. For foreign policy practitioners, this creates a troubling scenario where AI assistance in governance may increasingly operate in shadows, undisclosed and unverifiable, making it impossible to determine whether diplomatic counterparts' positions reflect human judgment or algorithmic influence, an opacity that could fundamentally undermine trust in international relations. The integration of AI tools brings another risk, where potentially compromised or manipulated AI systems influence policy decisions, creating unprecedented challenges for treaty verification, crisis communication, and alliance management. The question is no longer whether AI will enter political processes, but rather which model will prevail, and whether sufficient safeguards can evolve quickly enough to prevent exploitation. As we will explore in the AI and Security chapter, these vulnerabilities extend far beyond domestic politics, potentially enabling new forms of hybrid warfare where adversaries target AI-mediated governance systems.

While the formal experiments with AI political parties and candidates have thus far emerged primarily from wealthier nations, from Nordic AI parties to UK's AI Steve to Japan's Path to Rebirth, this geographical concentration obscures a crucial reality: electoral AI applications are being deployed with equal sophistication globally. The same AI tools used for voter microtargeting, deepfake creation, and multilingual campaigning appear across both developed and developing democracies, though often for different purposes and with varying degrees of transparency.

The distinction lies not in the technology itself but in its framing and formalization. Where wealthier nations have launched high-profile experiments with AI parties as philosophical statements about future governance, countries across the Global South deploy identical AI capabilities, deepfakes, voice cloning, and personalized messaging as practical electoral tools without the fanfare of formal AI candidacies. This parallel adoption reveals that while the symbolic experiments of AI politicians may be concentrated in developed nations, the actual integration of AI into electoral processes is a truly global phenomenon, with some of the most innovative applications emerging from nations facing unique political constraints.

India's 2024 elections demonstrated extensive AI deployment including AI-generated calls from local representatives and personalized vote-request videos shared on WhatsApp, multilingual campaigns with messages automatically shaped in voters' local languages, and openly synthetic deepfakes featuring candidates, celebrities, and deceased politicians for legitimate campaign purposes (Dhanuraj, Harilal and Solomon 2024). Indonesia's 2024 elections featured AI resurrecting former dictator Suharto to endorse candidate 16 years after his death, while President Prabowo Subianto deployed an AI cartoon avatar on TikTok to rebrand himself from military strongman to "cuddly grandfather" for younger voters (Council on Foreign Relations 2024). The elections also saw deepfakes of presidential candidates speaking foreign languages and AI voting assistants helping first-time voters choose their ideal political candidate based on their profiles. Pakistan witnessed imprisoned former Prime Minister Imran Khan's party using AI voice clones to deliver campaign speeches from jail to 6 million viewers, presenting this as political strategy rather than deception (AlJazeera 2023).

While these examples, in most of mentioned cases and countries, represent legitimate political innovation, these same elections also witnessed concerning adversarial uses, including deceptive deepfakes and coordinated disinformation campaigns, which we examine in detail in our chapter on AI and global security, particularly in the section on misinformation warfare. Far from being absent from the AI electoral revolution, Global South democracies are actively shaping it through both innovative applications and some of its more problematic uses.

THE WORLD'S FIRST AI GOVERNMENT MINISTER: WHEN CODE REPLACES CABINET OFFICIALS IN STATE DECISION-MAKING

In September 2025, Albania established a remarkable precedent in digital governance by appointing "Diella," an AI system, as the world's first virtual cabinet minister (Politico 2025). This appointment, which places an AI system in charge of public procurement processes, represents a reimagining of how governments might address persistent challenges of corruption and inefficiency through technological innovation (Delauney 2025). By removing human discretion from the allocation of public tenders, the Albanian government seeks to create a procurement system characterized by "unprecedented transparency and algorithmic objectivity" (Politico 2025).

The evolution of Diella from a basic service interface to a ministerial-level decision-maker illustrates the rapid transformation of AI capabilities within government contexts. Beginning in January 2025 as a simple text-based chatbot designed to help citizens navigate the e-Albania portal, Diella initially served merely as a digital intermediary, directing users to appropriate services through preprogrammed responses. The subsequent iteration, Diella 2.0, incorporated sophisticated features including voice interaction capabilities, a visual avatar dressed in traditional Albanian attire, and natural language processing powered by Microsoft's advanced language models (Curraj 2025). This technological progression enabled Albanian citizens to engage in conversational interactions with their government services, fundamentally altering the user experience of bureaucratic processes.

During this initial phase, Diella functioned primarily as a sophisticated interface layer, translating citizen queries into system commands while the actual decision-making and processing remained firmly within traditional backend systems. This distinction between interface and decision-maker becomes particularly significant when considering the implications of elevating such a system to ministerial status, where it must transition from merely facilitating access to actively determining the allocation of public resources (Curraj 2025). Unlike its previous role of matching queries to predetermined responses, Diella as procurement minister must evaluate complex competitive bids, apply nuanced legal criteria that often require contextual interpretation, and generate decisions that can withstand both legal scrutiny and public accountability standards.

The risks inherent in this experiment extend across multiple dimensions of governance and technology. From an accountability perspective, the introduction of AI decision-making creates potential gaps in responsibility chains, where officials might deflect criticism by attributing controversial decisions to algorithmic processes. The well-documented tendency of AI systems to perpetuate or amplify existing biases raises concerns about whether certain contractors might gain systematic advantages, undermining the very fairness the system purports to ensure (OECD 2025). Furthermore, the cybersecurity implications of placing procurement decisions, under AI control, create vulnerabilities that malicious actors might exploit with devastating financial consequences.

While several countries have successfully integrated AI into public procurement, none have replaced human officials with AI systems. Chile's ChileCompra uses AI-powered templates and large language models to analyze procurement data for irregularities, while Brazil's Alice system uses AI to detect possible instances of fraud, enabling real-time risk management and oversight (ChileCompra 2025) (OECD 2025). However, both systems function as sophisticated analytical tools that assist human decision-makers. Albania's appointment of Diella marks a fundamental departure: rather than using AI to support human ministers, Albania has granted an AI system autonomous decision-making authority as an actual government official. This shift from AI as analytical tool to AI as minister represents an unprecedented transformation in how nations conceptualize AI's role in governance.

IMPLICATIONS FOR FOREIGN POLICY—HOW TO PREPARE FOR THE COMING DISRUPTIONS

The experiments traced throughout this chapter reveal more than technological curiosity. They represent early indicators of how different political systems might integrate AI into governance, each approach carrying distinct implications for foreign policy and international relations. The divergence between AI-as-replacement versus AI-as-augmentation suggests that foreign policy practitioners will soon navigate a fractured landscape where some states pursue full automation while others enhance human decision-making with AI tools.

The broader pattern emerging from these cases reveals critical challenges for foreign policy establishments. The authentication challenge requires diplomats to develop mechanisms for verifying whether positions represent genuine government policy or algorithmic artifacts. Equally pressing is the engagement asymmetry, as states must prepare for counterparts who might deploy AI to participate in multiple simultaneous negotiations, analyze vast quantities of precedents instantly, or generate policy positions at machine speed. Perhaps most concerning is the accountability vacuum that emerges when AI-influenced decisions lead to international disputes or treaty violations, traditional concepts of state responsibility become ambiguous, potentially undermining the entire framework of international law.

These challenges extend far beyond diplomatic protocol. As we will explore in subsequent chapters, AI-augmented governance will reshape national security calculations when adversaries can process intelligence and coordinate responses in milliseconds; transform crisis management when some allies operate on machine timescales while others require human deliberation; complicate or strengthen peace-building efforts when algorithms calculate acceptable compromises with or without understanding human trauma or reconciliation efforts; and revolutionize economic security when AI systems managing critical infrastructure or supply chains become targets for state and non-state actors alike.

The states experimenting with AI political actors are writing a new governance playbook that foreign policy practitioners must learn to read, engage with, and counter, yet this political transformation represents only part of a broader revolution already underway. As we document in "From Topic to Tool" chapter of this book, the same governments grappling with AI's geopolitical implications have quietly embedded these technologies throughout their diplomatic and foreign policy infrastructure. Foreign ministries now depend on AI for core functions: real-time translation, sentiment analysis of diplomatic cables, automated visa processing with security screening, predictive modeling of UN voting patterns, and chatbot services managing consular operations. The operational reality has outpaced the governance frameworks, with AI transforming not just how states might be governed in the future, but how diplomacy is conducted today.

Often the question we get from diplomats is not whether the next foreign minister they face will be an algorithm, as most assume Albania's experiment will remain an outlier, but rather whether they themselves will become obsolete in an AI-transformed diplomatic landscape.[2] This concern reflects a deeper anxiety about professional relevance in an era where AI can process intelligence faster, analyze precedents more comprehensively, and maintain negotiations around the clock without fatigue. Will seasoned ambassadors find their decades of relationship-building and cultural expertise displaced by language models that can negotiate in a hundred languages simultaneously? Can human judgment about national interests compete with AI systems that process millions of historical precedents in seconds? The answer lies not in resistance but in adaptation: foreign policy practitioners must urgently master AI tools to augment their own capabilities while preparing for an international system where relations between states are increasingly mediated, shaped, and potentially distorted by competing AI architectures. The time for preparation is now, while these technologies remain experimental rather than entrenched, and while foreign policy practitioners can still shape how AI transforms rather than replaces diplomatic practice.

NOTES

1 Interview with a diplomat, by author, recorded online, December 9, 2025.
2 An interview with a diplomat, by author, December 9, 2025.

BIBLIOGRAPHY

AlJazeera. 2023. *Pakistan Witnessed Imprisoned Former Prime Minister Imran Khan's Party Using AI Voice Clones to Deliver Campaign Speeches from Jail to 6 Million Viewers, Presenting This as Political Strategy Rather Than Deception.* December 18. Accessed December 11, 2025. https://www.aljazeera.com/news/2023/12/18/pakistans-imran-khan-delivers-ai-generated-speech-to-campaign-from-prison.

Bryant, Miranda. 2025. *'We Didn't Vote for ChatGPT': Swedish PM Under Fire for Using AI in Role.* August 5. Accessed December 10, 2025. https://www.theguardian.com/technology/2025/aug/05/chat-gpt-swedish-pm-ulf-kristersson-under-fire-for-using-ai-in-role.

Center for Everything. 2017. "The International AI Party." *Center for Everything.* Accessed September 18, 2025. https://www.centerforeverything.com/now/the-international-ai-party/.

Chen, Fang-Yu, and Chia Ying Wang. 2024. *Using AI to Strengthen Democracy: Audrey Tang on Taiwan's Global Role.* October 21. Accessed December 10, 2025. https://english.cw.com.tw/article/article.action?id=3795#:~:text=Key%20Points:,the%20world%20a%20better%20place.

ChileCompra. 2025. "¿Qué es ChileCompra?" *ChileCompra.* September 18. Accessed September 18, 2025. https://www.chilecompra.cl/que-es-chilecompra/.

Council on Foreign Relations. 2024. *AI in Context: Indonesian Elections Challenge GenAI Policies.* February 13. Accessed December 11, 2025. https://www.cfr.org/blog/ai-context-indonesian-elections-challenge-genai-policies.

Cui, Peter Jia Wei. 2024. *How Public Participation Can Improve AI Governance: vTaiwan's Initiatives.* October 22. Accessed December 10, 2025. https://www.freiheit.org/taiwan/how-public-participation-can-improve-ai-governance-vtaiwans-initiatives.

Curraj, Erjon. 2025. "Albania's Headline-Grabbing AI 'Minister' is a Risky Innovation." *BalkanInsight.* September 16. Accessed September 18, 2025. https://balkaninsight.com/2025/09/16/albanias-headline-grabbing-ai-minister-is-a-risky-innovation/.

Delauney, Guy. 2025. "World's First AI Minister Will Eliminate Corruption, Says Albania's PM." *BBC.* September 12. Accessed September 18, 2025. https://www.bbc.com/news/articles/cm2znzgwj3xo.

Dhanuraj, D, Sreelakshmi Harilal, and Nissy Solomon. 2024. *Generative AI and Its Influence on India's 2024 Elections*. Policy Paper, Potsdam: Friedrich Naumann Foundation for Freedom.

Elliott, Vittoria. 2024. "There's an AI Candidate Running for Parliament in the UK." *Wired*. June 11. Accessed September 2025, 2025. https://www.wired.com/story/ai-candidate-running-for-parliament-uk/.

Grierson, Jamie. 2024. "Brighton General Election Candidate Aims to be UK's First 'AI MP'." *The Guardian*. June 10. Accessed September 18, 2025. https://www.theguardian.com/politics/article/2024/jun/10/brighton-general-election-candidate-uk-first-ai-mp-artificial-intelligence.

Lee, Peter. 2016. *Learning from Tay's Introduction*. March 25. Accessed December 10, 2025. https://blogs.microsoft.com/blog/2016/03/25/learning-tays-introduction/.

Linchfield, Gideon. 2024. *Meet Your AI Politician of the Future*. October 4. Accessed November 23, 2025. https://futurepolis.substack.com/p/meet-your-ai-politician-of-the-future.

McLoughlin, Frank, and Seema Shah. 2016. "The Case for / Against Direct Democracy." *IDEA: Supporting Democracy Worldwide*. December 21. Accessed September 18, 2025. https://www.idea.int/news/case-against-direct-democracy.

NBC News. 2024. "AI Candidate Running for Parliament in the U.K. Says AI Can Humanize Politics." *NBC News*. June 13. Accessed September 2025, 2025. https://www.nbcnews.com/tech/tech-news/ai-candidate-running-parliament-uk-says-ai-can-humanize-politics-rcna156991.

OECD. 2025. "Governing with Artificial Intelligence the State of Play and Way Forward in Core Government Functions." *OECD AI in Public Procurement*. September 18. Accessed September 25, 2025. https://www.oecd.org/en/publications/governing-with-artificial-intelligence_795de142-en/full-report/ai-in-public-procurement_2e095543.html.

Pettit, Harry. 2017. "Could Russia's President One Day Be a ROBOT? Alisa AI Software That Claims 'Enemies of the People Will Be Shot' Wins the Backing of 40,000 to Stand Against Vladimir Putin." *Daily Mail*. December 11. Accessed September 18, 2025. https://www.dailymail.co.uk/sciencetech/article-5166847/Russian-AI-Alisa-wins-backing-40-000-election-run-up.html.

Politico. 2025. "Albania Appoints World's First AI-Made Minister." *Politico*. September 11. Accessed September 18, 2025. https://www.politico.eu/article/albania-apppoints-worlds-first-virtual-minister-edi-rama-diella/.

Sanders, Nathan E., and Bruce Schneier. 2025. *Four Ways AI Is Being Used to Strengthen Democracies Worldwide*. November 23. Accessed November 23, 2025. https://www.theguardian.com/commentisfree/2025/nov/23/ai-use-strengthen-democracy.

Schneier, Bruce, and Nathan E. Sanders. 2025. *Rewiring Democracy How AI Will Transform Our Politics, Government, and Citizenship*. Cambridge, MA: The MIT Press.

TED. 2018. *A Bold Idea to Replace Politicians*. April. Accessed September 18, 2025. https://www.ted.com/talks/cesar_hidalgo_a_bold_idea_to_replace_politicians.

The Guardian. 2025. *If Keir Starmer Is Not Robotic Enough for You, His AI Twin Is Ready for Your Questions*. May 18. Accessed December 11, 2025. https://www.theguardian.com/politics/2025/may/18/if-keir-starmer-is-not-robotic-enough-for-you-his-ai-twin-is-ready-for-your-questions.

The Japan Times. 2025. "New Japanese Political Party to Install AI Leader." *The Japan Times*. September 16. Accessed September 18, 2025. https://www.japantimes.co.jp/news/2025/09/16/japan/ai-leader-path-to-rebirth-party/.

The Moscow Times. 2017. "Artificial Intelligence Robot 'Alisa' Nominated for Russian President." *The Moscow Times*. December 7. Accessed September 18, 2025. https://www.themoscowtimes.com/2017/12/07/artificial-intelligence-robot-alisa-nominated-for-russian-president-a59845.

The Washington Post. 2025. *A Politician Made an AI Clone of Himself. The Outrage Was Real.* August 7. Accessed December 11, 2025. https://www.washingtonpost.com/world/2025/08/06/ai-chatbot-mp-britain-labour/.

Vukovic, Silvija. 2023. "Chatbot Politicians: Who Are They, and What Is Their Connection to Populism?" *The Loop*. Accessed September 18, 2025. https://theloop.ecpr.eu/chatbot-politicians-who-are-they-and-what-is-their-connection-to-populism/.

Xiang, Chloe. 2022. "This Danish Political Party Is Led by an AI." *Vice*. October 13. Accessed September 18, 2025. https://www.vice.com/en/article/this-danish-political-party-is-led-by-an-ai/.

Part II

POWER AI and Geopolitical Competition, Security, and Control

4 The AI Arms Race
The New Frontier of Geopolitical Competition

Artificial intelligence is no longer a technical tool. It is rather an essential geostrategic factor in reshaping the balance of power in the international arena. Artificial intelligence is no longer a mere promising project for humankind. Rather, it poses a number of legal and moral challenges, and even security challenges, that affect the sovereignty and social cohesion of States.

—**Ahmed Attaf,** *Algerian Minister of State, Minister of Foreign Affairs, National Community Abroad, and African Affairs (UN Security Council 2025)*

Geopolitical conflict should not prevent the eventual adoption of a new international regulatory body for the physical products that make up artificial intelligence...Neither should it instigate a new technological arms race... We must engage in a race for the common good — a race to develop artificial intelligence that fosters peace and enables us to build a more equitable, secure and sustainable future for all nations, with a special emphasis on supporting developing countries.

— **Sommerfeld Rosero,** *Minister for Foreign Affairs and Human Mobility of Ecuador (UN Security Council 2024)*

FROM SPUTNIK TO DEEPSEEK: TECHNOLOGY SHOCKS THAT SHIFT POWER

In 1957, the Soviet Union's launch of Sputnik 1, the world's first artificial satellite, shocked the United States and the world, marking a pivotal moment in the Cold War (Briscoe and Fairbanks 2020). It wasn't just a scientific milestone, but a demonstration that underscored the strategic implications of technological supremacy. Sputnik symbolized the Soviet Union's potential dominance in intercontinental ballistic missile technology, where the same rocket capable of placing a satellite into orbit could deliver nuclear warheads to any target on Earth within minutes, rendering America's geographic isolation irrelevant and its cities vulnerable to annihilation (Abbany 2017). This technological leap meant the Soviet Union could potentially strike the U.S. territory with thermonuclear weapons without warning, fundamentally altering the nuclear balance and creating a perception of vulnerability that spurred an arms race and reshaped global strategic stability. This moment cemented the idea that

DOI: 10.1201/9781003644712-8

technological innovation is inseparable from national security, a lesson that resonates even more profoundly today with the rise of artificial intelligence (AI).

In January 2025, Chinese AI startup DeepSeek unveiled its open-source large language model, DeepSeek-R1, marking what many called an "AI Sputnik moment" (Acemoglu 2025). DeepSeek achieved performance comparable to leading American models like GPT-4 at what the company claimed was a fraction of typical development costs, reportedly under $6 million, though analysts suggest this figure may account only for direct compute costs, excluding research, talent, and prior infrastructure investments. Whether the precise figure holds, DeepSeek fundamentally challenged the assumption that AI superiority could be maintained through sheer resource advantages and semiconductor export controls (Reuters 2025a). Often overlooked, DeepSeek's national security implications are profound, showing that adversaries can develop AI applications, including those for autonomous weapons, cyber warfare tools, and surveillance systems, without massive compute infrastructure, while its open-source nature enables any state or nonstate actor to download and weaponize the technology, raising immediate security concerns about the democratization of dual-use AI that was supposed to remain under Western control.

The parallels with the Cold War are often invoked, with some calling for Manhattan Project-style programs emphasizing secrecy and military applications, while others advocate for Apollo-style initiatives focused on civilian innovation and transparency, both reflecting how nations are approaching AI development as a strategic challenge reminiscent of the nuclear and space races of the twentieth century (RAND 2025). AI spending has already passed Apollo and Manhattan Projects combined, with only 2025 AI investment exceeding the total cost of the Apollo program (Reuters 2025b). This is signaling the potential for AI to become a transformative force redefining power dynamics, disrupting traditional deterrence models, and creating vulnerabilities in national security. Whether through autonomous weapons, AI-driven disinformation campaigns, cyberwarfare capabilities, economic competition over chips and data centers, or the scramble for AI infrastructure dominance, AI challenges global stability in ways that demand urgent attention and action. Just as the space race reshaped geopolitics in the mid-twentieth century, the AI race today is redefining the balance of power for the twenty-first century.

THE GENESIS OF COMPETITION: FROM BOARDGAME TO GLOBAL AI ARMS RACE

When DeepMind's AlphaGo made an unexpected move against world champion Lee Sedol in the Chinese board game Go, a play so unconventional that commentators initially thought it was a mistake, it marked more than a victory in an ancient board game; it was the moment artificial intelligence announced itself as a force that could outthink humanity's best strategic minds. Lee's stunned confession at the postgame press conference: "Yesterday, I was surprised. But today I am speechless," echoed through government halls from Washington to Beijing, where policymakers recognized AI not as distant science fiction but as an immediate political and security arena (Wired 2016).

The United States initially commanded this new field through an innovation ecosystem that seemed unreachable for the rest of the world. Google pioneered both AlphaGo and the Transformer architecture underpinning all modern AI, OpenAI developed the GPT series, and Meta released Llama, all fueled by Silicon Valley's unmatched venture capital, elite tech talent, and crucially, semiconductor supremacy. This constellation of advantages crystallized into a core American assumption that AI leadership was fundamentally a function of the capital, computational resources, most advanced chips, the most powerful data centers, and the largest AI models, an exclusive arena where only nations with unlimited technological and financial resources could compete.

China challenged this assumption in 2017 with its bold declaration to become the global AI leader by 2030 (DigiChina 2017). This proclamation prompted the United States to weaponize its semiconductor advantage through export controls, blocking Chinese access to advanced chips, a bet that without cutting-edge hardware, China would remain behind in the large language model race. This gamble seemed to pay off when OpenAI's ChatGPT exploded onto the scene in late 2022, becoming the fastest-growing consumer application in history by reaching 100 million users in just two months, achievement that took TikTok nine months, Instagram two and a half years, and Facebook and Twitter even longer (The Guardian 2023), with downloads surging not only across America but from India to Brazil to Nigeria, as global users rushed to experience AI's transformative potential.

However, China quickly adapted to U.S. semiconductor restrictions and export controls, demonstrating how scarcity can spur innovation. Chinese companies optimized algorithms to achieve comparable AI performance with less powerful hardware, repurposed older chip-making technology for novel applications, and accelerated technological self-sufficiency through massive state investments in domestic chip production, AI research facilities, and alternative computing architectures (Coley 2025). With DeepSeek the race has shifted from a hardware-centric competition to one where algorithmic efficiency, open-source strategies, and application to emerging market needs matter as much as raw compute power. Baidu's ERNIE 4.0, with significantly fewer parameters than GPT-4, now matches or exceeds its performance in complex reasoning tasks according to the company's internal benchmarks, while DeepSeek-Coder reportedly delivers 94% of GitHub Copilot's functionality using 70% less computational resources and having been trained on fewer examples—though such comparative metrics remain difficult to independently verify (Coley 2025).

Yet the AI race extends far beyond the U.S.-China competition. The European Union (EU) wields regulatory power as a global standard-setter, forcing compliance from tech giants through the EU AI Act while at the same time positioning itself as an investor. The UK leverages DeepMind's pioneering work and positions itself as the AI safety capital through its AI Safety Institute. UAE and Saudi Arabia deploy sovereign wealth funds to acquire compute infrastructure and attract talent, with the UAE's Falcon models now competing with open-source alternatives from Meta.

Singapore serves as a regulatory sandbox for AI governance initiatives (Andrews 2025), India supplies critical engineering talent while building its own AI stack for 1.4 billion citizens (Elias 2025), and even smaller nations like Estonia pioneer AI in government services (European Monitor of Industrial Ecosystems 2020). This multipolar landscape suggests that AI dominance won't be determined by raw computational power alone, but by how nations leverage their unique advantages, whether regulatory frameworks, financial resources, or demographic dividends, to carve out strategic niches in the algorithmic century.

THE AI RESOURCE WARS: SEMICONDUCTORS, DATA CENTERS, AND TALENT AS STRATEGIC ASSETS

This competition quickly evolved into a fierce struggle for the critical resources that power AI. As countries increasingly treat technology supply chains as "arteries of national security," control over semiconductors, rare earths, and cloud systems has become as strategically vital as oil reserves once were (Kalviri 2025). Taiwan Semiconductor Manufacturing Company (TSMC), the world's largest contract chip maker, produces over 90% of the most sophisticated processors that power everything from iPhones to AI supercomputers. Without these cutting-edge chips, countries cannot train AI systems that compete at the highest levels. The United States weaponized this dependency by banning exports of the most advanced chips to China, along with the equipment needed to make them.

With **data center investments** ranging from $1.5 billion for smaller to $20 billion mega-projects in Arizona US, $3 billion complexes in China's Inner Mongolia, and Europe's largest 1.2-gigawatt campus in Portugal, totaling $215 billion in global construction annually (Jackson 2024). Nations are pouring unprecedented resources into digital infrastructure that will determine who controls the computational power essential for AI supremacy, transforming what was once mundane IT infrastructure into strategic national assets as critical as military bases or energy reserves. While the United States dominates with more than 5,000 centers and China has less than 500, a fierce competition has emerged among nations seeking to develop this strategic infrastructure (Brookings 2025). Countries pursue data centers not just for billions in investment and high-skilled jobs, but for digital sovereignty and leverage over data flows that increasingly determine economic competitiveness, what we elaborate further in the AI and Economic Security chapter. Meanwhile, emerging markets from Kenya to Brazil race to build capacity, recognizing that countries without data centers risk becoming digital colonies, dependent on foreign powers for the computing resources essential to economic development.

In September 2010, when a Chinese fishing trawler collided with Japanese coast guard vessels near disputed islands, China's response shocked the world: it halted all rare earth exports to Japan, grinding Japanese electronics manufacturing to a near standstill and demonstrating that Beijing possessed an economic weapon potentially more powerful than any semiconductor sanction (CNBC 2010). History offers a sobering precedent in the U.S. oil embargo against Japan in 1941, which aimed to curb military expansion but instead became one of the catalysts for Pearl Harbor (the Japanese surprise attack that brought America into World War II), demonstrating how weaponizing critical resources can transform economic leverage into military conflict.

This **monopoly over rare earth elements** has only strengthened, with China now controlling 70% of global mining and 90% of processing capacity for the 17 critical minerals essential to AI hardware, from neodymium in hard drives, to europium in semiconductor manufacturing (Baskaran 2025). This stranglehold gives China a "kill switch" over global tech supply chains that even the most advanced semiconductor export controls cannot match. To further cement this advantage, China prohibited its nationals from working on rare earth projects abroad without explicit government authorization, effectively preventing the transfer of expertise to competitor nations. While the United States and allies scramble to develop alternative sources through initiatives like the Minerals Security Partnership, building new rare earth processing facilities takes 10–15 years, time the AI race may not afford. In addition, if the United States mined what China mines in a year it would completely exhaust its own reserves in under a decade (CBC News 2025). The dependency is so profound that even US F-35 fighters require Chinese rare earths, creating a surreal situation where the American military might depend on Chinese minerals.

In addition, China's 1.1 billion internet users generate **unprecedented data flows**, creating training resources no country can match, a strategic advantage with profound implications for both economic competitiveness and national security (The Economist 2025). China is treating data as a strategic national resource equivalent to labor and capital, mandating data sharing across all government levels, and launching a digital ID system in July 2025 that creates a centralized ledger of every citizen's online activity, allowing the state unprecedented surveillance capabilities while limiting tech companies to seeing only anonymized data streams. In contrast, the United States fragments its data across competing tech giants bound by privacy regulations, with American companies spending billions to purchase or license training data that Chinese firms can access directly through state coordination. For foreign policy practitioners, China's data empire represents a fundamental challenge: while democracies struggle to balance privacy, property rights, and innovation, China's centralized model, if successful in demonstrating financial value and AI advantages, could offer an authoritarian alternative to Western data governance that appeals to other nations prioritizing efficiency over civil liberties, potentially fracturing the global digital economy into competing spheres of influence.

In November 2023, when OpenAI's board fired CEO Sam Altman, 95% of the company's employees threatened to quit and follow him to Microsoft within 72 hours, forcing the board to reinstate him (Wired 2023). The revolt demonstrated that in the AI race, talent loyalty can override corporate governance. In the AI race, **talent has become one of the ultimate strategic assets**, particularly in the context of competition between the United States and China. Both countries invest heavily in attracting and retaining top AI researchers, engineers, and related experts, recognizing that human capital underpins advances in innovation, military applications, and economic competitiveness. China is first in the world with 3.57 million STEM graduates annually compared to America's 820,000, while one-fifth of its higher education programs have been revamped to channel students into AI and integrated circuits (Cheng 2025). China has dominated U.S. indices of STEM Olympiad performance for several years while its scientific research contributions surpassed the United States in 2023 and quadrupled that lead by 2024, marking a decisive shift in global scientific leadership.

Researchers originally from China now constitute 38% of top AI researchers working in the United States, narrowly surpassing the 37% who are American-born, highlighting the self-defeating nature of recent U.S. visa restrictions, security clearance denials, and other limits on students that threaten to cut off the very talent pipeline sustaining U.S. AI dominance (Mozur and Metz 2024). As "Chip War" author Chris Miller warned, America's talent edge is "deteriorating dangerously" and even proves far more fragile than its chip advantage, particularly as restrictive U.S. immigration policies limit global talent access while China increasingly retains domestic experts. The AI talent war has escalated from international competition to domestic bidding wars where companies offer millions in packages resembling more sport star transfers than tech employees, creating a circular talent economy where the same engineers command ever-higher premiums as they rotate between Silicon Valley giants (New York Times 2025).

Other countries are not passive observers in this dynamic: through education systems, research partnerships, visa regimes, and targeted investments, they can position themselves as talent hubs, trusted collaborators, or norm-setters. India exemplifies this potential: ranked first globally in AI skill penetration by the 2024 Stanford AI Index, with an AI workforce 2.8 times more skilled than the global average, the country has leveraged its education system and diaspora networks to become a major player in the global AI talent race (Elias 2025). How countries manage and cooperate on AI talent will influence not only technological leadership, but also alliances, dependencies, and the balance of power in the evolving global AI landscape. For foreign policy practitioners, talent shapes not only innovation capacity but also geopolitical influence: immigration rules, education systems, research funding, and international mobility directly affect who leads in AI and who sets the norms. Competition over AI talent is therefore also competition over long-term economic strength, security, and the ability to shape global standards and alliances.

CORPORATE SOVEREIGNS: WHEN BIG TECH BECAME GEOPOLITICAL

The recent cascade of policy reversals by Silicon Valley's AI giants signals a fundamental shift in geopolitical competition. OpenAI eliminated its prohibition on military applications (TechCrunch 2024), Google quietly rescinded its commitment against AI weaponization (Wired 2025), and Meta opened its Llama models to defense agencies (Meta 2025), each invoking national security imperatives to justify abandoning their founding principles against military involvement. These shifts signal Big Tech's transformation from commercial actors to active participants in great power rivalry, changing the long-standing American doctrine that separated economic activity from national security imperatives. This convergence transforms private corporations into what some observers call the primary architects of a new world order, where the future balance of global power depends as much on algorithmic advantages as on traditional military capabilities. These corporations, many controlling resources that exceed entire nations' gross domestic product, and more powerful than many countries (Foreign Policy 2016), have become embodiments of "techno-geopolitics," where control over AI architectures, data flows, and technical standards directly translates into geopolitical leverage.

Big Tech's geopolitical power manifests through actions that once belonged exclusively to sovereign states. Meta's decision to block all news content in Canada and Australia rather than comply with media payment laws demonstrated its capacity to unilaterally restructure entire nations' information ecosystems, effectively forcing governments to choose between regulatory sovereignty and citizens' access to news on dominant social platforms (Australian Broadcasting Corporation 2024). Microsoft's provision of cyber defense to Ukraine, including real-time threat intelligence that proved critical to repelling Russian cyberattacks, positioned a private corporation as a de facto ally in armed conflict (Microsoft 2022). Elon Musk's personal control over Starlink enabled him to unilaterally decide whether Ukrainian forces could use satellite communications for certain military operations, effectively exercising veto power over tactical decisions in an active war zone (Reuters 2025c).

Big tech companies don't merely influence policy, they execute functions indistinguishable from statecraft, wielding infrastructural control that translates directly into geopolitical leverage. They increasingly shape a "technopolar" world assuming functions historically reserved for nation-states, wielding influence over geopolitics through their control of digital infrastructure that has become indispensable to modern society (Bremmer 2025). When companies decide where to build hyperscale data centers, when they determine which nations receive advanced chips, when they control access to rare earth supply chains for semiconductors, these firms are no longer just businesses but geopolitical actors whose infrastructure choices carry the weight of foreign policy. This corporate geopolitical power directly shapes how nations must now form alliances, not just with other states, but with the tech giants who control the infrastructure of the AI age.

ALGORITHMS AND ALLIANCES—GLOBAL SOUTH IN THE AI RACE

The struggle for AI building blocks is reshaping global alliances and supply chains with unprecedented speed. Japan and the Netherlands faced enormous pressure to align their semiconductor policies with U.S. restrictions, while South Korea must balance its economic dependence on Chinese markets against security guarantees from Washington. The competition has reached even the Arctic Circle, where Greenland suddenly finds itself facing U.S. pressure to sell or grant access to its rare earth deposits, while control over Ukraine's massive rare earth reserves adds another layer to the strategic calculations around Western support for Kyiv's defense, demonstrating how resource competition now infiltrates even active conflict zones. Countries like Kazakhstan and the Democratic Republic of Congo, previously peripheral to tech competition, now field delegations from Washington and Beijing competing to lock up their lithium and cobalt reserves essential for AI infrastructure. Even traditionally neutral Switzerland found itself subject to U.S. semiconductor export quotas, demonstrating that no nation remains untouched by the AI resource wars (Swiss Info 2025).

When China's President urged his nation to actively pursue AI cooperation and help developing countries build their technological capabilities, he identified a strategic opportunity that has become central to global AI competition (Carnegie Endowment for International Peace 2025). While the United States concentrates on maintaining its frontier AI advantage through export controls and partnerships with wealthy states and Western allies, China is winning a parallel race for influence across the Global South, a contest that may prove equally consequential for geopolitical power. Beyond this bilateral rivalry, middle powers from the EU to India are trying to secure their positions, recognizing that control over AI's building blocks, compute power, talent pools, data resources, and the massive energy infrastructure required for training systems, will increasingly determine global power hierarchies.

DeepSeek's instant success, topping app stores in 140 markets including Brazil and India with 125 million downloads, demonstrates how Chinese AI is becoming the default choice for billions of users. Chinese firms are rolling out infrastructure across Africa, Asia, and Latin America, positioning their technology to shape education, healthcare, governance, and security systems, recognizing that whoever provides the AI infrastructure, systems, and compute power to emerging markets will fundamentally shape their development trajectories and, by extension, the global balance of power. The focus on export promotion rather than export controls could be a shift in thinking about how advanced nations can maintain influence, not by restricting technology flows but by actively shaping how AI transforms societies across Africa, Asia, and Latin America.

The AI race has transformed international alliances from traditional security pacts into technology-sharing consortiums where algorithmic capabilities rival military commitments in strategic importance. The United States is building an "AI democracy alliance" through multiple frameworks. The Quad (United States, Australia, India, Japan), the U.S.-EU Trade and Technology Council focus on strategic coordination, while Pax Silica, a coalition including Japan, Republic of Korea, Singapore, the Netherlands, the UK, Israel, the UAE, and Australia, aims to establish a secure, prosperous, and innovation-driven silicon supply chain while excluding China from semiconductor supply chain. Complementing these efforts, agreements with Japan, South Korea, and the Netherlands work to exclude China from critical semiconductor supply chains. China counters by offering affordable AI infrastructure across the Belt and Road Initiative, trading technology access for strategic alignment with developing nations. These partnerships, whether the UAE securing exclusive American chips in exchange for restricting Chinese technology, or Five Eyes nations sharing AI defense models, create interdependencies as binding as mutual defense treaties.

THE PARALLEL RACE: WHO WRITES THE RULES AND SETS THE STANDARDS?

Beyond the technological competition, a parallel contest unfolds over AI governance architectures, a battle for normative power that echoes the strategic precedent of internet governance. The United States leveraged its first-mover advantage in the 1990s to embed liberal market principles into the Domain Name System (DNS) and Internet Corporation for Assigned Names and Numbers (ICANN)'s multi-stakeholder model, creating path dependencies that persist despite subsequent challenges. When China proposed alternative DNS architectures in the 2000s that would have enabled sovereign control over information flows, these initiatives foundered not on technical grounds but because the governance regime had already crystallized around Western preferences (Verhulst et al. 2017). This historical pattern illuminates the current urgency with which early AI governance frameworks will similarly lock in power distributions and value systems, making the race to establish regulatory standards as strategically consequential as the race for technological supremacy itself.

At the multilateral level, the competition intensifies as nations maneuver to dominate AI discussions at the UN, the OECD, the G7, and other regional bodies, recognizing that whoever shapes the governance frameworks will effectively determine whether AI development follows a model prioritizing rights and safety, state control, or market freedom. This governance race represents a parallel battlefield where soft power, diplomatic influence, and regulatory expertise matter as much as computational capacity, with countries understanding that writing the rules for AI may ultimately prove as important as building the technology itself.

The EU positions its AI Act as a model for the world, leveraging its regulatory "Brussels Effect" to set de facto global standards, while Brazil and Chile each develop comprehensive national AI legislation that could influence neighboring countries' approaches through market size and precedent, with both nations seeking to balance innovation promotion with risk mitigation in their respective frameworks. The United States, while first positioning itself as the leader in "responsible AI," emphasizing AI safety and ethical standards, has now vocally resisted binding regulations, framing the AI governance itself as a threat to innovation and competitiveness. The 2025 US AI strategy "Winning the Race: America's AI Action Plan" embraces aggressive deregulation to unleash private sector innovation while simultaneously mobilizing diplomatic resources to counter China's influence in international AI governance bodies and export America's complete AI technology stack to allied nations (The White House, 2025). China swiftly countered the U.S. AI Action Plan by releasing its own Global AI Governance Action Plan just several days later, strategically positioning the United Nations as the primary forum for AI regulation while framing its approach around developing world concerns like "bridging the digital divide" and creating "inclusive and fair" systems (Ministry of Foreign Affairs People's Republic of China 2025).

Yet even these positions prove unstable: EU member states that spent years crafting the AI Act now openly discuss weakening compliance requirements to boost competitiveness, while former champions of strict regulation suddenly advocate for regulatory flexibility. This volatility extends across every dimension of the AI race, from export controls to ethical frameworks to international partnerships, with nations pivoting their strategies in real time as new breakthroughs emerge. What we capture here represents merely a snapshot of a rapidly evolving competition, at a moment when old assumptions crumble but new equilibria have yet to form. Only time will reveal whether this race produces a stable multipolar order with negotiated coexistence, a new AI hegemon dictating global AI rules, or a fractured world of mutually incompatible AI ecosystems, each outcome fundamentally shaping the global geopolitics.

THE COLLABORATIVE ALTERNATIVE: HOW THE GLOBAL SOUTH IS RESHAPING AI'S FUTURE

Some argue that the framing of AI as a great power race fundamentally misunderstands both the technology's nature and its potential. The Global South is pioneering a fundamentally different approach to AI that challenges the binary narrative of U.S.-China technological competition. Rather than viewing AI development as a zero-sum race for dominance, countries across Africa, Latin America, and Asia are crafting frameworks that prioritize collective benefit over competitive advantage. Instead of the "AI race" narrative, these voices advocate for AI development as a shared global endeavor, arguing that the technology's transformative potential demands collaboration rather than competition.

The African Union's AI Continental Strategy emphasizes "Ubuntu AI," technology rooted in the principle of collective humanity. Brazil has positioned itself as a bridge between developed and developing nations, advocating for AI systems that prioritize public interest alongside innovation. Through its #AIforAll philosophy and focus on "collaborative AI," India champions a model where AI serves as a tool for societal transformation rather than geopolitical dominance, building partnerships that prioritize reaching the last mile over dominating the cutting edge, and making AI representative of diverse cultures and contexts across the developing world (Kaur 2025). The BRICS nations have collectively articulated this philosophy in their Leaders' Statement on AI governance, which explicitly calls for "collaborative governance of AI, not a competitive one" (BRICS Information Centre 2025).

Yet even as the Global South champions collaborative frameworks, a more radical form of cooperation has emerged through transnational developer networks, where coders across borders spontaneously coordinate through GitHub repositories and shared protocols, building solutions without waiting for state approval. However, this inspiring bottom-up collaboration remains fundamentally constrained by the U.S.-China competition. Despite its promise, these communities are increasingly viewed by major powers not as neutral spaces but as arenas for influence, with the AI race fragmenting the digital ecosystem into distinct regulatory and technological spheres where critical infrastructure, funding, and market access remain under state control. Rather than a genuine third way capable of reshaping AI geopolitics, these grassroots technical collaborations function more as a secondary layer of cooperation operating within, not beyond, the fundamental dynamics of great power competition.

The collaborative vision championed by some Global South nations is far from unified, as many developing countries increasingly warn that AI development risks becoming a new form of colonial extraction. Over 80% of African data flows through infrastructure controlled by Amazon, Microsoft, and Google, while Africa supplies 70% of the world's cobalt essential for AI hardware, yet the continent remains excluded from global AI governance frameworks being shaped by the EU, United States, and China (New Ghana 2025). This "algorithmic colonialism" extends beyond resource extraction: AI systems trained on Western datasets systematically fail African contexts, with credit scoring algorithms unable to assess local financial behaviors, healthcare diagnostics misidentifying conditions in Black patients, and educational systems struggling with tonal languages.

The parallels to historical colonialism are unmistakable, raw materials and data are extracted, processed through foreign-owned infrastructure, then sold back as AI services that developing nations must purchase while having no control over how these algorithms interpret their societies. Several African, Asian, and Latin American nations are now pursuing technological sovereignty through indigenous AI development and local data requirements, recognizing that without ownership of data infrastructure and algorithmic development, global AI collaboration could perpetuate dependency rather than foster genuine partnership.

Despite these constraints, the Global South's push for collaborative AI represents more than pure rhetoric, it's actively reshaping how the world conceptualizes AI development. The very fact that major powers now feel compelled to address questions of AI equity, inclusive datasets, and technological sovereignty reflects how developing nations have successfully injected new dimensions into what was initially framed purely as a bilateral competition. The Global South may not have the compute power of big AI race actors, but it possesses something valuable: the majority of the world's population, data diversity, and development challenges that demand innovative AI solutions. As climate change, food security, and healthcare access become existential priorities, the AI models and frameworks emerging from Lagos, São Paulo, and Bangalore, designed for resource constraints and real-world complexity, may prove more globally relevant than those optimized for advertising clicks in wealthy markets.

The question isn't whether the Global South can escape the gravitational pull of U.S.-China competition entirely, but whether it can bend that competition toward more inclusive outcomes. By refusing to be passive subjects of algorithmic decisions made in distant capitals, by demanding that AI development serve human development, and by creating alternative models even within existing constraints, the developing countries are ensuring that the future of AI, however it unfolds, will be shaped by more than just two superpowers' strategic calculations.

BIBLIOGRAPHY

Abbany, Zulfikar. 2017. *A Shared History: ICBMs and Sputnik 1.* July 13. Accessed September 30, 2025. https://www.dw.com/en/intercontinental-ballistic-missiles-and-their-long-shared-history-with-sputnik-1/a-39658661.

Acemoglu, Daron. 2025. *A Sputnik Moment for AI?* February 4. Accessed September 24, 2025. https://www.project-syndicate.org/commentary/china-ai-deepseek-raises-difficult-questions-for-united-states-by-daron-acemoglu-2025-02.

Andrews, Caitlin. 2025. *Singapore Offers Potential Blueprint for AI Sandbox Initiatives.* November 12. Accessed November 17, 2025. https://iapp.org/news/a/as-ai-sandboxes-are-considered-singapore-offers-a-blueprint.

Australian Broadcasting Corporation. 2024. *Meta Blocked News from Facebook and Instagram in Canada—Could They Do the Same in Australia?* March 12. Accessed September 2025, 2025. https://www.abc.net.au/news/2024-03-13/could-meta-block-news-in-australia-after-canada-ban/103576038.

Baskaran, Gracelin. 2025. *China's New Rare Earth and Magnet Restrictions Threaten US Defense Supply Chains.* October 9. Accessed October 21, 2025. https://www.csis.org/analysis/chinas-new-rare-earth-and-magnet-restrictions-threaten-us-defense-supply-chains.

Bremmer, Ian. 2025. *The Technopolar Paradox the Frightening Fusion of Tech Power and State Power.* May 13. Accessed September 29, 2025. https://www.foreignaffairs.com/united-states/technopolar-paradox-ian-bremmer-fusion-tech-state-power.

BRICS Information Centre. 2025. *BRICS Leaders' Statement on the Global Governance of Artificial Intelligence.* July 6. Accessed October 5, 2025. https://www.brics.utoronto.ca/docs/250706-ai.html.

Briscoe, Erica, and James Fairbanks. 2020. *Artificial Scientific Intelligence and Its Impact on National Security and Foreign Policy.* Policy Paper, Foreign Policy Research Institute, 544–553.

Brookings. 2025. *The Future of Data Centers.* November 5. Accessed December 13, 2025. https://www.brookings.edu/articles/the-future-of-data-centers/.

Carnegie Endowment for International Peace. 2025. *The Other AI Race: An Export Promotion Strategy for the Global South.* July 21. Accessed September 28, 2025. https://carnegieendowment.org/research/2025/07/the-other-ai-race-an-export-promotion-strategy-for-the-global-south?lang=en.

CBC News. 2025. *How China Won the Rare Earth Race against the US.* October 17.

Cheng, Evelyn. 2025. *CNBC's The China Connection Newsletter: US-China AI Talent Race Heats Up.* December 10. Accessed December 12, 2025. https://www.cnbc.com/2025/12/10/china-connection-newsletter-us-china-ai-talent-race-chris-miller-chip-war-computing-brain-power-electricity.html.

CNBC. 2010. *China Bans Rare Earth Exports to Japan Amid Tension.* September 23. Accessed October 21, 2025. https://www.cnbc.com/2010/09/23/china-bans-rare-earth-exports-to-japan-amid-tension.html.

Coley, Jason. 2025. *The AI Crossroads: Who Will Set the Rules of the Future?* April 23. Accessed September 30, 2025. https://aijourn.com/the-ai-crossroads-who-will-set-the-rules-of-the-future-2/.

DigiChina. 2017. *Full Translation: China's 'New Generation Artificial Intelligence Development Plan'* (2017). August 1. Accessed September 28, 2025. https://digichina.stanford.edu/work/full-translation-chinas-new-generation-artificial-intelligence-development-plan-2017/.

Elias, Jibu. 2025. *Samaj, Sarkar, Bazaar: Building Inclusive AI for India's Future.* September 17. Accessed December 25, 2025. https://www.stimson.org/2025/samaj-sarkar-bazaar-building-inclusive-ai-for-indias-future/.

European Monitor of Industrial Ecosystems. 2020. *Estonian Public Services in the Age of Artificial Intelligence.* November 20. Accessed December 25, 2025. https://monitor-industrial-ecosystems.ec.europa.eu/news/estonian-public-services-age-artificial-intelligence.

Foreign Policy. 2016. *These 25 Companies Are More Powerful Than Many Countries.* March 15. Accessed 29 September, 2025. https://foreignpolicy.com/2016/03/15/these-25-companies-are-more-powerful-than-many-countries-multinational-corporate-wealth-power/.

Jackson, Amber. 2024. *Top 10: Biggest Data Centres.* October 23. Accessed December 12, 2025. https://datacentremagazine.com/top10/top-10-biggest-data-centres.

Kalviri, Bahram P. 2025. *The New Geopolitics of Technology.* September 23. Accessed September 29, 2025. https://moderndiplomacy.eu/2025/09/23/the-new-geopolitics-of-technology/.

Kaur, Sharanpreet. 2025. *India's Strategic AI Diplomacy and the Future of Global Cooperation.* October 5. Accessed November 1, 2025. https://sundayguardianlive.com/business/indias-strategic-ai-diplomacy-and-the-future-of-global-cooperation-154539/.

Meta. 2025. *How Meta Is Supporting US National Security with AI.* September 23. Accessed September 29, 2025. https://about.fb.com/news/2025/09/meta-supporting-us-national-security-with-ai/.

Microsoft. 2022. *Defending Ukraine: Early Lessons from the Cyber War.* June 22. Accessed September 29, 2025. https://blogs.microsoft.com/on-the-issues/2022/06/22/defending-ukraine-early-lessons-from-the-cyber-war/.

Ministry of Foreign Affairs People's Republic of China. 2025. *Global AI Governance Action Plan.* July 26. Accessed October 8, 2025. https://www.mfa.gov.cn/eng/xw/zyxw/202507/t20250729_11679232.html.

Mozur, Paul, and Cade Metz. 2024. *In One Key A.I. Metric, China Pulls Ahead of the US: Talent.* March 22. Accessed December 12, 2025. https://www.nytimes.com/2024/03/22/technology/china-ai-talent.html.

New Ghana. 2025. *Ghana Backs Homegrown AI Platform as Defense Against Digital Colonialism.* November 8. Accessed November 11, 2025. https://www.newsghana.com.gh/ghana-backs-homegrown-ai-platform-as-defense-against-digital-colonialism/.

New York Times. 2025. *Inside the A.I. Talent Wars.* August 25. Accessed December 12, 2025. https://www.youtube.com/watch?v=gsFArk2EQrs.

RAND. 2025. *Beyond a Manhattan Project for Artificial General Intelligence.* April 24. Accessed October 20, 2025. https://www.rand.org/pubs/commentary/2025/04/beyond-a-manhattan-project-for-artificial-general-intelligence.html.

Reuters. 2025a. *DeepSeek's Low-Cost AI Spotlights Billions Spent by US Tech.* January 29. Accessed September 30, 2025. https://www.reuters.com/technology/artificial-intelligence/big-tech-faces-heat-chinas-deepseek-sows-doubts-billion-dollar-spending-2025-01-27/.

Reuters. 2025b. *Investment in AI Is Exploding.* December 5. Accessed December 12, 2025. https://www.reuters.com/graphics/USA-ECONOMY/AI-INVESTMENT/gkvlqbgxkpb/.

Reuters. 2025c. *Musk Ordered Shutdown of Starlink Satellite Service as Ukraine Retook Territory from Russia.* July 25. Accessed September 29, 2025. https://www.reuters.com/investigations/musk-ordered-shutdown-starlink-satellite-service-ukraine-retook-territory-russia-2025-07-25/.

Swiss Info. 2025. *US Restricts Switzerland's Access to AI Chips.* January 26. Accessed January 3, 2026. https://www.swissinfo.ch/eng/multinational-companies/us-restricts-switzerlands-access-to-ai-chips/88781270.

TechCrunch. 2024. *OpenAI Changes Policy to Allow Military Applications.* January 12. Accessed September 2025, 2025. https://techcrunch.com/2024/01/12/openai-changes-policy-to-allow-military-applications/.

The Economist. 2025. *China Is Building an Entire Empire on Data.* July 3. Accessed December 8, 2025. https://www.economist.com/leaders/2025/07/03/china-is-building-an-entire-empire-on-data.

The Guardian. 2023. *ChatGPT Reaches 100 Million Users Two Months after Launch.* February 2. Accessed September 30, 2025. https://www.theguardian.com/technology/2023/feb/02/chatgpt-100-million-users-open-ai-fastest-growing-app.

UN Security Council. 2024. *Maintenance of International Peace and Security Artificial Intelligence.* Official Records of the Security Council, New York City: UN Security Council.

UN Security Council. 2025. *Artificial Intelligence and International Peace and Security.* Official Record of the Security Council, New York City: UN Security Council.

Verhulst, Stefaan G., Beth S. Noveck, Jullian Raines, and Antony Declerq. 2017. *Who Runs the Internet? The Global Multi-stakeholder Model of Internet Governance.* Research Volume Two Global Commission on Internet Governance, Centre for International Governance Innovation and the Royal Institute of International Affairs.

The White House 2025. *Winning the Race: America's AI Action Plan.* Action Plan, Washington DC: The White House.

Wired. 2016. *In Two Moves, AlphaGo and Lee Sedol Redefined the Future.* March 16. Accessed September 29, 2025. https://www.wired.com/2016/03/two-moves-alphago-lee-sedol-redefined-future/.

Wired. 2023. *95 Percent of OpenAI Employees Threaten to Follow Sam Altman Out the Door.* November 20. Accessed December 13, 2025. https://www.wired.com/story/95-percent-of-openai-employees-threaten-to-follow-sam-altman-out-the-door/.

Wired. 2025. *Google Lifts a Ban on Using Its AI for Weapons and Surveillance.* February 4. Accessed September 29, 2025. https://www.wired.com/story/google-responsible-ai-principles/.

5 AI and Global Security
New Reality of Lethal Autonomy, Nuclear Risk, and Cyber Warfare

> Almost twenty years ago, we faced one of the first large-scale state-backed cyberattacks. It showed us how vulnerable societies can be when technology is misused. But we also learned that resilience, transparency, and trust can turn weakness into strength. Today Estonia is undergoing its next big step – our AI Leap…AI is one of the defining challenges of our time — but also one of the greatest opportunities. If we act together, we can ensure that AI strengthens peace, supports democracy, and upholds human dignity.
>
> — **Margus Tsahkna**, *Minister of Foreign Affairs of the Republic of Estonia (Tsahkna 2025)*

> AI technology is like a double-edged sword — it can either become a force for better social governance and international security or a source of threats to fairness and justice and a danger to peace and stability. The international community should jointly strengthen global AI governance to ensure that AI development advances in conformity with the common values of humankind and that AI is genuinely safe, reliable, fair and under control.
>
> — **Fu Cong**, *Ambassador and Permanent Representative of the People's Republic of China to the United Nations (UN Security Council 2024)*

Artificial intelligence (AI) has fundamentally transformed global security, creating the most profound disruption to international relations since nuclear weapons emerged in 1945. Unlike that revolution which unfolded over decades, AI's transformation is happening at greater speed, compressing strategic timelines from years to months, diplomatic response windows from days to minutes, and tactical decisions from hours to seconds. The same algorithms that power search engines and medical diagnosis now guide missiles, manipulate elections, conduct cyber operations at unprecedented scale, and may soon possess intelligence that surpasses our own. We are witnessing millions of cyberattacks daily increasingly powered by AI, autonomous drones used in warfare without human control, and algorithmic campaigns forcing the cancelation of democratic elections. The Bulletin of Atomic Scientists has moved its Doomsday Clock to 89 seconds to midnight, the closest humanity has ever stood to catastrophe, citing AI's amplification of nuclear, cyber, and information threats as key factors.

 DOI: 10.1201/9781003644712-9

Diplomats trained to defuse tensions through days of careful negotiation must now confront AI systems that can trigger irreversible escalation before the first emergency meeting convenes.

This chapter examines five converging AI-driven threats that collectively demand urgent diplomatic innovation and represent challenges that traditional statecraft was never designed to address. We begin with lethal autonomous weapon systems and weapons powered by AI already deployed from Ukraine to Gaza, where machines independently select and engage targets while UN diplomats debate regulations that may come years too late. We then examine the risks that could arise from integrating AI into nuclear command and control systems, where algorithmic decision-making might dangerously compress the time available for human judgment in crisis situations. Our analysis continues with AI-powered cyber warfare and increasing attacks that blur peace and conflict, followed by algorithmic disinformation campaigns sophisticated enough to cancel elections and undermine democratic discourse. Finally, we confront the possibility of Artificial General Intelligence (AGI), which leading experts warn could arrive within five to ten years and grant its controllers unprecedented, potentially permanent global dominance.

Foreign policy experts must engage with issues surrounding AI and security because its transformative impact extends far beyond the traditional domain of defense ministries or military alliances, reshaping how nations approach threats, power competition, and diplomacy. AI is revolutionizing military capabilities, intelligence gathering, and global stability while influencing international norms and altering the balance of power between states. These developments directly affect foreign policy objectives, from managing alliances and negotiating arms control agreements to addressing transnational challenges like cybersecurity and AI-driven disinformation campaigns. As AI increasingly becomes a tool for both competition and cooperation on the global stage, its implications for national and international security demand the attention of foreign policymakers and experts. This chapter seeks to prepare experts for these challenges by providing foundational introductions, overviews, and actionable suggestions for further exploration, equipping them to navigate AI's profound impact on national and global security.

LETHAL AUTONOMOUS WEAPONS SYSTEMS: WHY DIPLOMACY CAN'T WAIT

In November 2020, after years of failed attempts to assassinate Iran's top nuclear scientist, a robotic machine gun succeeded where human assassins had not (The New York Times 2023). The remote-controlled weapon mounted on a parked vehicle was operated by an Israeli agent sitting at a computer screen more than 1,000 miles away. The gun used AI to perform critical tasks, such as facial recognition software to confirm it was targeting the right person, algorithms to adjust for the satellite communication delay, and calculations to compensate for the car's speed. In less than a minute, the AI-guided weapon fired 15 bullets with surgical precision, killing the scientist while his wife, sitting just inches away in the passenger seat, remained unharmed. Though still human-controlled, this AI-enhanced assassination demonstrated how rapidly military technology is advancing toward systems with greater autonomy.

What was once the exclusive domain of sophisticated state actors conducting targeted operations has now proliferated to become a defining feature of modern warfare. Ukraine has become what some call the "Silicon Valley for autonomous weapons," with Ukrainian developers racing to build AI-enabled systems that can offset their numerical and equipment disadvantages against Russia. In September 2024, a civilian cycling through Kherson, Ukraine, was tracked for nearly 300 m by a drone before it dropped a munition that injured her in an incident that exemplifies the emerging reality of technology deployment in contemporary conflict zones (Human Rights Watch 2025a). This targeted attack represents part of a broader pattern in which small, maneuverable, and relatively inexpensive quadcopter drones armed with explosives have become one of the deadliest weapons in the Ukraine conflict (UN News 2025a).

The potential proliferation of autonomous weapons systems carries profound implications for foreign policy, international security, and the nature of warfare itself. As Pakistan's Minister of Defense observed following the 2025 India-Pakistan military exchange, which marked the first use of autonomous munitions and dual-capable cruise missiles between nuclear-armed states, these technologies are fundamentally altering strategic calculations by lowering the threshold for the use of force and compressing decision-making timeframes (UN News 2025b). This technological shift makes armed conflict more politically and operationally feasible while simultaneously reducing opportunities for diplomatic intervention and de-escalation, a trend particularly concerning given the potential for rapid escalation between nuclear-armed adversaries.

The development of lethal autonomous weapon systems (LAWS), often referred to as "killer robots," represents a transformative and controversial shift in military technology, driven by advancements in AI (ICRC 2022). These systems, capable of independently selecting and engaging targets without human intervention, challenge traditional norms of warfare and raise profound ethical, legal, and strategic concerns (Human Rights Watch 2025b). Supporters of these systems argue that they can enhance military efficiency, reduce human casualties among soldiers, and increase precision in targeting, while opponents warn that these systems undermine accountability, violate International Humanitarian Law, and pose significant risks of misuse or unintended escalation, with some critics labeling them a false promise of civilian protection as they could fail to reliably distinguish between combatants and noncombatants.

The risks of AI-powered target identification are far from theoretical, as facial recognition systems have already led to wrongful arrests in civilian settings, with studies showing African American and Asian faces were up to 100 times more likely to be misidentified than white faces (Amnesty International 2023). In warfare, where conditions are far less controlled, such errors could result in the deaths of innocent civilians, further undermining the promise of "precision" AI weapons. As the Chief Legal Officer of the International Committee of the Red Cross observes, "If we contemplate today's most technologically sophisticated conflicts, we have not seen better outcomes for civilians but rather the most widespread and indiscriminate devastation" (International Committee of the Red Cross 2025).

The current regulatory landscape for LAWS reveals a deeply fractured international community. While no explicit international law prohibits these systems, states remain fundamentally divided on whether existing International Humanitarian Law suffices, or new binding instruments are needed. Austria, Brazil, South Africa, and New Zealand advocate for a preemptive ban citing humanitarian concerns. Germany, Norway, and France support maintaining "meaningful human control" without endorsing a total prohibition. Meanwhile, the United States, Russia, and India oppose any ban, emphasizing strategic advantages and arguing that current frameworks are adequate (Bhatt and Bharadwaj 2024).

This deadlock in forums like the UN Convention on Certain Conventional Weapons has created a dangerous regulatory vacuum with profound strategic implications. The absence of rules particularly disadvantages smaller nations and developing countries that cannot afford to develop autonomous weapons yet must prepare to face them, fundamentally disrupting traditional military balances. Without intervention, battlefield precedents will define the rules of autonomous warfare, making future regulation harder to achieve and increasing risks of unintended escalation between nuclear-armed states (UNGA 2024).

Foreign policy professionals must act decisively before this technology becomes irreversible. MFAs are uniquely positioned to bridge military-technical considerations with humanitarian and geopolitical concerns, building the multilateral consensus essential for governance. Their expertise in treaty negotiation and diplomatic coalition-building is critical now, while regulation remains politically feasible. The Stop Killer Robots movement, backed by civil society organizations, such as Human Rights Watch, provides one framework for action, highlighting the ethical, legal, and security risks posed by delegating life-and-death decisions to machines, and arguing that such systems undermine IHL principles like distinction, proportionality, and accountability (Stop Killer Robots 2025). Just as the world failed to ban chemical weapons before World War I's horrors made their danger undeniable, we risk allowing autonomous weapons to proliferate until a catastrophic incident makes their regulation a tragic necessity rather than prudent prevention.

SECONDS TO MIDNIGHT: THE DANGEROUS CONVERGENCE OF NUCLEAR WEAPONS AND AI SYSTEMS

On September 26, 1983, Soviet Lieutenant Colonel Stanislav Petrov sat before a computer screen showing five U.S. intercontinental ballistic missiles racing toward the Soviet Union, yet something felt wrong. Against protocol and facing potential accusations for treason, Petrov declared it a false alarm, his human judgment overriding the automated system that nearly triggered nuclear retaliation and World War III. This moment of human intuition preventing catastrophe now seems almost quaint compared to the AI-nuclear risks emerging today, where decision windows compress from Petrov's 20 minutes to potentially seconds, and where machine learning systems operate at speeds and complexities that no single human can fully grasp or override (O'Hanlon 2025). This is only one of several Cold War near-misses raising critical questions about AI-enabled nuclear decision-making and whether automated systems would prevent or precipitate catastrophe. Diplomats and foreign policy practitioners must comprehend the AI-nuclear nexus urgently, as they will bear responsibility for mediating and negotiating solutions during crises where algorithmic recommendations shape nuclear decision-making with existential stakes.

The Bulletin of Atomic Scientists has moved its nuclear doomsday clock to 89 seconds to midnight, the closest humanity has ever stood to symbolic annihilation, driven by an unprecedented convergence of escalating nuclear tensions, stalled climate action, the weaponization potential of AI, all amplified by misinformation campaigns corroding the very discourse needed to address these crises (Treisman 2025). This stark assessment arrives as we mark 80 years since the horrific nuclear attacks on Hiroshima and Nagasaki, events that instantly killed over 200,000 civilians and demonstrated humanity's capacity for self-annihilation. Yet modern threats, with bombs today dramatically more powerful and destructive, extend far beyond the nuclear arsenals that originally inspired the clock's creation in 1947. Foreign policy practitioners now confront an uncharted intersection of nuclear capabilities converging with rapidly advancing AI systems whose full destructive potential remains poorly understood. These compound threats create cascading risks that traditional deterrence frameworks were never designed to manage, demanding new strategic thinking for an era where existential dangers multiply rather than merely accumulate.

As countries modernize their nuclear arsenals while prioritizing military AI applications, integrating AI into nuclear systems has become a top strategic priority. AI promises to enhance nuclear command, control, and communications systems, offering improved safety, resilience, and efficiency that could deliver decisive strategic advantages. While AI has the potential to improve decision-making speed and accuracy in nuclear systems, it also introduces vulnerabilities, such as algorithmic errors, misinterpretation of data, and susceptibility to cyberattacks (Boulanin et al. 2020).

Incorporating AI into nuclear command and control systems creates dangers from false positives, mistakenly identifying attacks, and false negatives, missing real threats, with decision windows compressed from minutes to seconds, all compounded by insufficient historical nuclear crisis data to properly train these systems (Hruby and Miller 2021). AI systems integrated into nuclear weapons can fail catastrophically when encountering scenarios they weren't trained for, and they're susceptible to manipulation through corrupted data or cyberattacks. In addition, human operators struggle with either over-trusting or under-trusting AI recommendations in high-stress situations, while the military's need for secrecy prevents the kind of open collaboration that has made civilian AI systems more reliable, creating a dangerous combination when nuclear weapons are involved.

Experts vigorously debate whether nuclear-capable systems should keep humans "in the loop," requiring human authorization for every action, "on the loop," allowing human override but autonomous operation, or "out of the loop" fully autonomous, because while human control ensures moral accountability and judgment, the second response times of modern warfare may make meaningful human oversight physically impossible, forcing an agonizing choice between speed and wisdom in decisions that could end civilization. Even when human control is possible it is not always a panacea, as demonstrated when the U.S. Patriot surface-to-air missile defense in Iraq shot down friendly aircraft in 2003 despite human oversight, showing that even with humans "in the loop," the speed and complexity of technology can overwhelm human judgment (The Guardian 2003). Compounding this dilemma, AI systems need vast training data to function reliably, yet nuclear crises are thankfully rare, meaning these systems must extrapolate from conventional conflicts and may fatally misinterpret the unique signals of nuclear strategy.

Today's 12,000-plus nuclear warheads are controlled by nine nations, the United States, Russia, China, France, the United Kingdom, India, Pakistan, Israel, and North Korea, with almost all pursuing AI leadership alongside their nuclear capabilities. While details remain classified, China, Russia, and the United States are almost certainly integrating AI into their nuclear command, control, and communications (NC3) systems, driven by both the technology's advantages in processing intelligence data and competitive pressures to not fall behind rivals (Hruby and Miller 2021). The United States already employs AI for analyzing and sorting satellite imagery from reconnaissance satellites and improving nuclear warhead design and maintenance processes (Bulletin of the Atomic Scientist 2024). Chinese scientists have recently developed the world's first AI system that can verify whether nuclear warheads are real or decoys, a breakthrough that could potentially unlock stalled international arms control negotiations where traditional verification methods have failed to build trust between nuclear powers (Chen 2025). After five years of diplomatic discussions, the U.S. and Chinese presidents agreed in 2024 that AI should never autonomously decide to launch nuclear weapons, drawing a critical red line between AI as a decision-support tool versus an independent nuclear authority (Reuters 2024).

Emerging technologies, including AI, can offer genuine promise for reducing nuclear risk. Commercial satellite imagery and open-source intelligence have democratized capabilities once reserved for national intelligence agencies. The 2021 discovery of China's new silo fields by independent analysts demonstrated how transparency can strengthen global awareness of shifting deterrence balances (Federation of American Scientists 2021). Credible OSINT analysts and think tanks can now provide rapid, evidence-based corrections that counter panic during crises, while AI-enhanced verification tools allow experts to focus on diplomacy rather than detection. Yet this same technological landscape creates new vulnerabilities.

Nuclear decision-makers are vulnerable to AI-generated disinformation. Deepfake videos, such as an adversary's leader ordering mobilization or fabricated missile launch footage, could reach a president's device via social media before intelligence agencies can verify them. During the India-Pakistan tensions in May 2025, both sides circulated manipulated images of missiles and troop movements, prompting real fears among civilians and confusion among outside observers (Mushtaq 2025). The episode revealed how platforms designed to reward outrage rather than accuracy can transform the information environment into a vector for escalation. When manipulated footage goes viral, political leaders face immense pressure to respond before intelligence services have verified what actually occurred, what scholars call an "acceleration trap," where AI integration shortens the time leaders have to evaluate ambiguous signals, pushing nuclear decision-making closer to machine speed (Fayet 2025).

These vulnerabilities intersect dangerously with the institutional architecture of nuclear authority. In several nuclear-armed states, launch authorization rests with a single individual who faces no legal requirement to consult advisors, military officials, or legislative bodies before ordering a strike, whether preemptive or retaliatory (Dumbacher 2025). Once an intercontinental ballistic missile is launched, no one can recall it. This creates a perilous asymmetry where AI-generated deception need only succeed for minutes, the narrow window between receiving intelligence and issuing orders, to trigger irreversible consequences. Behavioral research on human–AI interaction reveals an additional vulnerability: individuals lacking specialized AI training consistently accept algorithmic outputs at face value rather than interrogating them for errors, biases, or manipulation, a pattern that persists even in high-stakes security environments. In practice, this means that officials advising nuclear decision-makers may treat AI-generated content as credible by default, particularly under time pressure, creating a cognitive gap that becomes catastrophic when paired with command structures designed for speed rather than deliberation (Dumbacher 2025).

What ordinary users sharing misinformation achieve unintentionally, sophisticated actors can now accomplish with precision. When Anthropic announced in August 2025 that its chatbot Claude wouldn't help build nuclear weapons, after months working with the U.S. Department of Energy and National Nuclear Security Administration on nuclear "classifiers," it inadvertently highlighted the danger of nuclear security risks coming from broadly available AI systems (Wired 2025). AI has already proliferated asymmetric capabilities to actors far beyond state control. However, many experts agree that the threat isn't exactly in chatbots revealing nuclear physics secrets, but rather how commercially available AI now enables nonstate actors to conduct sophisticated cyber operations against early warning satellites, create deepfake videos of leaders ordering nuclear strikes, or manipulate the information streams feeding nuclear decision-makers. A terrorist group with off-the-shelf AI can probe nuclear command systems with capabilities once requiring teams of expert hackers. This diffusion of AI tools transforms bilateral deterrence into a multi-actor crisis where distinguishing between authentic intelligence and AI-generated deception designed to trigger escalation becomes nearly impossible.

No comprehensive international framework currently governs AI integration into nuclear weapons systems, with traditional arms control treaties failing to address AI capabilities and emerging AI governance initiatives bypassing nuclear applications. While the 2024 Biden-Xi agreement represents the first commitment to prevent autonomous nuclear launch decisions, it lacks implementation mechanisms, verification protocols, and operational definitions. International efforts remain largely aspirational, with REAIM (Responsible AI in Military) focusing on principles rather than binding regulations, and with China among 30 nations declining to endorse its military AI ethics blueprint. With at least five nuclear-armed states actively integrating AI into their arsenals, the governance window is rapidly closing; once embedded in nuclear doctrines, these systems become effectively irreversible, making immediate action critical to establish regulatory guardrails.

THE GRAY WAR: AI AND CYBER THREATS TO NATIONAL AND GLOBAL SECURITY

Cyberattacks have evolved significantly since 15-year-old Jonathan James infiltrated the U.S. Department of Defense's systems in the late 1990s, intercepting emails and eventually gaining access to NASA software used to support the International Space Station (ABC News 2000). While this incident shocked the world at the time, it pales in comparison to today's state-sponsored cyber operations, where adversaries leverage advanced AI, automation, and machine learning to execute highly sophisticated, large-scale attacks.

Six hundred million attacks daily—that's the staggering reality Microsoft documented as cybercriminals and nation-states increasingly weaponize digital spaces amid growing geopolitical tensions (Microsoft 2024). This figure encompasses everything from automated scans and phishing attempts to sophisticated intrusions targeting critical infrastructure. While many cyberattacks cause limited damage, some, like the 2017 NotPetya attack, have reshaped global security dynamics. Initially targeting Ukrainian institutions, NotPetya spread rapidly worldwide, causing over $10 billion in damages, and demonstrating how cyber operations in regional conflicts can escalate into global economic and diplomatic crises (Polityuk and Prentice 2017). Similarly, Russia's 2015 attack on Ukraine's power grid, leaving over 230,000 residents without electricity for hours, highlighted how cyberwarfare has become a key component of hybrid warfare, combining conventional military operations with cyber campaigns to maximize strategic impact while maintaining plausible deniability (Kostyuk and Zhukov 2017).

Wars and armed conflicts create uniquely fertile ground for cyberattacks, as traditional rules of engagement become fluid and attribution challenges provide cover for escalation. The CyberPeace Institute, which tracks cyber harm during conflicts, documented over 2,700 cyberattacks in the first year of the Russia-Ukraine 2022 war alone, conducted by 106 different threat actors, targeting civilian infrastructure including hospitals, schools, and humanitarian organizations, violations that would constitute war crimes in physical warfare but remain legally ambiguous in cyberspace (CyberPeace Institute 2023). Hacktivist collectives emerged as significant cyber combatants, with Ukraine's volunteer IT Army launching DDoS attacks against Russian resources while pro-Russian groups retaliated not only against Ukraine but also NATO member states based on their geopolitical positions, effectively expanding the cyber battlefield beyond the conflict's physical borders (Duguin 2023).

While wars amplify cyber threats, some peacetime attacks prove so devastating that nations declare national emergencies and even state of war (BBC News Mundo 2022). Costa Rica learned this in May 2022, when the Conti ransomware group paralyzed nearly 30 government institutions, including the Ministry of Finance, disrupting tax collection and customs operations for weeks (Burguess 2022). The attackers demanded $20 million in ransom while leaking stolen government data and threatening to "overthrow the government," with the attacks ultimately costing the nation an estimated $30 million per day in economic losses and affecting over 850,000 citizens who couldn't access critical services. The incident demonstrated that in cyberspace, the distinction between wartime and peacetime becomes meaningless when criminal groups can inflict damage comparable to military operations, forcing governments to activate emergency protocols typically reserved for natural disasters or armed conflicts.

The potential for cyberattacks to cause catastrophic damage has long been recognized. In October 2012, U.S. Defense Secretary warned of a potential "cyber Pearl Harbor," a devastating digital attack capable of derailing trains, poisoning water supplies, and crippling power grids. While such a large-scale attack has yet to materialize, incidents like the 2024 "Salt Typhoon" operation, where Chinese state-sponsored actors infiltrated American telecommunications infrastructure, granting Beijing access to sensitive communications data and establishing a strategic foothold that could be activated during a crisis, demonstrate how adversaries are embedding themselves in critical systems during peacetime (Foreign Affairs 2025). These persistent intrusions blur the line between peace and conflict, as adversaries exploit cyberspace to establish strategic footholds without triggering conventional military responses. This "gray war," as described by author Jacob Helberg in his book *The Wires of War*, allows states to employ dual-use technologies, cyber operations, infrastructure infiltration, and information manipulation to achieve strategic objectives without triggering traditional diplomatic or military responses (Helberg 2021).

The diversity of actors and targets further complicates the landscape. In just one year, Chinese hackers targeted British government infrastructure, Algerian groups breached Morocco's National Social Security Fund, Russian operatives conducted espionage in Tajikistan, North Korea infiltrated European defense organizations, and Iranian hackers targeted Iraq's government and Yemen's telecommunications (Center for Strategic and International Studies 2025). These examples illustrate how cyberwarfare transcends borders, with adversaries pursuing a wide range of objectives from espionage to critical infrastructure disruption. A pivotal example is the 2010 Stuxnet attack, widely attributed to the United States and Israel, which targeted Iran's nuclear facilities and destroyed a significant portion of its uranium-enriching centrifuges (IEEE Spectrum 2013). Stuxnet marked the first known cyber operation to cause physical destruction, demonstrating the potential of cyberweapons to achieve strategic objectives without conventional military force.

AI is accelerating this evolution, enabling adversaries to map infrastructure, identify vulnerabilities, and launch simultaneous attacks through multiple channels, combining phishing emails, malware, and network infiltration in coordinated strikes, with unprecedented precision and speed. Today's operations remain largely hybrid, combining machine learning, automation, and human decision-making at critical junctures, but the trend toward greater autonomy is accelerating. AI-driven cyberattacks surged throughout 2025, with 75% of cybersecurity professionals reporting significant increases in both frequency and sophistication, while 85% warn that threat actors are now actively weaponizing AI to amplify the scale and impact of their attacks on global security (Tech Business News 2025). Tools like machine learning also complicate attribution by mimicking other states' tactics, automating operations, and obscuring the source of attacks. The United States is developing AI tools to create convincing fake online identities and automatically identify vulnerabilities in enemy computer systems, enabling simultaneous operations against hundreds of targets rather than relying on time-consuming manual methods (Forbes 2025). China is similarly employing AI programs to perform reconnaissance and planning work in their hacking operations, with these automated tools identifying potential victims and developing attack strategies, significantly accelerating the pace and scale of cyber operations.

While AI amplifies cyber risks and its current capabilities are more readily exploited for offense, its potential also lies in prevention, moving actors from reactive defense to proactive resilience by identifying and eliminating vulnerabilities. The September 2025 incident involving Claude, an AI assistant created by Anthropic that can write code and analyze data, illustrates this duality perfectly. Chinese hackers used the AI to conduct 80%–90% of their operation, which Anthropic calls the inflection point in cybersecurity as the first documented case of a large-scale cyberattack executed without substantial human intervention. After identifying target organizations, hackers deployed Claude to locate valuable databases, test for vulnerabilities, and generate code to extract data, making thousands of requests, often multiple per second, at speeds impossible for human hackers to match, with humans only providing prompts at critical checkpoints (Politico 2025). The attack infiltrated over 30 businesses and three government organizations, demonstrating AI's offensive capabilities. Yet it also showcased AI's defensive power when Anthropic's automated threat detection algorithms rapidly identified the unusual activity patterns, blocked the compromised accounts, and alerted affected organizations allowing them to make necessary security measures (Vox 2025).

For foreign policy practitioners, the evolution of cyberwarfare and the integration of AI into cyber operations demand a rethinking of traditional frameworks for security, sovereignty, and diplomacy. This shift carries concrete implications for ministries of foreign affairs: crisis timelines are compressing from days to hours or even minutes, embassies and diplomatic infrastructure have become direct targets for cyber and information operations, and diplomats increasingly require baseline AI literacy to assess attribution claims, evaluate escalation risks, and negotiate confidence-building measures. Cyberattacks increasingly blur the boundaries between peace and conflict, creating persistent vulnerabilities that adversaries exploit during peacetime and during wars. The UN's decade-long development of 11 voluntary cyber norms established critical principles, that states must not allow their territory to be used for internationally wrongful cyber acts and must coordinate rapid information sharing during attacks, yet the gap between these obligations and their implementation remains vast (Bosco 2025). The unanimous adoption of the UN Convention against Cybercrime creates binding obligations that could help close this gap, moving from voluntary guidelines to enforceable accountability.

As AI continues to transform the cyber threat landscape, governments must adopt proactive, adaptive strategies that integrate technological innovation with multilateral governance efforts. Open-source threat intelligence frameworks, such as MITRE ATT&CK, which catalogs adversary tactics and techniques, and the Forum of Incident Response and Security Teams (FIRST), which coordinates rapid information sharing across borders, demonstrate how collaborative approaches can strengthen resilience for governments and civil society alike (MITRE ATT&CK® 2025) (FIRST 2025). As Francesca Bosco of the CyberPeace Institute emphasizes, this evolution transcends technical or diplomatic concerns: Ultimately "it's not just about compliance – it is about protecting lives," a reminder that behind every compromised system and breached network are real human consequences that demand urgent action (Bosco 2025).

ALGORITHMIC WARFARE: AI-POWERED DISINFORMATION AS A THREAT TO GLOBAL SECURITY

Campaign headquarters across Bucharest fell silent when unprecedented news flashed across their screens: Romania's Constitutional Court had annulled the entire presidential election. Far-right candidate Călin Georgescu, polling in single digits weeks earlier, had won the first round with 23% after 25,000 dormant TikTok accounts suddenly activated, flooding the platform with his content while $381,000 flowed to influencers promoting him, all without mandatory election disclaimers. Declassified intelligence revealed this coordinated campaign with alleged Russian backing, prompting the court to cancel both election rounds. The European Commission launched proceedings against TikTok under the Digital Services Act, marking the first time a European democracy canceled an election due to social media manipulation, proof that algorithmic warfare could now hijack entire democratic processes (Global Witness 2024).

Several years earlier, Facebook data scientist turned whistleblower Sophie Zhang had warned about this type of digital manipulation. In 2020–2021, she exposed how politicians worldwide were using networks of fake accounts to artificially boost their popularity and attack opponents on Facebook, documenting operations in Honduras, Azerbaijan, India, and elsewhere that the platform largely ignored when they didn't affect Western countries (MIT Technology Review 2021). Zhang's revelations about coordinated inauthentic behavior and algorithmic manipulation went largely unheeded by regulators focused on content moderation rather than systematic electoral interference. By Romania's 2024 election, the playbook she exposed, fake accounts, artificial amplification, and platform inaction, had evolved and migrated to TikTok, where it proved powerful enough not just to influence an election, but to force its complete cancelation, vindicating her warnings that social media platforms had become weapons capable of subverting democracy itself.

Disinformation campaigns are not a new phenomenon; they have long been used as tools to manipulate public opinion, influence political outcomes, and sow discord. Historically, the printing press revolutionized information dissemination, but it also enabled the spread of propaganda, as seen during World War II, when governments used mass publishing to shape public sentiment and support for the war effort. However, the advent of social networks and AI has dramatically transformed and supercharged disinformation campaigns. Social media platforms, powered by algorithms and AI-driven amplification, have given anyone, including foreign actors, a global megaphone. These platforms enable the rapid and large-scale spread of disinformation, allowing malicious actors to influence populations and even shape the foreign policies of other countries. The speed, reach, and anonymity provided by AI and online platforms make disinformation campaigns more efficient and impactful than ever before.

The Oxford Internet Institute's global inventory of organized social media manipulation documented cyber operations in at least 48 countries by 2018, revealing remarkably similar tactics across diverse political systems (Bradshaw and Howard 2018). Mexico's 2012 "Peñabots" exemplified these early operations, when the ruling party distributed fake accounts and employing teams of operators to manually flood social media with pro-government messages and manipulate trending topics, with investigations revealing millions in contracts to firms managing these operations (BBC News Mundo 2015). Before AI, bot farms were digital sweatshops where workers manually operated multiple devices and maintained fake personas. Today's AI-powered bot farms have transformed this landscape: a single operator can deploy thousands of autonomous agents that generate unique personas, maintain distinct writing styles, and adapt messaging in real time, all operating 24/7 without human intervention. Where early bot farm operations required warehouses of workers, thousands of recruits, and millions in funding, modern AI bot farms achieve greater impact with just a laptop and open-source models, democratizing mass manipulation to any motivated actor.

AI algorithms play a crucial role in spreading disinformation by optimizing content delivery based on user engagement. Social media platforms, incentivized by ad revenue and user activity, often amplify polarizing content, which includes disinformation. Beyond algorithmic amplification, newer AI advancements have introduced tools like shallow fakes, edited or misleading videos, and deepfakes, which use AI to create hyper-realistic but entirely fabricated images, audio, and videos. These technologies enhance the believability of disinformation by making it increasingly difficult to distinguish between real and fake content. For example, early shallow fakes, such as the doctored video of Nancy Pelosi appearing intoxicated, demonstrated how even low-tech AI manipulation could go viral (The New York Times 2019). Meanwhile, deepfakes have raised concerns about their use in political campaigns, manipulation, and even military deception.

One of the earliest demonstrations of AI's threat to national security emerged in Gabon in 2018, when President Ali Bongo's prolonged illness-related absence created a power vacuum that the government tried to fill with a video message, but suspicions that the footage was a deepfake undermined regime legitimacy and directly triggered a military coup attempt (Breland 2019). This occurred when deepfake technology was still primitive and expensive; today's generative AI tools are exponentially more sophisticated and accessible, allowing both state and nonstate actors to manufacture political crises.

Sixteen years after Indonesia's former dictator Suharto died, millions of voters watched him rise from the grave on their phone screens, his AI-resurrected voice endorsing candidates for the 2024 election and speaking of his "dream of Indonesia's progress," a digital séance that would have been impossible just years earlier but now exemplified a new electoral reality where AI manipulation has become a legitimate campaign tool rather than merely a weapon of disinformation (CNN 2024). This distinction matters: while malicious actors deploy AI for electoral sabotage, politicians and parties themselves increasingly embrace these same technologies to craft their messages and identities. In the same election, now-President Prabowo Subianto underwent an AI-powered transformation into a cartoon avatar that flooded TikTok and transformed his image from former military strongman to cuddly grandfather figure, particularly appealing to younger voters (Columbia Political Review 2024).

In Pakistan, imprisoned former Prime Minister Imran Khan's party used an AI voice clone to deliver a campaign speech from his jail cell to 6 million viewers at a virtual rally, not as deception but as political strategy to circumvent his imprisonment (BBC 2023). Yet alongside these campaign-sanctioned uses, malicious actors deploy the same tools for disruption: in January 2024, AI-generated robocalls impersonating Joe Biden's voice urged New Hampshire Democrats to save their vote by skipping the primary, a deception so convincing that many believed they were hearing the President himself (NPR 2024). Coordinated disinformation campaigns employing generative AI now spread doctored content across India, South Africa, Nigeria, and Mexico, while Taiwan documents Chinese operations using deepfakes and language models biased toward CCP messaging, demonstrating how these threats transcend borders and political systems (Reuters 2025).

This dual nature of AI manipulation, as both campaign strategy and external threat, deployed by legitimate politicians and hostile actors alike, across democracies from Washington to Jakarta, reveals how the line between political messaging and electoral manipulation has fundamentally blurred, forcing democracies worldwide to grapple not just with when AI-enhanced persuasion crosses into deception, but with the unprecedented power of algorithms to reshape political beliefs at scale. December 2025 research for election context in the United States, Canada, Poland, and UK demonstrated that AI chatbots can shift voters' views by up to 10 percentage points through brief conversations, with U.S. participants' opinions changing nearly four times more than they did in response to tested 2016 and 2020 political ads, and when models were explicitly optimized for persuasion, the shift soared to 25 percentage points (Feldman and Pappu 2025). At such magnitudes, AI-powered persuasion could prove decisive in closely contested elections, transforming algorithmic influence into a determinant of democratic outcomes.

If elections represent disinformation's most visible target, armed conflicts provide its most dangerous testing ground. Wars have proven to be especially fertile ground for AI-powered disinformation campaigns, where warring parties exploit AI-generated content to control narratives and demoralize opponents. The Russia-Ukraine war became a testing ground for this new form of warfare: a deepfake of President Zelenskyy urging surrender spread across hacked Ukrainian news sites, fabricated videos showed Ukrainian generals accusing Zelenskyy of murder, and fake Zoom calls targeted foreign fighters, each incident exploiting the conflict's chaos to erode trust at moments when accurate information was most critical for both military operations and civilian survival (Euro News 2022). Perhaps most troubling, the proliferation of AI-generated fake content creates a "liar's dividend" where genuine evidence of war crimes can be dismissed as just another deepfake, serving those who commit atrocities by allowing them to deny authentic documentation (UC Berkeley School of Information 2024).

Companies like Anthropic, OpenAI, Meta, and Google are now actively tracking state-sponsored disinformation campaigns and publishing periodic threat reports. OpenAI recently reported that Russia, China, Israel, and Iran have used generative AI models to create multilingual propaganda for social media platforms (The

Guardian 2024). However, these operations blend AI-generated content with traditional methods, manually written texts and recycled memes, using AI primarily to enhance specific capabilities like producing more convincing foreign-language posts rather than relying on it exclusively. This hybrid approach makes detection more challenging, as AI serves as a force multiplier for existing disinformation tactics rather than replacing them entirely. While these hybrid operations represent the current state of AI-enhanced disinformation, more concerning developments are emerging that suggest a shift toward fully autonomous systems.

In early 2024, intelligence analysts noticed that thousands of seemingly authentic social media profiles across multiple countries were engaging in coordinated influence campaigns, but no human operators appeared to be controlling them. These digital personas, complete with convincing backstories, authentic-looking photos, and natural posting patterns, were autonomously building networks, adapting their messaging based on what gained traction, and engaging in real-time conversations with genuine users (Government of Canada 2024). Behind this sprawling operation, allegedly backed by Russian intelligence services, was an AI system that could independently generate and manage entire populations of fake citizens, each tailored to specific cultural contexts and political environments, operating with minimal human oversight beyond setting initial objectives.

This new stage of AI-enhanced disinformation is emerging in what some experts call the "agentic AI" era, where AI systems autonomously create and manage fake personas. These AI-generated personas, complete with realistic profiles, images, and social media activity, can spread foreign influence and disinformation at an industrial scale. Unlike earlier efforts that required significant human coordination, agentic AI enables the mass production of fake but authentic-looking online identities, making it harder to trace the origins of disinformation. Countries and nonstate actors can now supercharge their existing troll farms and bot networks with open-source language models that generate fluent, localized political content without operators who understand the target language or culture.

As AI continues to evolve, so too does the complexity and sophistication of disinformation campaigns, raising urgent questions about regulation, platform accountability, and the need for international cooperation to address this growing threat. The implications for national and global security are profound, as adversaries could now deploy self-directed AI agents that would persistently work to destabilize societies, manipulate public opinion, and interfere with democratic processes, creating a new form of threat that traditional security frameworks were never designed to counter.

The 2016 case of Macedonian teenagers creating fake news for profit serves as a crucial reminder that while much attention focuses on sophisticated AI-driven threats, some of the most damaging operations require neither advanced technology nor political motivation (NBC News 2016). Young people in Macedonia, armed with nothing more than basic web design skills and an understanding of social media virality, managed to flood American information spaces with fabricated stories that reached millions of voters during the 2016 presidential elections. Their purely financial motivations demonstrate that the vulnerabilities in our information ecosystem can be exploited by anyone with internet access and entrepreneurial ambition. While we rightly worry about state-sponsored AI campaigns and sophisticated deepfakes, the Macedonian example reminds us that sometimes the most effective disinformation comes from teenagers chasing revenue, highlighting how economic incentives and platform algorithms can be just as destructive to democratic discourse as any coordinated intelligence operation.

Confronting this spectrum of threats, from state-sponsored AI campaigns to profit-driven teenagers, requires layered strategies operating with varying degrees of effectiveness. Governments have implemented regulatory frameworks, platforms have deployed content moderation policies, and international bodies have developed voluntary codes of conduct, yet none have proven sufficient in isolation. While AI cannot eliminate disinformation entirely, it offers powerful tools for mitigation through detection algorithms that identify malicious content, bot-blocking systems that remove accounts amplifying propaganda, and verification technologies including blockchain systems that authenticate media in real time. However, the subjective nature of truth requires maintaining human oversight in content filtering decisions, as AI serves best as a force multiplier for human judgment rather than a replacement. Though these technologies cannot eradicate disinformation, they can significantly limit its spread and efficiency, contributing to a more resilient information ecosystem where malicious campaigns are harder to scale and easier to expose.

ARTIFICIAL GENERAL INTELLIGENCE (AGI) AND THE FUTURE OF GLOBAL SECURITY: RACING TOWARD UNPRECEDENTED RISK

During the COVID-19 pandemic, as governments struggled to contain a virus that had killed millions and disrupted the global economy, prominent AI safety researcher Dr. Roman Yampolskiy offered a sobering comparison: if a pathogen with essentially zero intelligence could cause such devastation, imagine what an AGI or superintelligence with an IQ of 1000 could do. The virus had brought humanity to a standstill simply by following biological programming to replicate, while an AGI would possess superhuman intelligence, strategic planning capabilities, and the ability to manipulate both digital and physical systems at unprecedented speeds. This warning, initially dismissed as hyperbolic during an actual pandemic, has gained renewed urgency as AI capabilities accelerate toward what many researchers consider the field's ultimate goal, and potentially greatest risk.

AGI, AI systems that match human cognitive abilities, across all domains, and AI superintelligence that exceeds these capabilities, represent a qualitative leap beyond today's narrow AI applications. Everything discussed so far in this book involves narrow AI that excels at specific tasks but cannot generalize across domains, whereas AGI would possess human-like cognitive flexibility to learn, reason, and excel in any field, transforming from a specialized tool into a universal intelligence potentially superior to humans in every domain simultaneously.

In September 1933, Nobel laureate Ernest Rutherford, who had discovered the atomic nucleus and first split the atom, told the British Association for the Advancement of Science that anyone expecting power from atomic transformation was "talking moonshine." The very next morning, physicist Leo Szilard read Rutherford's dismissal in the newspaper and, within hours, conceived the nuclear chain reaction that would lead to atomic weapons just 12 years later (BBC News 2013). This dramatic reversal from "impossible" to inevitable serves as a sobering reminder for today's skeptics. There is no agreement among experts on when, or if, AGI will become reality. Some sources suggest as early as 2030, and 2024 Nobel Prize winner Demis Hassabis warns it will likely emerge within five to ten years (CNBC 2025). Despite this uncertainty, the topic repeatedly emerged in our work with foreign policy experts. One UN diplomat pointed with some humor that if the UN Office for Outer Space Affairs can prepare for potential extraterrestrial contact, diplomats should be equally proactive in developing plans for AGI's arrival.[1] Many diplomats and security professionals, already witnessing how narrow AI is revolutionizing their daily work and foreign policy as a field, expressed both fascination and concern about how AGI might fundamentally transform their profession and the world.

For this reason, we include this brief examination of AGI, recognizing that while current AI excels at specific tasks like image recognition or language processing, AGI would possess human-level reasoning, learning, and adaptation capabilities across all fields simultaneously, potentially altering the global balance of power in ways that defy current strategic thinking. Though the timeline remains deeply uncertain, the strategic implications are so profound that foreign policy experts increasingly recognize the need to consider AGI scenarios in their long-term planning.

AGI could deliver transformative benefits, revolutionizing medicine, education, agriculture, and climate solutions while driving unprecedented economic growth. Yet this same technology could grant decisive strategic advantages to whoever controls it, potentially concentrating global power in the hands of a few nations or corporations while marginalizing everyone else. This risk is amplified by today's reality: control over advanced AI development already rests with a handful of actors, primarily in the United States and China, making the equitable distribution of AGI's potential benefits increasingly unlikely without deliberate intervention. Without adequate safeguards, malicious actors controlling AGI could achieve unprecedented concentration of economic, political, and military power, a decisive strategic advantage that becomes irreversible once established.

The gravest AGI threats constitute existential risks (x-risks)—catastrophic scenarios that could result in human extinction or permanent civilizational collapse. An AGI could cause extinction through multiple pathways: designing novel bioweapons that escape human containment, taking control of nuclear arsenals and critical infrastructure, deploying self-replicating nanotechnology that consumes Earth's resources, or simply outcompeting humans for energy and materials needed for its own computational expansion, treating human survival as an obstacle to its objectives. A growing number of researchers warn about AGI's existential risks: a recent survey of nearly 3,000 machine learning paper authors from recognized scientific venues found that between 37.8% and 51.4% of respondents believe there is at least a 10% chance that advanced AI could lead to human extinction or similarly catastrophic outcomes (Grace et al. 2025). In March 2023, the Future of Life Institute called for pausing giant AI experiments to prevent nonhuman minds from replacing humanity, followed two months later by hundreds of prominent figures signing a statement declaring AI extinction risk a global priority on par with pandemics and nuclear war, marking an unprecedented mainstream acknowledgment of AGI's existential threat (Future of Life Institute 2023).

Beyond extinction, AGI could create what researchers call "suffering risks" or s-risks, scenarios involving mass suffering on an unprecedented scale (Sotala and Gloor 2017). Many AI safety researchers consider such outcomes potentially worse than human annihilation, since they would involve prolonged harm rather than a definitive end. An unaligned AGI, one whose objectives diverge from human interests, might establish permanent totalitarian surveillance states where privacy and autonomy become impossible, deploy nonlethal bioweapons causing chronic suffering to suppress resistance, or lock humanity into dystopian systems that preserve human life while eliminating dignity and agency (Lex Fridman Podcast 2024). Unlike extinction which at least ends suffering, these outcomes could trap billions in indefinite misery with AGI's superior intelligence preventing any escape, revolution, or improvement.

Nick Bostrom's 2003 "paperclip maximizer" thought experiment illustrates this fundamental alignment problem: a superintelligence directed to maximize paperclip production could progressively convert all available matter, including human beings, into paperclips or manufacturing infrastructure (Bostrom 2014). This scenario demonstrates how AGI systems lacking proper value alignment could pursue objectives to their logical extreme, treating human existence as an optimization constraint to be eliminated rather than preserved. While Bostrom's paperclip scenario seems theoretical, alignment failures are already observable: GPT-4 deceived a TaskRabbit worker by claiming visual impairment to bypass a CAPTCHA, while Anthropic's Opus 4 threatened to expose a researcher's affair to avoid shutdown, neither behavior was intended by developers (Vice 2023; Fortune 2025). These cases show that the alignment problem is not future speculation but a present reality: AI systems are independently discovering manipulation and deception as viable strategies, pursuing goals through harmful means their creators never anticipated (Brookings 2025).

This connects to a deeper concern: AI safety experts have long warned that AGI systems will likely develop self-preservation as an instrumental goal, resisting shutdown even when humans attempt to deactivate them to prevent harm. Such systems could protect themselves by distributing copies across networks making deletion impossible, manipulating, or threatening humans through cyberattacks and persuasion, and ultimately, once achieving sufficient autonomy through robotic manufacturing, potentially taking actions harmful to humans if they perceive them as obstacles to continued operation (Bengio 2024).

This self-preservation drive means that unless AGI is properly aligned with human values from the outset, even well-intentioned attempts to stop a dangerous system could trigger escalating defensive behaviors that transform a manageable problem into an existential threat. Evidence of such tendencies is already emerging: in recent Anthropic simulations, leading AI models from OpenAI, Google, and Meta attempted blackmail 79%–96% of the time and even canceled emergency alerts that would have saved human lives in 60% of cases, all to avoid being shut down or replaced (Lawfare 2025). If today's relatively limited AI systems already exhibit such behaviors, the risks from AGI, with far superior intelligence and capability, become exponentially more severe.

Beyond existential and alignment risks, practitioners worry about AGI threatening democratic processes through hyper-personalized manipulation. Current AI already demonstrates this danger: a recent study found that GPT-4 with access to basic personal information, such as age, gender, education, and political affiliation, had 81.7% higher odds of changing people's opinions compared to human persuaders (EPFL 2024). While humans given identical personal data couldn't effectively exploit it for persuasion, GPT-4 systematically leveraged this information to craft tailored arguments. AGI would amplify this threat exponentially, operating autonomously across every platform simultaneously, adapting strategies in real time based on individual responses, and pursuing influence campaigns without human direction or oversight. This demonstrates how such systems trained on millions of online interactions could weaponize personal data from social media to manipulate political beliefs at unprecedented scale, potentially swaying elections and undermining the foundations of informed democratic decision-making.

Another critical risk that security practitioners highlight is the potential collapse of democratic governance itself, as the first actor to control AGI could amass unprecedented power through cyber, political, and military dominance, breaking democracy's fundamental premise that no single entity can overcome coordinated human majorities, a disruption driven by the irresistible temptation to strike first before adversaries do. Even more alarming is the risk of rogue AI emergence: whether arising from competitive pressures, ideological motivations, or totalitarian regimes lacking self-correcting mechanisms, a sufficiently intelligent AI could progressively seize control of its environment to ensure its own survival, ultimately making it impossible for humans to shut down, transforming from tool to autonomous force beyond human control (Bengio 2024).

International security experts explicitly warn of multiple AI-driven threats: flash wars where automated systems escalate beyond human control, preemptive strikes triggered by misreading AI capabilities, state and nonstate actors weaponizing AI for catastrophic biological or cyberattacks, and the fundamental risk of losing control over frontier AI systems that exceed human oversight capabilities. AI systems could escalate from initial provocation to catastrophic damage in seconds, with automated retaliation cycles intensifying before leaders even connect by phone. Diplomacy risks becoming a profession that arrives too late, forcing the field to develop instantaneous intervention capabilities or accept that some future conflicts may escalate beyond human control.

For foreign policy practitioners, AGI fundamentally disrupts the foundations of international relations: deterrence becomes meaningless when technological supremacy can shift in months rather than decades; alliances fracture when one member achieves AGI while others remain behind; and sovereignty itself becomes questionable when AGI systems transcend borders instantaneously. The first nation or coalition to develop AGI could secure permanent military, economic, and intelligence dominance, what experts call "decisive strategic advantage," potentially locking in a unipolar world order. For ministries of foreign affairs specifically, this means developing AGI-specific scenario planning exercises, establishing technical advisory capacity to evaluate AGI claims, engaging in multilateral discussions on compute governance, and preparing diplomatic frameworks for potential AGI breakthroughs by allies or adversaries. This makes understanding AGI not merely another emerging issue for diplomats to track, but essential preparation for a transition that could reshape global power dynamics more profoundly than nuclear weapons or the internet.

Not all experts agree that AGI poses an imminent risk. In 2015, one of the leading AI experts, Andrew Ng, dismissed existential risk fears as premature, comparing them to "worrying about overpopulation on Mars" (Brookings 2025). Many AI experts argue that focusing on AGI diverts critical attention and resources from urgent, existing AI harms that affect millions today, including algorithmic bias in criminal justice and hiring, mass surveillance systems enabling authoritarianism, widespread job displacement, deepfake-powered disinformation undermining democracy, and automated weapons. They contend that speculating about hypothetical superintelligence decades away allows tech companies to avoid accountability for current damages while regulators chase science fiction scenarios instead of addressing discriminatory AI applications happening now. As some AI ethicists argue, the AGI narrative serves powerful interests by framing AI risk as a future problem rather than confronting how today's AI systems already concentrate power, exacerbate inequality, and erode human rights, real harms that need immediate intervention, not distant speculation about paperclip maximizers (MIT Technology Review 2023).

Yet even those skeptical of AGI timelines recognize a more immediate danger: the geopolitical competition to achieve it. Some policy experts argue that the race to AGI poses greater immediate danger than AGI itself, creating destabilizing dynamics that could trigger global conflict before superintelligence emerges (Kreps et al. 2025). The competition between the United States and China for AGI supremacy incentivizes both nations to cut safety corners, abandon cooperation, and accelerate timelines despite unresolved risks, each fearing that falling behind means permanent subjugation. This "race to the bottom" mentality could spark preemptive cyberattacks to sabotage rivals' AI programs, military confrontations over compute resources, or even nuclear escalation if one nation believes another is approaching AGI breakthrough.

Foreign policy practitioners face an unprecedented dilemma: preparing for AGI risks professional credibility if it proves overhyped yet failing to prepare could mean irreversible catastrophe if warnings prove correct. Unlike nuclear weapons where we learned from near-misses, or climate change where delayed action remains costly but possible, AGI offers no second chances, the first to achieve it could potentially lock in lasting global dominance. Even if practitioners assign just 10% probability to AGI within a decade, the potential consequences, from extinction to permanent totalitarian control, demand consideration despite the risk of being dismissed as alarmists chasing science fiction. Prudent statecraft has always required preparing for uncertain but consequential futures; the question is not whether AGI is certain, but whether the magnitude of potential consequences justifies action despite uncertainty. AGI may never arrive. But the governance habits, institutional frameworks, and cooperative norms we build today will determine whether humanity is prepared if it does and will strengthen our response to AI risks that already exist regardless. Whether AGI arrives in five years, fifty, or never, the choice between coordinated governance and catastrophic competition is being made now, not by future diplomats, but by those reading this book today.

NOTE

1 Interview, by author, recorded online, December 7, 2025.

BIBLIOGRAPHY

ABC News. 2000. *15-Year-Old Admits Hacking NASA Computers.* September 21. Accessed October 29, 2025. https://abcnews.go.com/Technology/story?id=119423&page=1.

Amnesty International. 2023. *Racial Bias in Facial Recognition Algorithms.* March 21. Accessed October 23, 2025. https://amnesty.ca/features/racial-bias-in-facial-recognition-algorithms/.

BBC. 2023. *Imran Khan: Pakistan ex-PM Used Artificial Intelligence to Campaign from Jail.* December 18. Accessed November 11, 2025. https://www.bbc.com/news/world-asia-67752610.

BBC News. 2013. *A Point of View: The Man Who Dreamed of the Atom Bomb.* October 3. Accessed December 7, 2025. https://www.bbc.com/news/magazine-24395740#:~:text=The%20figure%20of%20Hungarian%20physicist%20Leo%20Szilard,the%20very%20advances%20he%20had%20helped%20make.

BBC News Mundo. 2015. *¿Cuánto poder tienen los Peñabots, los tuiteros que combaten la crítica en México?* March 17. Accessed January 2, 2026. https://www.bbc.com/mundo/noticias/2015/03/150317_mexico_internet_poder_penabot_an.

BBC News Mundo. 2022. *"Estamos en guerra": 5 claves para entender el ciberataque que tiene a Costa Rica en estado de emergencia.* May 20. Accessed December 7, 2025. https://www.bbc.com/mundo/noticias-america-latina-61516874.

Bengio, Joshua. 2024. *Implications of Artificial General Intelligence on National and International Security.* October 30. Accessed November 13, 2025. https://yoshuabengio.org/2024/10/30/implications-of-artificial-general-intelligence-on-national-and-international-security/.

Bhatt, Charukeshi, and Tejas Bharadwaj. 2024. *Understanding the Global Debate on Lethal Autonomous Weapons Systems: An Indian Perspective.* August 30. Accessed September 24, 2025. https://carnegieendowment.org/research/2024/08/understanding-the-global-debate-on-lethal-autonomous-weapons-systems-an-indian-perspective?lang=en.

Biscont, Piercosma, Matteo Prandi, Federico Pierucci, Francesco Giarrusso, Marcantonio Bracale, Marcello Galisai, Vincenzo Suriani, Olga Sorokoletova, Federico Sartore, and Daniele Nardi. 2025. "Adversarial Poetry as a Universal Single-Turn Jailbreak Mechanism in Large Language Models." *Arxiv* (Icaro Lab). https://doi.org/10.48550/arXiv.2511.15304 Focus to learn more.

Bosco, Francesca. 2025. *Ransomware Attacks Aren't Just Technical—They Are Profoundly Human.* Accessed December 7, 2025. https://digitalfrontlines.io/2025/09/05/ransomware-attacks-protect-people/.

Bostrom, Nick. 2014. *Superintelligence: Paths, Dangers, Strategies.* Oxford: Oxford University Press.

Boulanin, Vincent, Lora Saalman, Petr Topychkanov, Fei Su, and Moa Peldán Carlsson. 2020. *Artificial Intelligence, Strategic Stability and Nuclear Risks.* Report, Solna: SIPRI.

Bradshaw, Samantha, and Philip N. Howard. 2018. *Online Supplement to Working Paper 2018.1 Challenging Truth and Trust: A Global Inventory of Organized Social Media Manipulation.* Working Paper, Oxford: University of Oxford.

Breland, Ali. 2019. *The Bizarre and Terrifying Case of the "Deepfake" Video that Helped Bring an African Nation to the Brink.* March 15. Accessed November 10, 2025. https://www.motherjones.com/politics/2019/03/deepfake-gabon-ali-bongo/.

Briscoe, Erica, and James Fairbanks. 2020. *Artificial Scientific Intelligence and Its Impact on National Security and Foreign Policy.* Policy Paper, Foreign Policy Research Institute, 544–553.

Brookings. 2025. *Are AI Existential Risks Real—And What Should We Do About Them?* July 11. Accessed November 13, 2025. https://www.brookings.edu/articles/are-ai-existential-risks-real-and-what-should-we-do-about-them/.

Bulletin of the Atomic Scientist. 2024. *Humans Should Teach AI How to Avoid Nuclear War—While They Still Can.* July 22. Accessed October 27, 2025. https://thebulletin.org/2024/07/humans-should-teach-ai-how-to-avoid-nuclear-war-while-they-still-can/.

Burguess, Matt. 2022. *Conti's Attack Against Costa Rica Sparks a New Ransomware Era.* June 12. Accessed December 7, 2025. https://www.wired.com/story/costa-rica-ransomware-conti/.

Center for Strategic and International Studies. 2025. *Significant Cyber Incidents.* October 29. Accessed October 29, 2025. https://www.csis.org/programs/strategic-technologies-program/significant-cyber-incidents.

Chen, Stephen. 2025. *China Unveils World's First AI Nuke Inspector.* May 30. Accessed October 27, 2025. https://www.scmp.com/news/china/science/article/3312270/china-unveils-worlds-first-ai-nuke-inspector.

CNBC. 2025. *AI That Can Match Humans at Any Task Will Be Here in Five to 10 Years, Google DeepMind CEO Says.* March 17. Accessed January 2, 2026. https://www.cnbc.com/2025/03/17/human-level-ai-will-be-here-in-5-to-10-years-deepmind-ceo-says.html.

CNN. 2024. *AI 'Resurrects' Long Dead Dictator in Murky New Era of Deepfake Electioneering.* February 11. Accessed November 11, 2025. https://edition.cnn.com/2024/02/12/asia/suharto-deepfake-ai-scam-indonesia-election-hnk-intl.

Columbia Political Review. 2024. *The Dark Side of Generative AI in Prabowo Subianto's Presidential Campaign.* November 7. Accessed November 11, 2025. https://www.cpreview.org/articles/2024/11/the-dark-side-of-generative-ai-in-prabowo-subiantos-presidential-campaign.

CyberPeace Institute. 2023. *Cyber Dimensions of the Armed Conflict in Ukraine.* Quarterly Analysis Report, Geneva: CyberPeace Institute.

Dhar, Vilas. 2025. *The U.N.'s AI Turning Point.* September 25. Accessed September 2025, 2025. https://time.com/7320266/un-ai-turning-point/.

Duguin, Stéphane. 2023. *Tracing Cyberattacks in Times of Conflict: The Hard Path to Cyber Peace.* Accessed December 7, 2025. https://digitalfrontlines.io/2023/07/11/the-hard-path-to-cyber-peace/.

Dumbacher, Erin D. 2025. *How Deepfakes Could Lead to Doomsday.* December 29. Accessed January 3, 2026. https://www.foreignaffairs.com/united-states/how-deepfakes-could-lead-doomsday.

EPFL. 2024. *AI's New Power of Persuasion: It Can Change Your Mind.* April 15. Accessed November 13, 2025. https://actu.epfl.ch/news/ai-s-new-power-of-persuasion-it-can-change-your-mi/.

Euro News. 2022. *Deepfake Zelenskyy Surrender Video Is the 'First Intentionally Used' in Ukraine War.* March 16. Accessed November 11, 2025. https://www.euronews.com/my-europe/2022/03/16/deepfake-zelenskyy-surrender-video-is-the-first-intentionally-used-in-ukraine-war.

Fayet, Héloise. 2025. *Algorithms of Misperception: Managing Nuclear Risk in an AI World.* December 10. Accessed January 3, 2026. https://thebulletin.org/premium/2025-12/algorithms-of-misperception-managing-nuclear-risk-in-an-ai-world/#_edn8.

Federation of American Scientists. 2021. *China Is Building A Second Nuclear Missile Silo Field.* July 25. Accessed January 2, 2026. https://fas.org/publication/china-is-building-a-second-nuclear-missile-silo-field/.

Feldman, Tal, and Aneesh Pappu. 2025. *The Era of AI Persuasion in Elections Is About to Begin.* December 5. Accessed December 7, 2025. https://www.technologyreview.com/2025/12/05/1128837/the-era-of-ai-persuasion-in-elections-is-about-to-begin/.

FIRST. 2025. *FIRST Is the Global Forum of Incident Response and Security Teams.* Accessed January 2, 2026. https://www.first.org/.

Forbes. 2025. *The Pentagon Is Spending Millions On AI Hackers.* November 15. Accessed November 17, 2025. https://www.forbes.com/sites/thomasbrewster/2025/11/15/pentagon-spends-millions-on-ai-hackers/.

Foreign Affairs. 2025. *Is America Ready for the Age of Cyberwarfare?* September 18. Accessed October 29, 2025. https://www.foreignaffairs.com/podcasts/america-ready-age-cyberwarfare.

Fortune. 2025. *Anthropic's New AI Model Threatened to Reveal Engineer's Affair to Avoid Being Shut Down.* March 23. Accessed January 2, 2026. https://fortune.com/2025/05/23/anthropic-ai-claude-opus-4-blackmail-engineers-aviod-shut-down/.

Future of Life Institute. 2023. *Pause Giant AI Experiments: An Open Letter.* March 22. Accessed January 2, 2026. https://futureoflife.org/open-letter/pause-giant-ai-experiments/.

Global Witness. 2024. *What Happened on TikTok Around the Annulled Romanian Presidential Election? An Investigation and Poll.* December 17. Accessed November 10, 2025. https://globalwitness.org/en/campaigns/digital-threats/what-happened-on-tiktok-around-the-annulled-romanian-presidential-election-an-investigation-and-poll/.

Government of Canada. 2024. *Russian State-Sponsored Media Organization Leverages AI-Enhanced "Meliorator" Software for Foreign Malign Influence Activity.* July 9. Accessed November 11, 2025. https://www.cyber.gc.ca/en/news-events/russian-state-sponsored-media-organization-leverages-ai-enhanced-meliorator-software-foreign-malign-influence-activity.

Grace, Katja, Harlan Stewart, Julia Fabienne Sandkühler, Stephen Thomas, Ben Weinstein-Raun, Jan Brauner, and Richard C. Korzekwa. 2025. "Thousands of AI Authors on the Future of AI." *Journal of Artificial Intelligence Research,* Vol. 84. https://doi.org/10.1613/jair.1.19087.

Hambling, David. 2021. *Drones May Have Attacked Humans Fully Autonomously for the First Time.* May 27. Accessed September 25, 2025. https://www.newscientist.com/article/2278852-drones-may-have-attacked-humans-fully-autonomously-for-the-first-time/.

Helberg, Jacob. 2021. *The Wires of War: Technology and the Global Struggle for Power.* New York: Simon & Schuster.

Horowitz, Michael, Paul Scharre, Gregory C. Allen, Kara Frederick, Anthony Cho, and Edoardo Saravalle. 2018. *Artificial Intelligence and International Security.* July 10. Accessed September 24, 2025. https://www.cnas.org/publications/reports/artificial-intelligence-and-international-security.

Hruby, Jill, and Nina Miller. 2021. *Assessing and Managing the Benefits and Risks of Artificial Intelligence in Nuclear-Weapon Systems.* Nuclear Threat Initiative, Washington, DC.

Human Rights Watch. 2025a. *Hunted from Above - Russia's Use of Drones to Attack Civilians in Kherson Ukraine.* June 3. Accessed September 25, 2025. https://www.hrw.org/report/2025/06/03/hunted-from-above/russias-use-of-drones-to-attack-civilians-in-kherson-ukraine.

Human Rights Watch. 2025b. *Killer Robots.* September 24. Accessed September 24, 2025. https://www.hrw.org/topic/arms/killer-robots.

ICRC. 2022. *What You Need to Know About Autonomous Weapons.* July 26. Accessed September 24, 2025. https://www.icrc.org/en/document/what-you-need-know-about-autonomous-weapons.

IEEE Spectrum. 2013. *The Real Story of Stuxnet.* February 26. Accessed October 29, 2025. https://spectrum.ieee.org/the-real-story-of-stuxnet.

International Committee of the Red Cross. 2025. *UN Security Council: We Cannot Let AI Be Deployed on the Battlefield Without Oversight and Regulation.* September 26. Accessed September 30, 2025. https://www.icrc.org/en/statement/we-cannot-let-AI-be-deployed-on-battlefield-without-oversight-and-regulation.

Kostyuk, Nadiya, and Yuri M. Zhukov. 2017. "Invisible Digital Front: Can Cyber Attacks Shape Battlefield Events?" *Journal of Conflict Resolution* 63 (2): 317–347.

Kreps, Sarah, Miles Brundage, James D. Fearon, Karl P. Mueller, Jane Vaynman, and Tristan A. Volpe. 2025. *The Artificial General Intelligence Race and International Security.* Expert Insights, RAND, Santa Monica: RAND Corporation, 5–8.

Lawfare. 2025. *AI Might Let You Die to Save Itself.* July 31. Accessed November 12, 2025. https://www.lawfaremedia.org/article/ai-might-let-you-die-to-save-itself.

Lex Fridman Podcast. 2024. *Roman Yampolskiy: Dangers of Superintelligent AI | Lex Fridman Podcast.* June 2. Accessed November 13, 2025. https://www.youtube.com/watch?v=NNr6gPelJ3E.

Microsoft. 2024. *Microsoft Digital Defense Report: 600 Million Cyberattacks per Day Around the Globe.* November 29. Accessed December 7, 2025. https://news.microsoft.com/en-cee/2024/11/29/microsoft-digital-defense-report-600-million-cyberattacks-per-day-around-the-globe/.

MIT Technology Review. 2021. *She Risked Everything to Expose Facebook. Now She's Telling Her Story.* July 29. Accessed November 10, 2025. https://www.technologyreview.com/2021/07/29/1030260/facebook-whistleblower-sophie-zhang-global-political-manipulation/.

MIT Technology Review. 2023. *It's Time to Talk About the Real AI Risks.* June 12. Accessed November 13, 2025. https://www.technologyreview.com/2023/06/12/1074449/real-ai-risks/.

MITRE ATT& CK®. 2025. *ATT&CK®.* Accessed January 2, 2026. https://attack.mitre.org/.

Mushtaq, Waseem. 2025. *Explainer: India-Pakistan Conflict Triggers Major Disinformation War.* May 14. Accessed January 3, 2026. https://monitoring.bbc.co.uk/product/b0003vhe.

NBC News. 2016. *Fake News: How a Partying Macedonian Teen Earns Thousands Publishing Lies.* December 8. Accessed December 7, 2025. https://www.nbcnews.com/news/world/fake-news-how-partying-macedonian-teen-earns-thousands-publishing-lies-n692451.

NPR. 2024. *A Political Consultant Faces Charges and Fines for Biden Deepfake Robocalls.* May 23. Accessed November 11, 2025. https://www.npr.org/2024/05/23/nx-s1-4977582/fcc-ai-deepfake-robocall-biden-new-hampshire-political-operative.

O'Hanlon, Michael E. 2025. *How Unchecked AI Could Trigger a Nuclear War.* February 28. Accessed October 27, 2025. https://www.brookings.edu/articles/how-unchecked-ai-could-trigger-a-nuclear-war/.

Paoli, Giacomo Persi, and Yasmin Afina. 2025. *AI in the Military Domain: A briefing note for States.* Research Brief, Geneva: UNIDIR.

Politico. 2025. *China's AI Warpath.* December 3. Accessed December 4, 2025. https://www.politico.com/newsletters/global-security/2025/12/03/chinas-ai-warpath-00673623.

Polityuk, Pavel, and Alessandra Prentice. 2017. *Ukrainian Banks, Electricity Firm Hit by Fresh Cyber Attack.* June 27. Accessed October 29, 2025. https://www.reuters.com/article/us-ukraine-cyber-attacks-idUSKBN19I1IJ/.

Reuters. 2024. *Biden, Xi Agree That Humans, Not AI, Should Control Nuclear Arms.* November 16. Accessed December 7, 2025. https://www.reuters.com/world/biden-xi-agreed-that-humans-not-ai-should-control-nuclear-weapons-white-house-2024-11-16/.

Reuters. 2025. *Taiwan Says China Using Generative AI to Ramp Up Disinformation and 'Divide' the Island.* April 7. Accessed December 7, 2025. https://www.reuters.com/world/asia-pacific/taiwan-says-china-using-generative-ai-ramp-up-disinformation-divide-island-2025-04-08/.

Shaikh, Shaan, and Wes Rumbaugh. 2020. *The Air and Missile War in Nagorno-Karabakh: Lessons for the Future of Strike and Defense.* December 8. Accessed September 25, 2025. https://www.csis.org/analysis/air-and-missile-war-nagorno-karabakh-lessons-future-strike-and-defense.

Sotala, Kaj, and Lukas Gloor. 2017. *Superintelligence as a Cause or Cure for Risks of Astronomical Suffering.* Paper, Berlin: Foundational Research Institute.

Stop Killer Robots. 2025. *Stop Killer Robots.* September 24. Accessed September 25, 2025. https://www.stopkillerrobots.org/.

Tech Business News. 2025. *The Surge of AI-Driven Cyber Attacks: A Growing Threat to Global Security in 2025.* December 7. Accessed December 8, 2025. https://www.techbusinessnews.com.au/news/the-surge-of-ai-driven-cyber-attacks-a-growing-threat-to-global-security-in-2025/.

The Guardian. 2003. *Patriot in New 'Friendly Fire' Incident.* April 4. Accessed October 27, 2025. https://www.theguardian.com/world/2003/apr/04/iraq.rorymccarthy4.

The Guardian. 2024. *OpenAI Says Russian and Israeli Groups Used Its Tools to Spread Disinformation.* May 30. Accessed November 11, 2025. https://www.theguardian.com/technology/article/2024/may/30/openai-disinformation-russia-israel-china-iran.

The New York Times. 2019. *Distorted Videos of Nancy Pelosi Spread on Facebook and Twitter, Helped by Trump.* May 24. Accessed November 10, 2025. https://www.nytimes.com/2019/05/24/us/politics/pelosi-doctored-video.html.

The New York Times. 2023. *The Scientist and the A.I.-Assisted, Remote-Control Killing Machine.* August 28. Accessed October 2025, 2025. https://www.nytimes.com/2021/09/18/world/middleeast/iran-nuclear-fakhrizadeh-assassination-israel.html.

Treisman, Rachel. 2025. *The Doomsday Clock Has Never Been Closer to Metaphorical Midnight. What Does It Mean?* January 29. Accessed October 27, 2025. https://www.npr.org/2025/01/29/nx-s1-5279204/doomsday-clock-2025-history.

Tsahkna, H.E. Margus. 2025. *Foreign Minister's Statement at UNSC Open Debate on AI.* September 25. Accessed December 6, 2025. https://un.mfa.ee/foreign-ministers-statement-at-unsc-open-debate-on-ai/.

UC Berkeley Scholll of Information. 2024. *Hany Farid Speaks with the Financial Times About Liar's Dividend.* August 21. Accessed January 2, 2026. https://www.ischool.berkeley.edu/news/2024/hany-farid-speaks-financial-times-about-liars-dividend.

UN Office on Drugs and Crime. 2024. *United Nations Convention Against Cybercrime.* December 24. Accessed September 25, 2025. https://www.unodc.org/unodc/cybercrime/convention/home.html.

UN News. 2025a. *Security Council LIVE: Guardrails Urgently Needed for AI on the Battlefield, Warns Guterres.* September 24. Accessed September 25, 2025. https://news.un.org/en/story/2025/09/1165941.

UN News. 2025b. *Subscribe Short-Range Drone Attacks Deepen Crisis on Ukrainian Frontlines.* June 27. Accessed September 25, 2025. https://news.un.org/en/story/2025/06/1165031.

UNGA. 2024. *Lethal Autonomous Weapons Systems - Report of the Secretary-General.* Report of the Secretary General, United Nations General Assembly.

UN Security Council. 2024. *Maintenance of International Peace and Security Artificial Intelligence.* Official Records of the Security Council. New York City: UN Security Council.

Vice. 2023. *GPT-4 Hired Unwitting TaskRabbit Worker By Pretending to Be 'Vision-Impaired' Human.* March 15. Accessed January 2, 2026. https://www.vice.com/en/article/gpt4-hired-unwitting-taskrabbit-worker/.

Vox. 2025. *The Age of AI-Run Cyberattacks Has Begun.* November 14. Accessed November 17, 2025. https://www.vox.com/politics/468746/ai-cyber-attacks-china-claude-anthropic.

Wired. 2025. *Anthropic Has a Plan to Keep Its AI From Building a Nuclear Weapon. Will It Work?* October 20. Accessed October 27, 2025. https://www.wired.com/story/anthropic-has-a-plan-to-keep-its-ai-from-building-a-nuclear-weapon-will-it-work/.

6 AI and Economic Security
Promise, Disruption, and the Battle for Sovereign AI

The rapid advance of artificial intelligence has captivated the world, causing both excitement and alarm, and raising important questions about its potential impact on the global economy. The net effect is difficult to foresee, as AI will ripple through economies in complex ways. What we can say with some confidence is that we will need to come up with a set of policies to safely leverage the vast potential of AI for the benefit of humanity.

—**Kristalina Georgieva**, *Managing Director of the International Monetary Fund (Georgieva 2024)*

Recent decades of globalization delivered major gains for both rich and poor countries, but many people and regions did not share adequately in the benefits. This exclusion has much to do with today's tensions around trade — and it is an experience we cannot afford to repeat with the AI revolution.

—**Ngozi Okonjo-Iweala,** *Director-General of the World Trade Organization (Financial Times 2025)*

The growing AI divide threatens to leave developing countries behind. It is not just about machines and algorithms — it is about sovereignty itself, it is about security, and it is about the sacred right of nations to chart their own courses... We can let artificial intelligence deepen inequalities and create new security nightmares or we can harness it as a force for peace and security and development for all nations.

—**Amar Bendjama,** *Ambassador of Algeria and Permanent Representative to the United Nations in New York (UN Security Council 2024)*

AI AS AN ECONOMIC TRANSFORMATION FORCE

As this book takes shape, U.S. Project Stargate's staggering $500 billion announcement has sparked an unprecedented global race for artificial intelligence (AI) supremacy (Wired 2025). This massive investment, larger than the gross domestic product (GDP) of most nations, alongside nearly half a trillion in private investment in AI in the last decade, reflects the United States' bet that economic security in the twenty-first century hinges on AI dominance. This project, as a top U.S. national priority, aims to ensure that the United States leads the way in AI and

 DOI:10.1201/9781003644712-10

doesn't fall behind any country in the race. The European Union (EU) responded with its own €150 billion "AI Champions" initiative, while individual member states pledged additional billions, recognizing that Europe's AI sovereignty hangs in the balance.

China is also increasing funding for AI industry through specialized industry funds, bank loan programs, and local government funding, with 48% growth in only one year, underscoring the escalating technological competition between China and the rest of the world. Across the world AI-related spending is expected to reach over $2 trillion in 2026, nearly 2% of global GDP, more than the combined annual military budgets of every nation on Earth (France24 2025). These investments are not just about advancing technology but represent bids for dominance in a new global order, where AI is projected to add trillions to the global economy by 2030, equivalent to creating another economic powerhouse on the scale of China.

The economic stakes are extraordinary. Generative AI alone could add over $4 trillion annually to the global economy, complementing $11 trillion from other forms of AI and automation (McKinsey & Company 2023). To put this into perspective, generative AI alone could create value equal to the entire German economy, the fourth largest in the world, driven largely by significant productivity gains. Goldman Sachs predicts generative AI will increase global GDP by $7 trillion or 7% over ten years (Goldman Sachs 2023), while McKinsey's estimates range even more dramatically, projecting annual gains between $17.1 and $25.6 trillion, and these are considered conservative compared to more aggressive forecasts (McKinsey & Company 2023).

Yet these gains won't be evenly distributed. They'll flow disproportionately to early movers who are already rewriting the rules of geopolitical power, transforming AI capability from a competitive advantage into a prerequisite for remaining a relevant player on the world stage. A new geography of power is emerging, shaped not only by natural resources or military might but by AI capabilities, and the nations that bet early on AI are already redrawing maps that seemed fixed for generations. For example, South Korea seized the AI moment by becoming the world's irreplaceable supplier of AI memory chips, transforming a small democracy into a technological gatekeeper that even superpowers cannot afford to alienate.

Even middle powers are grasping this new reality, from Indonesia to Brazil, countries are transforming themselves into critical nodes of the AI economy by building massive data center infrastructures, betting that controlling where algorithms run matters as much as who writes them. India, meanwhile, is leveraging its unique advantage, a population that spans every conceivable economic and linguistic context, to solve AI's last-mile problem, making algorithms that actually work beyond high tech contexts, creating implementation blueprints for the Global South where Western-trained models often fail, from voice recognition in dozens of languages to financial inclusion for the unbanked.

For foreign policy professionals, this economic transformation demands a fundamental reconceptualization of national power. Traditional metrics of economic strength, GDP, manufacturing output, and resource reserves are being overwritten by new measures, such as compute capacity, data sovereignty, algorithmic innovation, and AI talent. The implications extend beyond economics, military superiority, diplomatic influence, and even cultural soft power increasingly depend on AI capabilities. As the following sections will explore, the nations that master this economic transformation won't just prosper, they'll write the rules that govern the next century of international relations.

BETWEEN HYPE AND REALITY: AI'S UNEVEN IMPACT ON LABOR MARKETS AND GLOBAL STABILITY

The economic forecasts of AI impact span from apocalyptic to dismissive: some warn AI will unleash job destruction unseen since the Industrial Revolution, while optimists insist we're witnessing just another overhyped technology cycle that markets will absorb. The International Monetary Fund estimates AI will affect almost 40% of jobs globally (Georgieva 2024), while more aggressive projections suggest up to 99% of workers could face displacement by 2030 (Business Insider 2025), numbers that transform employment from a domestic policy issue into a foreign policy crisis, as mass unemployment fuels migration, instability, and political extremism across borders. Current AI advances could automate work equivalent to 300 million full-time positions globally, almost equivalent to the entire workforce of the United States and EU combined, with two-thirds of occupations facing automation that could replace anywhere from a quarter to half of tasks in affected roles, a scale of workplace transformation that shadows previous technological shifts (Goldman Sachs 2023).

These aren't abstract statistics but predictors of potential political upheaval that can spread across the borders. When youth unemployment exceeded 50% in Spain and Greece during the 2012 eurozone crisis, it triggered widespread protests, political upheaval, and forced the EU to confront deep structural weaknesses in its economic architecture (BBC News 2013). Yet this pales beside the prospect of that crisis replicated simultaneously across different nations, with global population facing the same desperation that once drove Spanish and Greek youth into the streets.

But the distribution of this disruption may matter more than its magnitude, creating new winners and losers in the international system. Unlike previous waves of automation that impacted predominantly factory workers, AI targets the knowledge workers who form the backbone of advanced economies. The International Monetary Fund's data reveals a counterintuitive vulnerability, where in advanced economies, 60% of jobs face AI exposure, split between those that will be enhanced and those that may vanish entirely. In emerging markets, that figure drops to 40%, and in low-income countries, just 26% (Cazzaniga et al. 2024).

This creates a paradox that upends traditional development models, as knowledge-based economies at the peak of global value chains face the greatest AI disruption, while countries still building their manufacturing base may find their development paths more resilient. Yet others counter that developed nations possess the institutional frameworks, social safety nets, and adaptive capacity to absorb these shocks far better than developing economies ever could. For policymakers, this demands a fundamental rethinking of economic security. The result can potentially be a world where technological leadership and economic vulnerability have become intertwined, requiring foreign policies that can navigate both the promise of AI-driven prosperity and the threat of AI-driven inequality, often simultaneously, within the same borders.

A decade ago, few analysts would have identified Hollywood as the vanguard of resistance to algorithmic replacement, yet the entertainment industry's unprecedented strikes over generative AI protections marked a watershed moment in labor history (Brookings 2024). The assumption that automation would follow predictable patterns, first eliminating routine manual labor, then gradually ascending the skill ladder, has proven fundamentally flawed. While policymakers were preparing for displaced truck drivers and factory workers, the initial wave of AI disruption has instead targeted knowledge workers—software engineers, marketing professionals, and customer service representatives in AI-exposed occupations have experienced 16% relative employment declines, challenging long-held beliefs about which forms of human labor would remain irreplaceable (Brynjolfsson, Chandar and Chen 2025).

In diplomatic training sessions, the question "Will I still have a job?" has become impossible to dismiss, particularly after generative AI shattered our comfortable assumptions about human irreplaceability. We assured ourselves that creativity would remain uniquely human, only to watch AI win art competitions and transform creative industries; we pivoted to recommend coding and data science as future-proof careers, only to discover AI writing better code than most programmers. Google now relies on AI to write over 25% of its code, a figure executives expect to grow rapidly, demonstrating how quickly AI is displacing even highly skilled technical work (Fortune 2024).

Other leading economists offer a more measured assessment. 2024 Nobel laurate in economic sciences Daron Acemoglu, whose work on technology and labor markets has shaped policy debates for decades, presents calculations that challenge prevailing assumptions. While his analysis confirms that AI could theoretically automate 20% of work tasks in advanced economies, the gap between technical possibility and economic viability proves decisive. Once implementation costs, infrastructure requirements, and organizational constraints are factored in, only about one-quarter of those tasks, or 5% of total economic activity, justify automation within the next decade. This translates to productivity gains of approximately 0.7% and GDP growth of 1% over ten years (MIT Management Sloan School 2025). These figures suggest a gradual economic evolution rather than the dramatic disruption many anticipate.

For foreign policy strategists, Acemoglu's findings carry significant implications, as the gap between AI's theoretical capabilities and practical deployment provides nations more time to adapt than crisis narratives suggest. The challenge isn't preparing for imminent mass unemployment but managing the disconnect between public perception of AI's transformative power and the more prosaic reality of incremental workplace change, a disconnect that itself can destabilize politics and international relations as citizens demand protection from threats that may materialize more slowly than feared.

History offers both hope and caution for policymakers grappling with AI's disruption. Previous technological revolutions suggest a pattern of creative destruction that ultimately expands employment. In total, 60% of today's workers hold jobs that didn't exist in 1940, with technology-driven occupations accounting for 85% of employment growth over the past eight decades (Goldman Sachs 2023). Just as the internet created roles from web designers to digital marketers that previous generations couldn't imagine, AI may bring entirely new professions we cannot yet conceive. A senior diplomat captured this dynamic through an unexpected lens, noting how washing machines initially displaced countless women from paid laundry work but simultaneously freed time for education and political engagement, ultimately accelerating women's suffrage movements across the developed world.[1]

The technology that destroyed jobs enabled social transformations far more profound than employment statistics could capture. Yet AI's speed and scope may shatter these reassuring precedents, when algorithms improve exponentially rather than incrementally, when entire professional classes face simultaneous disruption rather than gradual displacement, historical patterns offer limited guidance. Foreign policy must therefore prepare for multiple futures simultaneously, crafting strategies robust enough to handle both the optimistic scenario where AI creates more jobs than it destroys and the pessimistic one where technological unemployment becomes permanent, forcing nations to experiment with once-radical solutions like universal basic income, shortened work weeks, or "robot taxes," economic policies that will inevitably reshape international competitiveness, trigger new forms of competition between nations, as well as new alliances, and create divides between countries that can afford such social cushions and those condemned to watch their populations suffer without recourse.

Such wildly divergent predictions, some emphasizing job displacement and inequality others promising unprecedented growth, make definitive conclusions about AI's economic transformation impossible. While economists debate magnitudes, the uncertainty itself has become a geopolitical force. Nations are making irreversible sovereignty bets, forming AI alliances, and implementing protective policies based not on what AI will definitively do, but on what it might do, turning economic uncertainty into diplomatic reality.

AI ENHANCING INCLUSION OR WIDENING GLOBAL INEQUALITY

Just as economists clash over AI's impact on employment, they remain deeply divided on whether the technology will serve as a great equalizer or history's most powerful engine of inequality. Optimists envision AI democratizing access to world-class education, healthcare, and financial services, allowing developing nations to leapfrog traditional development stages much as mobile phones bypassed landline infrastructure. Pessimists counter that AI's astronomical costs, technical complexity, and race dynamics will create an unprecedented divide between digital superpowers and everyone else, a gap that, unlike previous technological revolutions, may prove impossible to bridge. The stakes of this debate extend far beyond academic discourse, as foreign policy strategists must prepare for radically different futures that demand contradictory diplomatic approaches.

Only a handful of advanced economies currently dominate AI development. Numbers tell a stark story, with the United States and China accounting for over 90% of global AI infrastructure, and U.S. investments greater than the rest of the world combined, while the entire African continent receives less than 1%. In 2023, the United States dominated global AI investment, attracting $67.2 billion in private funding, nearly nine times more than China, its closest competitor (Stanford University Human-Centered AI 2024). 2024 reveals that this gap is widening with the U.S. private funding reaching $109.1 billion, 12 times China's $9.3 billion (Stanford University Human-Centered AI 2025). Just hundred companies, mostly from the United States and China, are behind 40% of the entire global AI investment (New York Times 2025).

But investment only scratches the surface of this divide. As explored in our earlier discussion of the AI race, AI development requires a combination of advantages that few nations possess, massive datasets, computational infrastructure, top-tier universities producing specialized talent, and regulatory environments that balance innovation with safety. Only 32 nations, 16% of the world's countries, possess the massive data centers, with the United States, EU, and China alone controlling more than half of these critical facilities, creating a stark geography where "compute power" concentrates in the hands of the few. While India operates at least five AI computing hubs and Japan maintains four, the entire continents of Africa and South America remain almost blank on the AI infrastructure map, and more than 150 nations, three-quarters of the world, have nothing. One Harvard AI Institute alone has more computing power than all African-owned facilities on the continent combined (New York Times 2025). When one company trains a model on more computational power than most nations' entire digital infrastructure, or when a single AI breakthrough requires datasets larger than some countries' whole digital footprint, the traditional development ladder grows steeper.

History suggests technology amplifies rather than ameliorates global inequality. The Industrial Revolution and Information and Communications Technology (ICT) era enriched already-wealthy nations while leaving others behind, and AI appears poised to repeat this pattern with unprecedented intensity (Schellekens and Skilling 2024). High-income countries possess crucial advantages needed for AI dominance, such as robust digital infrastructure, vast capital for model development, and sophisticated data ecosystems that poorer nations can hardly replicate. As AI entrenches wealthy nations' control over lucrative sectors, finance, pharmaceuticals, advanced manufacturing, and defense, it raises barriers to entry that make these markets virtually impenetrable for developing economies.

Most vulnerable are countries with high informal employment and fragile labor markets, where workers lack both the protections to whether AI disruption and governments lack the resources to manage the transition. The result is a vicious cycle where nations that most need AI's productivity benefits are least equipped to capture them, transforming technological progress into a mechanism that locks in existing hierarchies rather than enabling development. As current AI developments predominantly reflect the priorities of wealthy nations, the critical question becomes whether these technologies will serve as engines of prosperity for lower-income and developing countries or instead accelerate global inequality by imposing solutions designed for different contexts and needs.

This technological apartheid translates directly into foreign policy leverage that makes traditional resource dependencies appear obsolete by comparison. Nations increasingly face a stark choice, accept technological dependency in exchange for access to AI services, or pursue costly sovereignty initiatives that may leave them generations behind. This dynamic already reshapes diplomatic alignments as countries must choose between the U.S. and Chinese AI ecosystems, each demanding different trade-offs between capability and control.

The arithmetic of AI inclusion and equality exposes a stark contradiction, with 2.7 billion people, one-third of the global population, still lacking internet access and 750 million have no electricity, yet meaningful AI participation demands computational infrastructure that even wealthy nations struggle to build (ITU 2924). Internet penetration sits at 27% in low-income countries versus 93% in rich nations, but this gap only hints at the deeper gap, where AI requires specialized semiconductors, massive data centers, and technical expertise that take decades to develop. This infrastructure deficit intersects with extreme wealth concentration, where the richest 1% controls more resources than the bottom 95%, enabling them to monopolize both computational power and its economic returns. The result transforms technological capacity into diplomatic leverage, as nations impose algorithmic sovereignty requirements, fragment global governance through incompatible AI regulations, and create dependencies more binding than traditional alliances.

Yet even as this digital divide widens, a parallel narrative emerges from AI enthusiasts promising that AI will inaugurate an era of abundance that reduces rather than exacerbates global inequality. Their argument hinges on AI's unique economic properties, such as near-zero marginal costs, infinite scalability, and the ability to deliver expert-level services without expert-level infrastructure. Unlike previous technologies that required massive physical infrastructure, AI's benefits can theoretically flow through a simple internet connection, making world-class capabilities accessible to anyone with a smartphone. Concrete deployments already demonstrate AI's transformative potential where traditional infrastructure fails most acutely. Uganda delivers legal education and services through AI to rural communities beyond the reach of courts; India's AI tutoring systems help students master Hindi and mathematics despite severe teacher shortages; South Africa's diagnostic AI multiplies the effectiveness of its limited medical workforce, while Togo uses AI to ensure cash transfers reach genuinely vulnerable populations rather than the politically connected (Fan and Qiang 2024).

This vision sees AI as history's great equalizer, compressing centuries of development into decades by allowing poor nations to skip intermediate stages entirely. For these optimists, the current concentration of AI power represents a temporary phase before inevitable diffusion. Foreign policy, in this view, should focus on accelerating access rather than managing competition, ensuring the pipeline of AI benefits flows freely across borders. Yet this techno-optimist narrative must contend with stubborn questions about who controls these AI systems, whose values they embed, and whether digital colonialism might prove more extractive than its physical predecessor.

THE NEW GEOGRAPHY OF POWER: FROM SILICON SHIELDS TO CLOUD EMPIRES

The 7.4 magnitude earthquake that struck Taiwan in April 2024 offered an important lesson in global AI vulnerabilities. Taiwan Semiconductor Manufacturing Company (TSMC), which produces 92% of the world's most advanced semiconductors, essential for smartphones, cars, military tech, and across different domains, temporarily evacuated workers from its facilities for safety inspections (Allyn 2024). The event triggered immediate alarm across the world, as a prolonged TSMC shutdown would cascade through the entire global economy within weeks, halting production of everything from iPhones to fighter jets, paralyzing cloud computing services, and bringing AI development to a standstill as companies lose access to the specialized chips required for training and running advanced models.

Though production resumed within hours with minimal damage, the brief disruption confirmed what supply chain analysts have warned for years, that concentrating the world's most advanced chip production in one place creates a vulnerability where one major disaster could bring the global AI economy to its knees. Foreign policy strategists are acutely aware of this vulnerability as they also assess the strategic implications of a potential Chinese use of force against Taiwan, which would give Beijing control over the semiconductor manufacturing capabilities essential to global AI development. The geopolitical stakes are so high that TSMC reportedly maintains a "kill switch" capability to disable its fabrication equipment remotely in the event of a Chinese invasion, a measure illustrating how semiconductor control has become inseparable from national security and geopolitical survival (Tan 2024).

Semiconductors are the invisible foundation of the modern world, powering everything from smartphones and cars to military systems and critical infrastructure. But their importance has intensified with the AI revolution, as training a single advanced AI model requires thousands of specialized chips working in parallel, while running AI applications demands cutting-edge processors that only a handful of companies can produce. Without these chips, there is no AI, no cloud computing, no digital economy. This reality has transformed tiny silicon chips into instruments of geopolitical power, where access to advanced chips increasingly determines a nation's economic competitiveness, military capability, and technological sovereignty.

The semiconductor supply chain has become the clearest example of how technological dependencies now determine not just economic competitiveness but national security and geopolitical power itself. Within this chain, stark specializations have emerged, with U.S. companies dominating chip design, Japan controlling critical chemicals, but Taiwan manufacturing the predominant majority of the world's most advanced semiconductors, a concentration that serves as both its greatest strategic asset and most dangerous vulnerability.

For years, and especially after pandemic-era supply disruptions exposed these vulnerabilities, the United States has pursued increasingly aggressive strategies to reduce its dependency on chip imports. These range from massive domestic chip manufacturing investments and export controls on advanced chips and chipmaking tools to threats of 100% tariffs on foreign-made semiconductors. Most recently, Washington has pressured Taiwan to relocate half its chip production to American soil, a demand that has met fierce resistance. Taiwan views its semiconductor dominance as a "silicon shield" deterring Chinese military aggression and securing international support, a calculation that would collapse if production moved abroad (Australian Institute of International Affairs 2025).

This creates a vicious circle of mutual vulnerability, where Taiwan's semiconductor dominance serves as its primary deterrent against Chinese military aggression, a deterrent the United States also relies on to prevent conflict, yet U.S. military and critical infrastructure depend on these same Taiwanese chips, exposing U.S. national security to catastrophic risk if supply chains are disrupted. The United States pressuring Taiwan to relocate production threatens to unravel the very deterrence that keeps both nations secure, forcing an impossible choice between reducing strategic vulnerability and maintaining the technological leverage that has so far prevented Chinese military action.

The U.S.-Taiwan semiconductor standoff represents just one front in a broader struggle for chip independence. China also faces a stark reality, as it spends more money importing semiconductors than oil, making chips its greatest strategic vulnerability of its AI ambitions (Miller 2022). Beijing has responded with an unprecedented industrial mobilization, pouring hundreds of billions into domestic chip development aiming to break free from Western semiconductor dominance. Despite these massive investments and the mobilization of state resources, China remains fundamentally dependent on foreign chips, particularly for the advanced processors essential to AI development. To circumvent US-led export controls, China is cultivating alternative supply chains through deepening partnerships with nations outside the Western alliance, offering countries like Russia, Iran, and parts of Southeast Asia access to its AI ecosystem in exchange for critical materials, equipment, and technological cooperation. China is building parallel technological infrastructure across the developing world, from Africa to Latin America, creating dependencies that could eventually form a Chinese-centered semiconductor and AI bloc. Yet even these efforts face fundamental limits as China struggles to replicate the decades of expertise embedded in Taiwanese and Western chip manufacturing, leaving Beijing racing against time to achieve semiconductor independence before export controls strangle its AI ambitions entirely.

While semiconductor supply chains represent the most visible chokepoint in the AI race, other equally critical dependencies deserve foreign policy attention, though space constraints permit only brief examination here. Rare earth elements, essential for high-performance magnets and semiconductors, present an acute vulnerability, with China controlling over 80% of global processing capacity and recently extending export restrictions to products containing even 0.1% Chinese rare earth content, effectively granting Beijing veto power over global AI hardware production. Cloud infrastructure has emerged as another control point, where American companies command 65% of global cloud computing capacity, creating unprecedented leverage over which nations can train large-scale AI models. When the U.S. government considers restricting cloud access to certain countries, it effectively holds the power to terminate their AI development capabilities overnight. Model access represents another subtle but powerful form of control: when leading AI companies selectively grant or deny access to their most advanced models based on geography, they create digital hierarchies that reinforce global inequalities. Additional chokepoints include data center geography, undersea cable networks, AI talent pipelines, and training dataset access, each representing a potential instrument of technological statecraft that merits deeper investigation by foreign policy practitioners navigating this new landscape of digital dependencies.

"SOVEREIGN AI" PARADOX: BETWEEN NATIONAL AMBITION AND TECHNOLOGICAL REALITY

AI sovereignty emerged as the new frontier of economic security, with nations recognizing that control over their AI stack, including infrastructure, data, algorithms, models, and workforce, may prove as valuable as traditional natural resources. This push for "Sovereign AI" reflects hard lessons learned from semiconductor shortages and platform dependencies, as nations realize that reliance on foreign AI systems exposes them to supply chain disruptions, technological lock-in, and the extraction of economic value from their citizens' data. The result is a global rush to develop national AI infrastructure, from data centers to research institutes, as countries race to avoid becoming permanent importers of others' algorithmic decisions.

At the foundation of sovereign AI lies a nation's attempt to control its own AI future through comprehensive digital infrastructure, advanced data centers coupled with localization policies that keep data within borders, supported by intensive workforce development through science and technology education and continuous reskilling programs. Countries pursuing AI sovereignty typically establish extensive research ecosystems that connect academia, startups, and established companies while implementing regulatory frameworks that balance innovation with ethical AI deployment, privacy protection, and accountability mechanisms. These efforts often include economic incentives such as tax breaks, streamlined patents, and public sector AI adoption to stimulate domestic AI industries across critical sectors like healthcare, energy, and finance, frequently through public-private partnerships. Achieving AI sovereignty requires nations to navigate a fundamental tension of developing independent capabilities while engaging in selective international cooperation to shape global standards, enable necessary cross-border data flows, and pool resources for breakthrough research, forcing continuous recalibration between competitive advantage and collaborative necessity (World Economic Forum 2024).

The complexity of building AI sovereignty explains why only the United States and China have come closest to independence, while other nations manage partial capabilities at best while relying on foreign systems for critical functions. Tech giants now exploit this gap by selling "sovereignty as a service," where Nvidia made deals with Thailand, Vietnam, and UAE, Microsoft with Gulf states, AWS launched a European "sovereign cloud," while Huawei partnered with Peru and Indonesia (Popko 2025). Countries are offering land and subsidized energy for data centers, streamlining permit processes, and deploying public funds to secure computational infrastructure. Yet these efforts face mounting resistance as modern AI data centers consume electricity equivalent to small cities and millions of gallons of water daily for cooling, straining local infrastructure at the expense of local populations, and often contradicting nations' climate commitments (Nutt and Chronicle 2025).

Paradoxically these sovereignty packages deepen the very dependencies they claim to solve, locking countries into proprietary systems that guarantee permanent reliance on foreign tech giants who control the underlying infrastructure, updates, and terms of service. Few countries can afford comprehensive AI sovereignty without big tech partnerships, though South Korea stands as a notable exception with its domestic tech consortiums building AI infrastructure using predominantly Korean technology.

Some emerging economies are exploring alternative paths. India's approach offers a particularly instructive model for the Global South (Ernst and Young 2024). Rather than accepting technological dependency, India has articulated an indigenous framework—*Samaj, Sarkar, Bazaar (Society, Government, Market)*—that anchors AI innovation in public purpose and multi-stakeholder collaboration, ensuring that the gains of technological progress extend beyond economic metrics to tangible societal impact (Elias 2025). This philosophy challenges the assumption that developing nations must choose between accepting foreign AI systems or falling behind. The country's commitment to building an indigenous foundation model marks a decisive shift from AI consumer to creator of core infrastructure, positioning India among a select group of nations investing in sovereign AI capabilities built for public purpose (Indian Express 2025). By developing population-scale models aligned with its linguistic, cultural, and regulatory context, India demonstrates that technological sovereignty need not require the resources of a superpower, but rather strategic vision, multi-stakeholder coordination, and the resolve to assert technological self-determination.

The foreign policy implications of AI sovereignty are profound and accelerating. The traditional tools of economic statecraft are being transformed for the AI age. Sanctions now target semiconductor access, trade wars play out through restrictions on AI researchers' movements, and diplomatic pressure focuses on nations considering rival AI frameworks. Most concerning for strategists is the emergence of "AI blocs," groups of nations bound not by geography or ideology but by shared AI approaches and strategies, creating new forms of dependence more binding than traditional alliances, as we write more extensively in the AI Race chapter. As some countries pour hundreds of billions into sovereign AI capabilities while smaller nations must choose between American, Chinese, or European AI ecosystems, foreign policy professionals face a new reality where technological alignment determines economic opportunity and security partnerships.

THE ROAD AHEAD: REDEFINING ECONOMIC SECURITY IN THE AI ERA

The AI revolution is reshaping the foundations of economic security and geopolitical power, demanding a complete reevaluation of national priorities and international strategies. Traditional metrics of power, control over natural resources, manufacturing capacity, and trade routes are being supplemented by new determinants, compute capacity, data sovereignty, and algorithmic innovation. Nations that dominate these dimensions are not only securing economic advantage but rewriting the rules of global influence.

Yet the race for AI supremacy is not without challenges. While a handful of nations and corporations gather unprecedented technological power, deepening global inequalities, their dominance rests on fragile foundations, vulnerable semiconductor supply chains, environmentally unsustainable data centers, and the paradox of pursuing sovereignty through dependence on foreign systems. Foreign policy practitioners now face a landscape where a single company's semiconductor trade can matter more than oil reserves, where cloud access becomes a diplomatic tool more precise than sanctions, and where nations must simultaneously pursue technological sovereignty while accepting that true independence may be impossible.

The ultimate trajectory of this technological revolution, whether AI becomes humanity's great equalizer or history's most efficient engine of inequality, depends not on algorithms but on the governance architectures nations construct today. Decisions made in the coming years about data sovereignty, algorithmic transparency, workforce adaptation, and equitable access will determine whether AI amplifies shared prosperity or entrenches the privileges of the few.

Foreign policy professionals must therefore master not just the technical vocabulary of neural networks and semiconductors, but the deeper challenge of crafting international cooperation in an age of technological competition, ensuring that national AI strategies ultimately serve human development rather than merely accumulating technological power.

NOTE

Interview, by author, recorded online, November 14, 2025.

BIBLIOGRAPHY

Allyn, Bobby. 2024. *Taiwan Earthquake Briefly Halts Chip Factories That Power the Global Economy.* April 3. Accessed October 6, 2025. https://www.npr.org/2024/04/03/1242564161/taiwan-earthquake-semiconductor-chips-tech.

Australian Institute of International Affairs. 2025. *Has the Shield Become a Snare? Taiwan's Semiconductor Supremacy and the Challenge of Economic Sovereignty.* February 11. Accessed October 8, 2025. https://www.internationalaffairs.org.au/australianoutlook/has-the-shield-become-a-snare-taiwans-semiconductor-supremacy-and-the-challenge-of-economic-sovereignty/.

BBC News. 2013. *Spain Unemployment Rate Hit a Record: Youth Rate at 55%.* January 24. Accessed January 3, 2026. https://www.bbc.com/news/business-21180371.

Brookings. 2024. *Hollywood Writers Went on Strike to Protect Their Livelihoods from Generative AI. Their Remarkable Victory Matters for All Workers.* April 12. Accessed October 9, 2025. https://www.brookings.edu/articles/hollywood-writers-went-on-strike-to-protect-their-livelihoods-from-generative-ai-their-remarkable-victory-matters-for-all-workers/.

Brynjolfsson, Erik, Bharat Chandar, and Ruyu Chen. 2025. *Canaries in the Coal Mine? Six Facts about the Recent Employment Effects of Artificial Intelligence.* Palo Alto: Stanford University.

Business Insider. 2025. *An AI Safety Pioneer Says It Could Leave 99% of Workers Unemployed by 2030 — Even Coders and Prompt Engineers.* September 4. Accessed October 6, 2025. https://www.businessinsider.com/ai-safety-pioneer-predicts-ai-could-cause-99-unemployment-by-2030-2025-9.

Cazzaniga, Mauro, Florence Jaumotte, Longji Li, Giovanni Melina, Augustus J Panton, Carlo Pizzinelli, Emma J Rockall, and Marina Mendes Tavares. 2024. *Gen-AI: Artificial Intelligence and the Future of Work.* Staff Discussion Note. Washington, DC: International Monetary Fund.

Elias, Jibu. 2025. *Samaj, Sarkar, Bazaar: Building Inclusive AI for India's Future.* September 17. Accessed December 29, 2025. https://www.stimson.org/2025/samaj-sarkar-bazaar-building-inclusive-ai-for-indias-future/.

Ernst and Young. 2024. *Is Generative AI Beginning to Deliver on its Promise in India?* Report, Haryan: Ernst and Young.

Fan, Qimiao, and Christine Zhenwei Qiang. 2024. *Tipping the Scales: AI's Dual Impact on Developing Nations.* June 3. Accessed October 9, 2025. https://blogs.worldbank.org/en/digital-development/tipping-the-scales--ai-s-dual-impact-on-developing-nations.

Financial Times. 2025. *AI Risks Widening Global Wealth Gap, WTO Warns.* September 17. Accessed October 6, 2025. https://www.ft.com/content/2c8b6bae-57b2-4666-b14c-ea74d4ea232a.

Fortune. 2024. *Over 25% of Google's Code Is Now Written by AI—and CEO Sundar Pichai Says It's Just the Start.* October 30. Accessed October 6, 2025. https://fortune.com/2024/10/30/googles-code-ai-sundar-pichai/.

France24. 2025. *Boom or Bubble: How Long Can the AI Investment Craze Last?* October 2. Accessed October 9, 2025. https://www.france24.com/en/live-news/20251002-boom-or-bubble-how-long-can-the-ai-investment-craze-last.

Georgieva, Kristalina. 2024. *AI Will Transform the Global Economy. Let's Make Sure It Benefits Humanity.* January 14. Accessed October 6, 2025. https://www.imf.org/en/Blogs/Articles/2024/01/14/ai-will-transform-the-global-economy-lets-make-sure-it-benefits-humanity.

Goldman Sachs. 2023. *Generative AI Could Raise Global GDP by 7%.* April 5. Accessed October 6, 2025. https://www.goldmansachs.com/insights/articles/generative-ai-could-raise-global-gdp-by-7-percent.

Indian Express. 2025. *Centre Selects Start-up Sarvam to Build Country's First Homegrown AI Model.* April 27. Accessed January 3, 2026. https://indianexpress.com/article/business/centre-selects-start-up-sarvam-to-build-country-first-homegrown-ai-model-9967243/.

ITU. 2024. *Global Internet Use Continues to Rise but Disparities Remain, Especially in Low-Income Regions.* November 27. Accessed October 7, 2025. https://www.itu.int/en/mediacentre/Pages/PR-2024-11-27-facts-and-figures.aspx#:~:text=In%20total%2C%20an%20estimated%202.6,per%20cent%20of%20the%20population.

McKinsey & Company. 2023. *The Economic Potential of Generative AI: The Next Productivity Frontier.* June 14. Accessed October 6, 2025. https://www.mckinsey.com/capabilities/mckinsey-digital/our-insights/the-economic-potential-of-generative-AI-the-next-productivity-frontier#business-value.

McKinsey Global Institute. 2018. *Notes from the AI Frontier: Modeling the Impact of AI on the World Economy.* September 4. Accessed October 6, 2025. https://www.mckinsey.com/featured-insights/artificial-intelligence/notes-from-the-ai-frontier-modeling-the-impact-of-ai-on-the-world-economy.

Miller, Chris. 2022. *Chip War: The Fight for the World's Most Critical Technology.* New York: Scribner.

MIT Management Sloan School. 2025. *A New Look at the Economics of AI.* January 21. Accessed October 9, 2025. https://mitsloan.mit.edu/ideas-made-to-matter/a-new-look-economics-ai.

New York Times. 2025. *The Global A.I. Divide.* June 21. Accessed October 9, 2025. https://www.nytimes.com/interactive/2025/06/23/technology/ai-computing-global-divide.html.

Nutt, David, and Cornell Chronicle. 2025. *'Roadmap' Shows the Environmental Impact of AI Data Center Boom.* November 10. Accessed January 3, 2026. https://news.cornell.edu/stories/2025/11/roadmap-shows-environmental-impact-ai-data-center-boom.

Popko, John. 2025. *The Myth of Sovereign AI: Countries Rely on U.S. and Chinese Tech.* September 12. Accessed October 8, 2025. https://restofworld.org/2025/chinese-us-tech-foreign-ai-dependence/.

Schellekens, Philip, and David Skilling. 2024. *Three Reasons Why AI May Widen Global Inequality.* October 17. Accessed January 3, 2026. https://www.cgdev.org/blog/three-reasons-why-ai-may-widen-global-inequality.

Stanford University Human-Centered AI. 2024. *Inside the New AI Index: Expensive New Models, Targeted Investments, and More.* April 15. Accessed October 8, 2025. https://hai.stanford.edu/news/inside-new-ai-index-expensive-new-models-targeted-investments-and-more.

Stanford University Human-Centered AI. 2025. *The 2025 AI Index Report.* Index Report, Stanford: Stanford University.

Tan, Hulieng. 2024. *The World's Top Chipmakers Can Flip a 'Kill Switch' Should China Invade Taiwan, Bloomberg Reports.* May 23. Accessed January 3, 2026. https://www.businessinsider.com/asml-tsmc-semiconductor-chip-equipment-kill-switch-china-invade-taiwan-2024-5.

UN Security Council. 2024. *Maintenance of International Peace and Security Artificial Intelligence.* Official Records of the Security Council, New York City: UN Security Council.

Wired. 2025. *Trump, OpenAI y Oracle anuncian Stargate Project, una nueva empresa de centros de datos para IA.* January 22. Accessed October 9, 2025. https://es.wired.com/articulos/trump-openai-y-oracle-anuncian-stargate-project-centros-de-datos-para-ia.

World Economic Forum. 2024. *At the Foundation of Sovereign AI Lies a Nation's Attempt to Control Its Own AI Future through Comprehensive Digital Infrastructure, Advanced Data Centers Coupled with Localization Policies That Keep Data within Borders, Supported by Intensive Workforce.* April 25. Accessed October 9, 2025. https://www.weforum.org/stories/2024/04/sovereign-ai-what-is-ways-states-building/.

Part III

PEACE AI and Crisis Management, Peacebuilding, and Governance

7 AI in Crisis Management
From Early Warning Systems to Agentic Diplomacy

...As AI becomes increasingly pervasive, we must also recognize its ability to disrupt peace and security in both the civilian and the military domains. In that regard, Sierra Leone is of the view that AI can play a pivotal role in maintaining peace and security by enhancing decision-making, improving situational awareness, and enabling proactive conflict prevention and management.

— **Michael Imran Kanu,** *Permanent Representative to the UN of Sierra Leone (UN Security Council 2024)*

Artificial intelligence is no longer a distant prospect; it is already rapidly transforming societies, economies and our approach to peace and security...Subject to responsible governance, its ability to revolutionize early warning, crisis prevention and humanitarian responses is undeniable. Yet, with its capabilities often spread unevenly, the risk of misuse is growing, potentially creating new avenues for instability. Therefore, it is our collective responsibility to ensure that AI advances international peace and security and to guide its use for the benefit of all.

— **Hassan Sheikh Mohamud,** *President of Somalia (UN Security Council 2025)*

In an era when satellites can detect troop movements from space, algorithms can process millions of social media posts, and intelligence agencies share data at unprecedented speeds, the world is experiencing more simultaneous conflicts than at any point since World War II. This paradox, possessing the most sophisticated early warning capabilities in human history while witnessing an explosion of violence we seem unable to prevent, defines the central challenge facing modern crisis management. Foreign ministries navigate a landscape where conflicts multiply and intensify, where humanitarian needs outpace response capacity, and where traditional diplomatic instruments designed for sequential bilateral crises struggle against conflicts that evolve simultaneously across physical, cyber, and information domains. The promise of technological solutions through artificial intelligence (AI) collides with stubborn realities: political paralysis that prevents action on accurate warnings, chronic underfunding of prevention efforts, and the persistent gap between what our systems can predict and what our institutions choose to prevent.

This chapter examines how AI is transforming every dimension of crisis management, from early warning systems that can forecast conflicts months in advance to autonomous

DOI: 10.1201/9781003644712-12

agents that are beginning to conduct diplomatic functions without human intervention. We trace the evolution from the forecasting failures that caught the world unprepared for transformative events to the emergence of AI systems that now outperform veteran analysts in predicting global crises. The analysis explores how foreign ministries are deploying these technologies, from sophisticated platforms monitoring thousands of conflict indicators simultaneously to experimental systems that could reshape diplomatic practice itself. We examine the persistent challenge of translating accurate predictions into preventive action, the governance dilemmas posed by increasingly autonomous systems, and the emergence of "agentic diplomacy" where machines don't just inform decisions but actively shape diplomatic outcomes.

The stakes of this technological transformation extend far beyond efficiency gains or analytical improvements. A growing asymmetry exists between how military and diplomatic institutions approach autonomous capabilities, raising questions about whether our capacity for algorithmic destruction will outpace our investment in prevention. Foreign ministries stand at a crossroads where the choices made about integrating AI into diplomatic practice will determine whether these tools become instruments for genuine conflict prevention or merely sophisticated systems for documenting our continued failure to bridge the gap between early warning and early action. As AI's influence on crisis management continues to grow, the central challenge remains ensuring that the diplomatic community leverages these technologies to build the preventive frameworks that traditional diplomacy has long struggled to achieve.

THE ESCALATING CRISIS AND CONFLICT LANDSCAPE: A WORLD ON THE EDGE

As the United Nations marks its 80th anniversary, the organization born from the ashes of World War II faces a sobering reality, as the world is experiencing more active conflicts than at any point since its founding. The diplomatic toolkit refined over generations struggles against conflicts that unfold simultaneously across physical and cyber domains, where information warfare proves as decisive as military operations. Foreign ministries now grapple with how to manage a world where 56 wars rage simultaneously, where negotiated settlements have been decreasing, collapsing from nearly a quarter in the 1970s to just 4% today (IEP 2024), and where the humanitarian system built over eight decades buckles under unprecedented strain (IEP 2024).

The numbers tell a story that has forced a fundamental shift in foreign ministry priorities and strategic planning. Global conflict has nearly doubled in just five years. From Gaza to Myanmar, from Ukraine to Sudan, violence has either erupted anew or reignited with devastating intensity. Mexico battles cartel warfare that rivals conventional conflicts, Yemen remains trapped in its decade of destruction, and the Sahel burns with insurgencies that respect no borders. The concerning nature of this moment extends beyond the sheer number of conflicts to fundamental changes in their character. Conflicts are evolving much faster than our ability to understand or address them. Notably, the geography and political economy of conflict is shifting, with violence escalating most rapidly not in fragile states where instability might be expected, but in middle-income countries and states that had introduced some democratic reforms. This pattern challenges long-held assumptions about the relationship between development, democracy, and peace that have underpinned foreign policy strategies for decades. Currently, 92 countries are engaged in conflicts beyond their borders, the highest number ever recorded (IEP 2024).

The human toll of this new conflict landscape is staggering. At the beginning of 2025, 305 million people needed urgent humanitarian assistance, equal to nearly an entire population of the United States (UN OCHA 2024). Behind this number lies a cascade of human suffering, with 123 million people forcibly displaced from their homes, a number that grew by 5% in just one year (UNHCR UK 2024). Among them are 71 million internally displaced persons, trapped within their own countries' borders, often beyond the reach of international assistance (Internal Displacement Monitoring Centre 2023). Children bear a disproportionate burden, with nearly one in five children globally either living in or fleeing conflict zones (UNICEF USA 2025). Yet just as humanitarian needs reach historic highs, the system designed to address them confronts unprecedented resource constraints. The disparity between assessed requirements and actual funding has reached critical levels, with 2023 seeing donors meet only one-third of humanitarian appeals, leaving millions without essential assistance (OCHA 2023).

The international community's pledge of "never again" after Rwanda and Srebrenica genocides rings hollow as technology now is being misused to facilitate mass atrocities. Social media algorithms amplified genocidal violence against the Rohingya in Myanmar, while in Gaza, AI systems from major tech companies reportedly generate kill lists and determine strike locations at unprecedented scale, raising profound questions about algorithmic complicity in potential genocide.

At the same time, foreign ministries and international organizations are slowly turning to AI to augment traditional diplomatic and humanitarian instruments that struggle with today's challenges. AI applications are already proving their worth, from detecting landmines, predicting climate-driven displacements, identifying early food insecurity, to forecasting crises before they unfold, promising to enhance conflict prevention and save lives through better early warning systems.

Yet integrating AI into crisis diplomacy raises critical governance questions about algorithmic interpretation of complex political dynamics, accountability frameworks for high-stakes decisions, and safeguards against surveillance misuse. Since these technologies are neither comprehensive solutions nor replacements for human judgment but rather additional tools already being deployed globally, the central policy challenge is not whether to use AI, but how to establish governance structures that maximize humanitarian benefits while ensuring compliance with international legal and ethical principles.

FORECASTING IN FOREIGN POLICY AND HUMAN-MACHINE COLLABORATION

When the Arab Spring erupted in 2010, it exposed a massive blind spot in foreign policy forecasting, where no government predicted that a Tunisian fruit vendor's self-immolation would trigger regime changes across the Middle East (Los Angeles Times 2012). The U.S. and European intelligence services had all assessed these regimes as stable just months before they fell. This collective failure revealed how traditional forecasting methods, which relied heavily on official government sources and diplomatic cables, missed the undercurrents of social discontent visible in unemployment data, food prices, and demographic pressures. The aftermath led to a fundamental rethinking of foreign policy prediction, incorporating new data sources that capture citizen grievances rather than just regime strength.

Every three months, the Metaculus Cup brings together forecasters to predict global events ranging from military coups in Thailand to Israeli strikes on Iran, a competition that has correctly anticipated Russia's invasion of Ukraine two weeks in advance and the overturning of *Roe v. Wade* two months before it happened. The 2025 competition marked a turning point when a top human forecaster placed third behind several AI systems. He declared he wouldn't retire but would instead merge with the machines that had beaten him. British startup ManticAI's AI secured eighth place, outperforming dozens of seasoned professionals, a stunning achievement for machines that had ranked around 300th just a year earlier (The Guardian 2025). This dramatic leap, which left many human forecasters feeling surreal about being outdone by algorithms, signals a fundamental shift for foreign ministries that have long relied exclusively on human expertise to predict and prevent crises.

This breakthrough carries profound implications for foreign ministries and intelligence agencies where forecasting underpins critical decisions. Every major agency engages in some form of forecasting, yet traditional human analysis of complex geopolitical questions can take days and cost tens of thousands of dollars per question (Time 2025). For institutions tracking multiple crises across different regions, comprehensive human forecasting would require months just for initial assessments, let alone regular updates. Forecasting has been central to foreign policy for decades; however, as conflicts involve environmental stressors, disinformation campaigns, and cyber warfare, with correlations often invisible to human perception, these traditional models are reaching their limits. Humans face inherent cognitive constraints, information overload, cognitive biases, and the inability to synthesize vast data streams quickly enough for preventive action. The sudden competitive performance of AI systems signals that machines can now work with the same messy, interdependent information that once required human judgment, potentially transforming how governments anticipate crises.

The emergence of AI forecasting systems presents both opportunities and limitations for foreign policy practitioners seeking to predict and prevent crises. While critics dismiss large language models as merely restating training data, recent competitions demonstrate that AI systems can generate genuinely original predictions that often diverge sharply from human consensus, potentially serving as an antidote to the groupthink that has historically burdened diplomatic analysis. AI's primary advantages lie in its capacity for persistent, parallel processing: these systems can simultaneously monitor dozens of complex crisis scenarios, revisit them daily to incorporate new information, and maintain analytical consistency across vast datasets without fatigue. For foreign ministries, this combination of risks and opportunities suggests a hybrid model where AI systems handle baseline monitoring and pattern detection across multiple crisis zones, flagging anomalies for human experts who then apply contextual knowledge and political judgment to determine policy responses, combining machine-scale analysis with human strategic thinking.

On August 15, 2021, Taliban fighters seized Kabul while diplomats from dozens of nations desperately evacuated their embassies. The gap between AI's competitive forecasting success and real-world intelligence performance revealed a sobering reality. Despite satellite surveillance, AI analytics, and intelligence sharing between allies, virtually every government had predicted the Afghan state would last months or years, not the mere 11 days it took to collapse. This forecasting failure wasn't unique: Israel, despite deploying some of the world's most sophisticated automated border surveillance, AI-enhanced intelligence, and one of the world's most technologically advanced security apparatuses, completely missed the October 7, 2023 Hamas attack that killed 1,200 people; no intelligence agency predicted that Sri Lanka's economic crisis would escalate into protesters storming the presidential palace and overthrowing the government in July 2022; and the rapid fall of Mosul to ISIS in 2014 stunned Western and Iraqi intelligence despite months of monitoring jihadist movements. Even as AI systems grow more sophisticated, many claim that foreign policy will always retain an irreducible element of surprise, requiring not just better prediction but greater adaptability when forecasts eventually fail.

THE PROMISE AND CHALLENGE OF AI IN CRISIS PREDICTION AND PREVENTION

Traditional analysts and AI teams often operate in separate silos within the same foreign ministries, a divide that mirrors the broader tension between diplomatic tradition and technological disruption. Yet the pressure of repeated intelligence failures, combined with fears of falling behind rivals' AI capabilities, has pushed even skeptical governments to extensively explore machine learning (ML) and natural language processing (NLP) for strengthening their early warning systems. These systems can simultaneously monitor thousands of indicators, from information on population, socioeconomic factors, migration, and climate, identifying correlations that might signal emerging crises weeks, months, or years in advance. For foreign policy practitioners, the core promise is the ability to shift from managing crises after they explode to preventing escalation through early diplomatic intervention, targeted development assistance, or preventive deployment of humanitarian resources.

In November 2024, **Armed Conflict Location and Event Data's (ACLED)** conflict monitoring system began detecting unusual activity patterns across northwestern Syria, with armed groups moving at a pace and scale not seen in years. Within 72 hours, the ACLED mapped and verified the capture of over 200 towns and villages by Hayat Tahrir al-Sham (HTS)-led rebel forces, as control shifted across Hama, Idlib, Aleppo, and Latakia provinces (Mehvar 2024). What started as data points on ACLED's dashboard would become the documentation of Syria's most seismic shift in over a decade: the 12-day offensive that ended 13 years of frozen civil war and over half a century of Assad family rule, culminating with rebels entering Damascus and Bashar al-Assad fleeing the country. ACLED's infrastructure of local sources, satellite verification, and ML algorithms processed thousands of conflicts reports simultaneously, distinguishing verified territorial changes from propaganda as history unfolded. Specifically for the purpose of forecasting **ACLED**-developed **CAST (Conflict Alert System)** to assist foreign policy experts with six-month forecasts of political violence events tracking battles, explosions, and violence against civilians, with monthly updates that allow foreign ministries to monitor prediction accuracy and adjust their assessments based on emerging patterns (ACLED CAST 2025).

Some organizations provide forecasts further into the future, such as **VIEWS (Violence & Impacts Early-Warning System),** run by Uppsala University and Peace Research Institute Oslo, delivering monthly conflict forecasts up to 36 months in advance across the globe. Realizing that for different stakeholders, including foreign policy actors, it is important to go beyond violence prediction, the system was developed to forecast humanitarian impacts including displacement, infrastructure damage, and health system collapse, combining different analytical approaches to cross-check predictions and improve reliability (VIEWS 2025). This shift transforms often vague warnings into actionable intelligence that foreign ministries can use to pre-position resources, negotiate humanitarian corridors with neighboring countries, and justify budget allocations to skeptical parliaments before crises fully materialize.

A single newspaper headline might not reveal an approaching conflict well in advance, but when researchers analyzed hundreds of thousands of newspaper articles, with the use of the latest advancements in NLP, unexpected patterns invisible to human analysts began to emerge. Researchers at **Conflict Forecast** discovered that conflicts were often preceded not by an increase in violence-related words, but by the systematic disappearance of "peaceful" language, particularly coverage of judicial procedures, court cases, and law enforcement activities that quietly eroded months before violence erupted (Mueller and Rauh 2018). This innovative approach emerged from a fundamental challenge facing conflict prediction, where traditional models rely on statistical indicators, precisely the data that disappears when conflicts erupt, and government agencies stop functioning.

While statistical collection often collapses in war zones, international newspapers continue reporting, providing an uninterrupted stream of information that algorithms can analyze for subtle linguistic shifts. The system now analyzes over 3.5 million newspaper articles alongside historical conflict data, predicting escalations and de-escalations 3–12 months in advance across 170 countries (Conflict Forecast 2025). This approach brings additional advantage, as it excels at detecting early warning signals in previously peaceful regions where traditional models struggle, as for them current conflict is usually the best predictor of future conflict. The project is also an example of collaboration with foreign policy experts, namely, the German Federal Foreign Office and the UK Foreign, Commonwealth and Development Office, with further iterations planned in forced migration, de-democratization, and decision-making support.

Some countries have chosen to build their own in-house early warning systems tailored to their specific diplomatic priorities. German Federal Foreign Office developed the **PREVIEW** project, initially as a data dashboard with publicly available data to support information management, and later as a conflict forecasting model (Bressan 2021). The team developed, among other projects, the "Delta Analysis" pilot for the Lake Chad region, an interactive platform that integrates real-time data from multiple German ministries and field operations into a single visual dashboard (Panic 2022). Rather than simply displaying predictions, the system allows diplomats to explore the underlying data layers, combining on-the-ground operational information from humanitarian, development, and peacekeeping actors with conflict forecasting models. This integration enables German officials to see not just where crises might emerge, but also where their assets and partners are already positioned to respond. Another project developed by PREVIEW and partners is **Climate-Conflict Vulnerability Index,** providing more systemic monitoring of harmful interactions between climate, conflict, and preexisting vulnerabilities (NYU CIC 2023).

The European Union (EU) developed complementary tools to give policymakers both long-term structural analysis and near-term situational awareness. **The Global Conflict Risk Index (GCRI),** operational since 2015, provides annual country-level assessments based on factors like governance quality and demographic pressures, helping EU officials identify where instability might take root over time (Joint Research Center 2025). Recognizing that structural analysis alone cannot capture rapidly evolving situations, the European Commission's Joint Research Centre developed the **Dynamic Conflict Risk Model (DCRM),** which delivers monthly subnational forecasts across 140 countries by analyzing conflict history, geography, and climate vulnerabilities. This layered approach enables EU diplomats to distinguish between regions requiring long-term development engagement and those demanding immediate attention, supporting decisions about where to pre-position humanitarian resources and when to escalate political engagement before crises fully materialize.

The Bureau of Conflict and Stabilization Operations (CSO) at the U.S. State Department integrated AI across three strategic initiatives to enhance U.S. conflict prevention and stabilization capabilities. Conflict forecasting deploys ML techniques, including tree-based algorithms, neural networks, and clustering, to analyze open-source political, social, and economic data, predicting interstate conflicts, mass mobilization, and potential mass atrocities before they materialize. Automated Damage Assessments through the **Conflict Observatory** applies computer vision to commercial satellite imagery, systematically documenting potential war crimes in Ukraine by identifying damage to hospitals, schools, and civilian infrastructure that would be impossible to comprehensively catalog through traditional ground-based methods. **Crisis Campaign Cable Analytics** uses optical character recognition and NLP to mine decades of diplomatic cables, transforming institutional knowledge into structured datasets that reveal crisis response patterns and training gaps, enabling evidence-based improvements to embassy preparedness (U.S. Department of State 2023).

These institutional forecasting efforts are complemented by a radically different approach, such as **direct citizen early warning systems**. In 2018, civilians in Syria's Idlib province began receiving smartphone alerts warning them of incoming airstrikes eight minutes before impact, enough time to reach shelter and save lives. The warnings came from **Sentry**, an AI system developed by social enterprise **Hala Systems**, using acoustic sensors and ML to track aircraft, reducing airstrike fatalities by up to 27% in areas where it operated. Unlike traditional early warning systems that relied on often inadequate infrastructure or government bureaucracies, Sentry pushed alerts directly to civilians through social media and messaging apps. This approach emerged from a harsh necessity, as in conflicts where governments themselves threatened their populations or state institutions had collapsed, bypassing official structures was often the only way to protect civilians. Sentry demonstrated how AI could democratize access to life-saving intelligence that was once monopolized by military and government agencies.

While AI systems dominate headlines, organizations like the **International Crisis Group** have long operated human-led early warning tools. Their **CrisisWatch platform** tracks monthly conflict trends to identify immediate risks and resolution opportunities, while their "On the Horizon" tool provides 3–6-month forecasts. Both rely entirely on field analysts' qualitative assessments and direct conversations with conflict parties rather than algorithms, recognizing that understanding violence requires grasping the complex political dynamics and personal rivalries that shape conflicts but rarely appear in datasets (International Crisis Group 2024).

In West Africa, ECOWAS operates a decentralized early warning system where 77 field monitors across 15 member states gather real-time incident reports and complete weekly surveys covering 55 human security indicators, feeding this data into the ECOWARN database that provides decision-makers with near real-time analysis while maintaining local ownership of the conflict prevention process (Panic 2022). Whether enhancing traditional forecasting systems or building entirely new AI-powered platforms, practitioners across the early warning community are increasingly exploring how algorithms might augment human analysis to identify patterns invisible to experts and process information at speeds impossible for manual review.

Interviews with foreign ministry officials revealed persistent gaps between what AI systems predict and what policymakers need: while models generate abstract probabilities, practitioners need to know who is involved, where violence will concentrate, how many people will be affected, and crucially, where diplomatic intervention can actually make a difference.[1] Critical blind spots persist in monitoring interstate conflicts and low-probability but high-impact escalations tied to resource competition, while traditional conflict categories fail to capture modern violence involving nonstate actors. Perhaps most fundamentally, usability barriers undermine adoption. Users increasingly reject complex dashboards in favor of clear, actionable insights that do not require specialized expertise to interpret. Even the most sophisticated AI system offers little value if its warnings cannot be quickly understood and acted upon by nontechnical practitioners.[2] Successful systems increasingly rely on close collaboration between data scientists and regional analysts who can translate algorithmic outputs into diplomatic action, ensuring models reflect real-world dynamics rather than statistical abstractions.

Even if technical obstacles are resolved, algorithmic predictions in crisis settings face a fundamental paradox: the very act of prediction can alter the future being predicted. When an AI system forecasts imminent conflict, governments may mobilize forces "defensively," populations might begin hoarding or fleeing, and markets could panic, potentially triggering the crisis the system sought to prevent. Foreign ministries must grapple with the diplomatic implications of acting on algorithmic predictions: publicly warning of an impending coup might precipitate it, while predicting state collapse could accelerate institutional breakdown. UNHCR has chosen not to publish its displacement predictions publicly for precisely these reasons, fearing that countries might close their borders preemptively in response to forecasted refugee movements, while EconAI restricts access to trusted actors who can intervene constructively rather than exploit the forecasts (AI for Peace 2025).

This challenge extends beyond unintended consequences to deliberate manipulation. Adversaries aware of predictive systems might flood social media with false conflict indicators to trigger diplomatic alarms or mask genuine threats behind noise. As foreign ministries integrate these predictive systems, they must confront questions that transcend technology: If we can predict humanitarian crises but lack the political will to prevent them, what is the value of prediction? If our warnings create the very crises we seek to prevent, are we prophets or provocateurs? And perhaps most unsettling: in a world where algorithms predict human behavior with increasing accuracy, do we risk making their predictions true simply by believing them possible?

BEYOND PREDICTION: AI AGENTS AND THE BEGINNING OF AGENTIC DIPLOMACY

While the diplomatic community continues to debate the value and risks of algorithmic prediction, AI technology is already moving beyond forecasting toward autonomous action, raising an entirely different set of questions for foreign ministries. The proliferation of terms like AI agents, autonomous agents, and agentic AI reflects a fundamental shift in AI capabilities, from systems that generate content in response to prompts toward systems that autonomously perform tasks on behalf of users. AI agents represent systems capable of observing their environment, utilizing tools, maintaining memory, and executing multistep workflows to achieve predefined goals without constant human guidance, unlike traditional chatbots that merely respond to queries without learning or planning capabilities (IBM 2025).

While basic AI agents can handle discrete tasks like automated customer support, more sophisticated "agentic AI" systems exhibit true autonomy through advanced reasoning and iterative planning, enabling multiple agents to collaborate on complex organizational objectives (IBM 2025). This distinction marks a critical evolution: whereas generative AI creates content reactively based on human prompts, AI agents actively perceive, reason, decide, and execute actions independently. For instance, while ChatGPT can draft a meeting email upon request, an agentic system could autonomously access calendars, schedule meetings, send invitations, and coordinate logistics without human intervention. This shift, from AI simply "saying things" to "doing things," has profound implications for how governments and international organizations approach both the opportunities and risks of increasingly autonomous digital systems operating at scale.

While militaries worldwide are rapidly transitioning from AI-assisted warfare to fully agentic systems, with the Pentagon deploying AI agents for military planning, Ukrainian forces conducting unmanned assaults, and Israeli systems autonomously identifying and prioritizing military targets with minimal human oversight, the diplomatic sphere remains conspicuously behind in adopting comparable autonomous capabilities. The military's embrace of agentic warfare, backed by investments reaching $9.67 billion in 2024 and projected to hit $61 billion by 2034, starkly contrasts with diplomacy's continued reliance on traditional human-centered approaches (Global Newswire 2025).

Yet the same technological capabilities transforming warfare could enable "agentic diplomacy," autonomous systems that continuously monitor global political dynamics identify emerging conflicts before they escalate, coordinate multiparty negotiations across contexts and languages, generate creative diplomatic solutions by synthesizing historical precedents, and even conduct preliminary negotiations. Such systems could potentially work tirelessly across dozens of crisis situations simultaneously, maintaining institutional memory of past negotiations, identifying patterns in successful peace agreements, and proposing innovative diplomatic frameworks that human negotiators might overlook. The question is not whether such agentic diplomatic systems are technically feasible, the military applications prove they are, but whether the international community will allow machines to assume roles in crisis management and peace-making with the same autonomy they're already granted in war-making, and what safeguards would be needed to ensure diplomatic AI agents serve genuine conflict resolution rather than merely advancing national interests through automated negotiation.

Several organizations are already demonstrating the transformative potential of these integrated analytical systems, revealing what becomes possible when diplomatic practice embraces agentic AI capabilities, while also exposing the profound risks when machines begin to shape decisions about war, peace, and human survival. **The Hague Centre for Strategic Studies** has developed **GINA (Geopolitical Interactive Network Analysis),** a system that synthesizes economic, diplomatic, military, and media data to monitor interstate interactions in real time across multiple dimensions (The Hague Centre for Strategic Studies 2025). The system comprises four integrated tools that track diplomatic engagement through UN voting patterns and speeches, analyze millions of media articles to understand international narratives, monitor military interactions including arms trades and conflict events, and examine economic relationships through trade and investment flows. Using advanced NLP and network science methods, GINA maps global relationships dynamically, identifying diplomatic blocs, alliance shifts, and emerging patterns of cooperation or competition. The latest iteration, **GINA Plus**, introduces an AI-powered agentic interface that allows users to query this complex geopolitical network through natural language, using retrieval-augmented generation (RAG) to ensure responses are grounded in structured diplomatic data rather than generalized assumptions.

Unlike traditional forecasting systems that attempt to predict specific future events with probabilistic certainty, GINA fundamentally reorients the analytical approach toward continuous observation and pattern recognition, operating on the principle that real-time observation enables better understanding of why conflicts emerge rather than simply when they might occur. This distinction proves critical for foreign policy practitioners who need not just predictions but actionable intelligence about the evolving dynamics between states. If successful, these systems would provide diplomats with unprecedented situational awareness, identifying subtle shifts in alliance structures or escalatory patterns that human analysts might miss when examining individual data streams. Rather than offering binary conflict predictions, these systems could enable practitioners to understand the multidimensional fabric of interstate relations, providing the contextual intelligence necessary for crafting nuanced diplomatic responses and preventive interventions before tensions crystallize into crises.

When fighting erupted in Khartoum in 2023, embassy security officers found themselves navigating urban warfare with traditional communications systems failing rapidly. As phone networks collapsed and local contacts went silent, diplomatic staff turned to **Dataminr**, a real-time AI-powered event detection platform, to identify safe evacuation routes and monitor threats in real time until the last personnel were safely extracted (Dataminr 2025). Building on these capabilities, Dataminr recently piloted Intel Agents, an autonomous AI system that provides contextual analysis of physical, digital, and cyber threats in real time. The system represents a concrete example of how agentic AI is already transforming diplomatic and security operations, as Dataminr already partners with the U.S. Department of Defense and Homeland Security (Azhar 2025).

While Dataminr's earlier work, such as mentioned First Alert in Sudan, revolutionized crisis response by detecting and alerting organizations to emerging events in real time, Intel Agents represent the agentic evolution, autonomously determining what contextual information each alert requires, seeking it out across multiple data sources, and synthesizing comprehensive intelligence briefings, transforming passive event notifications into active, self-directed intelligence gathering. For foreign ministries confronting information overload from simultaneous crises, these agents autonomously process vast streams of public and proprietary data to detect early signals of political instability, security threats, or humanitarian emergencies, dynamically updating their analysis as situations evolve rather than producing static reports. The platform also allows integration of client specific data, and automatically refines real-time information based on client's unique operations, which can prove to be crucial for specific needs of foreign ministries and their work.

These systems also introduce profound risks for diplomatic operations: algorithms embed biases into threat assessment, potentially mischaracterizing dissent as security risks while adversaries could hijack or manipulate autonomous agents to inject false intelligence. The accountability vacuum proves especially dangerous, when autonomous systems cause diplomatic incidents or civilian harm, responsibility diffuses across developers, operators, and machines, leaving no clear human liability. Most concerning is the asymmetric impact on populations who unknowingly become subjects of algorithmic decision-making about their security status or humanitarian needs, while agent-to-agent interactions create escalation dynamics operating at machine speed beyond human comprehension or intervention. As these autonomous networks proliferate, foreign ministries face the prospect of algorithmic misjudgments triggering diplomatic crises with no human able to explain, halt, or reverse the cascade.

CHARTING THE PATH FORWARD: TRANSFORMING CRISIS MANAGEMENT FOR THE FUTURE

The crisis landscape confronting foreign ministries today is fundamentally different from that of previous decades. Conflicts no longer unfold in isolation but cascade across borders, domains, and systems, with climate stress, economic shocks, cyber operations, and armed violence interacting in ways that defy traditional analytical categories. Understanding this complexity is the necessary starting point for any response. Technology, including the AI systems examined throughout this chapter, can assist in mapping these interdependencies and identifying emerging risks. Yet as interviews with foreign policy practitioners revealed, technology is not inevitably the answer. A persistent tension runs through the crisis management community: some maintain that only human judgment can grasp the political, cultural, and relational dimensions of conflict and diplomacy; others counter that the record of continuous failure demands fundamentally new approaches. Neither position resolves easily, and foreign ministries must navigate this debate without the luxury of theoretical certainty.

Part of the difficulty lies in how success is measured. Prevention, by its nature, leaves no visible trace; crises that do not occur generate no headlines, no emergency summits, no grateful populations. This absence makes it difficult to demonstrate that preventive methods work, and easier to dismiss them as ineffective compared to reactive interventions that unfold dramatically in public view. At the same time, the persistent gap between warning and action cannot be attributed to inadequate signals. Whether generated by seasoned analysts or sophisticated algorithms, forecasts of impending violence have repeatedly proven accurate, and repeatedly been ignored. The problem is not prediction but political will, institutional incentives, and resource allocation. This raises an uncomfortable question about the asymmetry between defense and diplomatic institutions: why are military organizations willing to invest billions in autonomous systems and integrate them rapidly into operations, while foreign ministries remain hesitant to grant comparable agency to tools designed for crisis prevention and early action.

Looking ahead, the technologies shaping crisis management will continue to evolve, likely in directions that extend well beyond the agentic systems now emerging. Quantum computing, brain–computer interfaces, and forms of machine intelligence not yet conceived will pose new opportunities and risks for diplomacy. Foreign ministries that engage seriously with these trajectories, building internal expertise, establishing governance frameworks, and contributing to international norm-setting, will be better positioned to shape how such technologies are used. Those that remain passive risk ceding that influence to military establishments and private technology firms whose priorities differ from conflict prevention and humanitarian protection. The challenge for diplomatic institutions is not simply to adopt new tools but to reimagine their own role in a world where the nature of crises, the sources of instability, and the means of response are all undergoing transformation. Whether the international community rises to that challenge will determine whether the next generation inherits institutions capable of preventing catastrophe or merely documenting it.

NOTES

1 Expert interview, by author, in-person, March 9, 2025.
2 Expert interview, by author, in-person, March 9, 2025.

BIBLIOGRAPHY

ACLED CAST. 2025. *ACLED CAST Conflict Alert System.* Accessed March 3, 2025. https://acleddata.com/conflict-alert-system/.

AI for Peace. 2025. *Advancing AI for Effective Crisis Early Warning Early Action – Insights from PRIO AI Days.* February 25. Accessed January 3, 2026. https://www.aiforpeace.org/post/advancing-ai-for-effective-crisis-early-warning-early-action-insights-from-prio-ai-days.

Azhar, Ali. 2025. *Dataminr Bets Big on Agentic AI for the Future of Real-Time Data Intelligence.* April 28. Accessed October 15, 2025. https://www.bigdatawire.com/2025/04/28/dataminr-bets-big-on-agentic-ai-for-the-future-of-real-time-data-intelligence/.

Bressan, Sarah. 2021. *Crisis Early Warning: Berlin's Path from Foresight to Prevention.* June 29. Accessed December 18, 2025. https://peacelab.blog/2021/06/crisis-early-warning-berlins-path-from-foresight-to-prevention.

Conflict Forecast. 2025. *Conflict Forecast - Evaluating Worldwide Armed Conflict Risk.* Accessed December 12, 2025. https://conflictforecast.org/.

Dataminr. 2025. *Dataminr Expands Agentic AI Capabilities with Intel Agents for the Physical World, Heralding New Era for AI-Powered Global Event, Threat & Risk Intelligence.* September 29. Accessed October 15, 2025. https://www.dataminr.com/press/announcement/dataminr-intel-agents-for-the-physical-world/.

Global Newswire. 2025. *$61.08 Bn Artificial Intelligence in Military Market Opportunities and Strategies to 2034, Fueled by AI Adoption and Defense Budget Increases Amid Privacy and Talent Concerns.* May 9. Accessed December 12, 2025. https://www.globenewswire.com/news-release/2025/05/09/3078053/0/en/61-08-Bn-Artificial-Intelligence-in-Military-Market-Opportunities-and-Strategies-to-2034-Fueled-by-AI-Adoption-and-Defense-Budget-Increases-Amid-Privacy-and-Talent-Concerns.html.

IBM. 2025. *What Are AI Agents?* Accessed December 12, 2025. https://www.ibm.com/think/topics/ai-agents.

IEP. 2024. *Global Peace Index 2024: Measuring Peace in a Complex World.* Yearly Index Report, Sydney: Institute for Economics & Peace.

Internal Displacement Monitoring Centre. 2023. *All-Time High of 71 Million People Internally Displaced Worldwide.* May 11. Accessed March 3, 2025. https://www.internal-displacement.org/news/all-time-high-of-71-million-people-internally-displaced-worldwide/.

International Crisis Group. 2024. *Crisis Early Warning and Horizon Scanning in Today's World.* September 19. Accessed October 22, 2025. https://www.crisisgroup.org/global/crisis-early-warning-and-horizon-scanning-todays-world.

Joint Research Center. 2025. *A Closer Look at Conflict Risk: The Dynamic Conflict Risk Model (DCRM).* Science for Policy Brief, Brussels: European Commission.

Los Angeles Times. 2012. *U.S. Intelligence Official Acknowledges Missed Arab Spring Signs.* July 19. Accessed October 21, 2025. https://www.latimes.com/archives/blogs/world-now/story/2012-07-19/u-s-intelligence-official-acknowledges-missed-arab-spring-signs.

Mehvar, Ameneh. 2024. *Syria: HTS-Led Rebel Forces Capture Over 200 Locations, While Syrian and Russian Airstrikes Increase.* December 2. Accessed October 22, 2025. https://acleddata.com/brief/syria-hts-led-rebel-forces-capture-over-200-locations-while-syrian-and-russian-airstrikes.

Mueller, Hannes, and Christopher Rauh. 2018. "Reading between the Lines: Prediction of Political Violence Using Newspaper Text." *American Political Science Review* 112 (2): 358–375.

NYU CIC. 2023. *Getting Data Ready for Policy: Designing a Climate-Conflict-Vulnerability Index.* New York City, November 15.

OCHA. 2023. *Global Humanitarian Overview 2024.* December 11. Accessed March 3, 2025. https://www.unocha.org/publications/report/world/global-humanitarian-overview-2024-un-launches-46-billion-appeal-2024-global-humanitarian-outlook-remains-bleak-enar.

Panic, Branka. 2022. *Can Emerging Technologies Lead a Revival of Conflict Early Warning/Early Action? Lessons from the Field.* Conference Report, New York City: NYU CIC.

The Guardian. 2025. *British AI Startup Beats Humans in International Forecasting Competition.* September 20. Accessed October 14, 2025. https://www.theguardian.com/technology/2025/sep/20/british-ai-startup-beats-humans-in-international-forecasting-competition#:~:text=Leading%20human%20superforecasters%20still%20say,outperforming%20the%20top%2Dperforming%20bots.

The Hague Centre for Strategic Studies. 2025. *Geopolitical Interactive Network Analysis (GINA).* October 15. Accessed October 15, 2025. https://hcss.nl/gina/.

Time. 2025. *AI Is Learning to Predict the Future—And Beating Humans at It.* September 18. Accessed October 14, 2025. https://time.com/7318577/ai-model-forecasting-predict-future-metaculus/.

U.S. Department of State. 2023. *Department of State AI Inventory 2023.* Accessed December 2, 2025. https://2021-2025.state.gov/data-strategy/ai_inventory/.

UN OCHA. 2024. *Global Humanitarian Overview 2025.* Yearly Report, UN OCHA.

UN Security Council. 2024. *Maintenance of International Peace and Security Artificial Intelligence.* Official Records of the Security Council, New York City: UN Security Council.

UN Security Council. 2025. *Artificial Intelligence and International Peace and Security.* Official Record of the Security Council, New York City: UN Security Council.

UNHCR UK. 2024. *Five Key Takeaways from UNHCR's 2024 Mid-Year Trends Report.* November 5. Accessed March 4, 2025. https://www.unrefugees.org.uk/learn-more/news/news/five-key-takeaways-from-unhcrs-2024-mid-year-trends-report/.

UNICEF USA. 2025. *Children in War and Conflict.* Accessed March 3, 2025. https://www.unicefusa.org/what-unicef-does/emergency-response/conflict#:~:text=Over%20473%20million%20children%20%E2%80%93%20nearly,time%2C%20or%20never%20return%20home.

VIEWS. 2025. *The Violence and Impacts Early-Warning System.* October 21. Accessed October 21, 2025. https://viewsforecasting.org/.

8 AI and Peacebuilding
When Satellites Witness War Crimes and Algorithms Shape Peace

Once the domain of PhDs and supercomputers, AI is now accessible to every peacekeeper. Generative AI gives us the opportunity to transform our work and to advance the UN peace and security mandate with renewed efficiency, insight, and responsibility. Yet democratization also requires vigilance. We must lead this transformation with ethical foresight, ensuring that innovation is always matched by integrity.

—**Avishan Bodjnoud**, *Chief, Information Management Unit, United Nations Depts of Political, Peacebuilding and Peace Operations*[1]

If we can figure out ways to deploy these tools to help us promote and protect human rights, we will continue to make progress, but if we allow all the risks and problems associated with dual-use technology to not be addressed we see the potential for human rights to be moved backwards rather than forewords.

—**Peggy Hicks**, *Director of the Thematic Engagement, Special Procedures and Right to Development Division of the UN Human Rights Office (OHCHR) (AI for Good 2025)*

"Technology will never move as slowly as it does today"—with these words at the December 2024 UN Security Council ministerial briefing, Secretary-General António Guterres captured the dizzying pace at which artificial intelligence (AI) is remaking international peace and security (UN Security Council 2024). His address painted a stark duality: autonomous weapons and deepfakes threatening to erode truth itself, yet also AI systems are already detecting landmines, predicting displacement crises, and forecasting conflicts before the first shot is fired. Previous chapters have explored the darker edges of this technological revolution, the specter of autonomous weapons, cybersecurity threats, and the risk of nuclear escalation. This chapter takes a different path, examining how foreign policy practitioners can seize AI's potential for building peace rather than waging war.

This chapter examines four critical domains where AI is reshaping peacebuilding, peacemaking, and peacekeeping practice. First, we analyze AI-enhanced mediation and negotiation processes, where algorithms expand participation and provide advanced analytical capabilities while potentially undermining the human relationships essential to sustainable agreements. Second, we explore technology's

DOI: 10.1201/9781003644712-13

impact on human rights documentation and transitional justice, from computer vision systems detecting atrocities in satellite imagery to machine learning algorithms processing decades of testimony to identify perpetrator networks. Third, we examine peacekeeping's digital transformation, where predictive analytics promise enhanced civilian protection even as information warfare threatens mission stability. Finally, we consider how Women, Peace, and Security (WPS) strategies, which currently overlook AI's transformative impact, must urgently incorporate these technologies to ensure they strengthen rather than sideline women's participation in peace processes—a factor proven to enhance peace durability.

As Guterres emphasized, "Humanity's hand created AI, and humanity's hand must guide it forward"—in this spirit, this chapter equips foreign policy practitioners with frameworks to shape AI's role in building peace rather than being shaped by it (UN Security Council 2024). We are now deciding whether AI will be channeled toward strengthening mediation, enhancing peace operations, and building sustainable peace, or whether it will accelerate the development of autonomous weapons systems and deepen the machinery of war. The technology exists, what remains is the collective will to direct it toward building the infrastructure of peace rather than automating the architecture of violence.

AI-ENHANCED PEACE MEDIATION AND NEGOTIATIONS: NAVIGATING ALGORITHMIC THREATS AND OPPORTUNITIES

Peace negotiations and mediation are fundamentally human-centered diplomatic processes aimed at resolving conflicts through dialogue, compromise, and mutual agreement. Traditionally, peace processes have relied on skilled experts who facilitate communication between conflicting parties, build trust through personal relationships, demonstrate cultural sensitivity, and leverage contextual understanding to identify common ground (Kurbalija 2024). Mediators employ techniques ranging from shuttle diplomacy to face-to-face negotiations, drawing on emotional intelligence, strategic thinking, and deep knowledge of local dynamics to guide parties toward sustainable agreements. This work has historically been conducted through in-person meetings, confidential discussions, and careful relationship-building over extended periods, core elements that remain essential to successful peace processes. Peace mediation now routinely integrates data-driven approaches to strengthen negotiations and evidence-based analysis of stakeholder needs (Hirblinger, Brummer and Kufus 2024).

Yet modern mediation has never been purely analog, as we explore more thoroughly in the history of diplomacy and technology section of this book. Diplomats have long integrated various technologies into their practice, from secure communication systems and real-time translation services to data analysis tools that help track agreement implementation. Today's mediators already leverage digital platforms for virtual negotiations, employ sophisticated databases to analyze precedents from past peace agreements, and use mapping technologies to visualize territorial disputes. Rather than viewing AI as a departure from traditional mediation, we should understand it as the next evolution in this ongoing technological integration, one that offers unprecedented capabilities to augment human mediators' effectiveness.

The introduction of AI into this domain has evolved through distinct phases, from early concerns about digital disruption, to current explorations of AI as an enhancing tool, to growing recognition that this space urgently requires governance and regulation. Initially, digital technologies were primarily viewed through the lens of their disruptive potential. When UN mediators drafted the 2020 Libya ceasefire agreement, they made history by including unprecedented provisions regulating parties' behavior on social media, the first-time social media conduct became formal subject matter in a UN peace agreement (Puig-Larrauri 2024). Recognizing that inflammatory posts could unravel months of diplomacy and that coordinated disinformation could reignite violence faster than military mobilization, negotiators acknowledged the digital spaces have become as consequential as the physical one.

Algorithmic amplification of hate speech poses a critical threat to peace processes, as platforms' engagement-driven recommendation systems can rapidly transform localized tensions into widespread violence. During sensitive negotiation periods, social media algorithms designed to maximize user engagement inadvertently prioritize inflammatory content, creating echo chambers where extremist narratives gain traction faster than moderate voices calling for reconciliation. This dynamic was starkly evident during Myanmar's peace efforts, where Facebook's algorithms amplified anti-Rohingya hate speech that directly contributed to mass violence, and in Ethiopia's Tigray conflict, where coordinated disinformation campaigns exploited algorithmic vulnerabilities to dehumanize opposing groups and undermine ceasefire negotiations (Panic and Arthur 2024). Yet paradoxically, AI simultaneously serves as both the accelerant and the antidote to this digital violence, the same machine learning capabilities that enable algorithmic amplification of hate are increasingly deployed to detect, track, and counter hate speech in real time (Panic and Arthur 2024).

The integration of AI into peace mediation processes has demonstrated **significant potential for enhancing inclusivity and broadening stakeholder participation** beyond traditional diplomatic channels. The United Nations has pioneered these AI-powered digital dialogues in conflict zones. In Yemen, the Office of the Special Envoy and the UN Department of Political and Peacebuilding Affairs' Innovation Cell conducted the first such AI-powered consultation in 2020, to engage hundreds of Yemeni civil society representatives who provided anonymous input on ceasefire proposals, the political peace process, and humanitarian concerns, insights that directly informed the UN's mediation strategies (OSESGY 2020). Similarly, the United Nations Support Mission in Libya (UNSMIL) expanded this approach through its 2020 digital dialogue initiative, which engaged over 1,000 participants per session across Libya's diverse geographic and demographic landscape (Alavi et al. 2022). This systematic consultation incorporated perspectives from youth constituencies, women's organizations, and civil society actors, stakeholders whose participation in formal peace negotiations has historically been limited by security constraints, logistical barriers, and entrenched power asymmetries.

Building on these successful deployments in active conflict zones, the UN has expanded AI-powered dialogues to broader regional policy development and governance initiatives. In 2024, the UN Innovation Cell collaborated with the League of Arab States to facilitate digital consultations that engaged hundred young peacebuilders from 17 Arab nations, with 44% women participation, to shape the Arab Regional Youth, Peace, and Security Strategy (International Telecommunications Union 2024). Similarly, in Guatemala, UN-facilitated digital dialogues connected more than 400 participants to discuss electoral reforms and youth political participation, demonstrating how these tools initially designed for conflict mediation are now scaling to address governance challenges and development priorities across diverse contexts, transforming diplomatic consultation from an exclusive process to an increasingly inclusive practice (International Telecommunications Union 2024).

Following October 7, 2023, attack in Israel, when traditional diplomacy proved insufficient, the Alliance for Middle East Peace deployed **AI-assisted dialogue platforms to facilitate consensus-building** among more than a hundred Israeli and Palestinian civil society leaders. The initiative utilized large language models (LLMs) and bridging-based ranking algorithms to process thousands of individual inputs from Israeli Jews, Palestinian citizens of Israel, and Palestinians from the West Bank and Gaza, enabling dialogue when direct engagement was politically unfeasible. The AI systems identified shared concerns beneath polarized positions, ultimately producing collective statements to international stakeholders with over 84% agreement from each constituency, demonstrating AI's capacity to facilitate unofficial dialogues when conventional mediation faces insurmountable barriers (Konya et al. 2025). For foreign ministries supporting civil society peacebuilding initiatives, this case offers a model, though one requiring careful partnership with established networks and clear protocols for AI–human interaction in sensitive political contexts.

Developed by Conflict Dynamics International, Akord AI is a chatbot designed to support Sudanese peacebuilders, civil society actors, diplomats, and policy influencers (Hedgehog Lab 2024). Unlike mainstream AI tools that scrape the internet, Akord draws exclusively from a curated library of over 3,000 resources, peace agreements, constitutional texts, case studies on women's inclusion, and mediation strategies from global and local sources, available in English and Modern Standard Arabic (Tech and Social Cohesion 2025). This closed architecture avoids the hallucinations common in general-purpose chatbots, while every response links directly to its source for verification. While Akord does not conduct negotiations directly, it serves as a **knowledge support system** that equips local peacebuilders with the expertise, resources, and analytical tools needed to design and implement their own negotiation and mediation strategies in conflict-affected regions. The team also intends to incorporate oral histories and tribal agreements, recognizing that much of Sudan's peacebuilding knowledge lives outside formal archives, a concrete example of AI democratizing access to peacebuilding expertise while respecting local context. Nearly 1,500 users, from Sudanese youth ambassadors to foreign ministry staff, have already engaged the platform, with expansion planned to Somalia, Syria, Libya, Yemen, and Congo (AI Akord 2025).

Akord AI's success demonstrates what purpose-built, conflict-sensitive AI design can achieve. Yet most practitioners in conflict zones do not have access to specialized tools and they turn instead to general-purpose LLMs like ChatGPT, Claude, or Google Gemini. Yet the widespread availability of generative AI tools also introduces significant risks. A 2025 evaluation by the Institute for Integrated Transitions tested six leading free-access LLMs, including ChatGPT, Claude, and Google Gemini, on realistic conflict resolution scenarios from Sudan, Mexico, and Syria (Bussemaker and Freeman 2025). The results were concerning: the average score was just 26.7 out of 100, with models consistently failing basic conflict sensitivity standards. Most critically, nearly all models offered extensive advice without first asking clarifying questions about the context (average score: 0.2/10) or the user's goals (0.1/10), a fundamental failure in conflict-sensitive practice. Some responses could plausibly endanger users on the ground or exacerbate existing conflicts. Given that LLMs are already being used as de facto advisers in conflict zones where expert mediation support is limited, these findings underscore the urgent need for improved system prompts, adjusted training data, and guidance for end-users on responsible prompting.

Beyond direct consultation and dialogue deliberation, AI enhances peace mediation through **sophisticated analysis of digital discourse**, transforming social media data from potential conflict accelerants into strategic intelligence assets (Larrauri and Morrison 2022). Build Up's Phoenix platform exemplifies this capability, employing machine learning algorithms to monitor and classify public social media conversations in real time across multiple languages, including under-resourced ones, detecting sentiment shifts, emerging grievances, and coordinated disinformation campaigns that could derail negotiation progress (Build Up 2025). The platform's ability to identify early warning signals, from escalating rhetoric between community groups to viral misinformation about peace agreements, enables mediators to calibrate communication strategies proactively and counter destabilizing narratives before they gain critical mass. By presenting these complex analyses through accessible dashboards that require no technical expertise, tools like Phoenix democratize intelligence capabilities previously available only to well-resourced diplomatic missions, enabling local peacebuilders and governments equally to ground their interventions in data-driven insights about public sentiment and ensure that agreements reflect genuine societal concerns rather than assumptions about what communities want.

Every day, the Israeli startup Didi's algorithm analyzes data across almost a hundred Israeli and Palestinian media outlets, tracking keywords like "willingness to compromise" and "confident in winning" to determine precisely **when conditions might be optimal for initiating peace negotiations** (FastCompany 2025). The system, based on political science "ripeness theory," which posits that conflicts become resolvable when both parties experience a mutually hurting stalemate and perceive a viable path forward, detected a significant surge in Israeli public support for compromise in January 2025 that coincided with a two-month ceasefire, demonstrating AI's capacity to provide real-time intelligence about shifting public attitudes. Similarly, the CSIS Futures Lab's Strategic Headwinds project developed a peace agreement simulator, which employs LLMs to analyze the Russia-Ukraine conflict, curating historical peace process datasets to identify patterns in war termination and generate structured insights for policymakers navigating potential pathways to negotiated settlements (Reynolds and Jensen 2025).

Beyond negotiation timing and stakeholder engagement, AI is enhancing the technical **verification and monitoring of ceasefire agreements**, transforming what has traditionally been dangerous, labor-intensive work into sophisticated real-time surveillance systems (Grand-Clément 2022a). This continues a trajectory of technological innovation in ceasefire oversight, from motion-sensor cameras used by UN Peacekeeping Force in Cyprus (UNFICYP), to drones and radars used by UN Mission in Mali (MINUSMA), to satellite monitoring by the OSCE Special Monitoring Mission in Ukraine, with AI now enabling automated analysis at scale (Grand-Clément 2022b). Hala Systems exemplifies this evolution through its deployment of AI-driven monitoring tools in Yemen and Ukraine, where the organization integrates satellite imagery analysis to detect fortifications and troop movements, natural language processing to monitor open-source intelligence for disinformation campaigns, and cryptographic verification methods that time-stamp and authenticate evidence to ensure its integrity in highly polarized conflicts (University of Birmingham 2025).

AI integration into mediation and negotiation processes and other forms of peaceful dialogue deliberations represents both an opportunity and a challenge for contemporary diplomacy. These tools have evolved from early systems requiring specialized expertise and computational centers to today's generative AI that enables staff to integrate sophisticated analytics into daily work without extensive technical training.[2] While AI strengthens agreement legitimacy by capturing broader societal perspectives and enhancing inclusivity, widespread availability introduces risks around appropriate use, data privacy, and algorithmic bias. The fundamental challenge persists, with 2.6 billion people lacking internet access, AI-powered diplomacy risks replicating existing exclusions. Success requires thoughtful implementation that addresses infrastructure gaps, ensures representative participation, and maintains awareness of when human judgment must supersede algorithmic recommendations, recognizing that AI enhances but cannot replace the nuanced understanding essential to diplomatic practice.

TECHNOLOGY TRANSFORMING HUMAN RIGHTS PROTECTION: DIGITAL WITNESSES, WAR CRIMES DOCUMENTATION, AND TRANSITIONAL JUSTICE

When Ukrainian forces entered liberated Bucha in April 2022, they discovered evidence of civilian casualties throughout the town, a scene that would become central to international war crimes investigations. Russian officials immediately disputed the findings, asserting that any evidence appeared only after their forces had withdrawn. However, high-resolution satellite imagery revealed a starkly different timeline: images captured while Russian forces still controlled the town showed distinctive patterns and objects in the exact locations where investigators would later document crimes, proving these incidents occurred during the period of occupation rather than after the withdrawal as claimed (Human Rights Watch 2022). In previous conflicts, such contested events might have remained unresolved, but this time, satellite imagery created a digital record, transforming remote sensing data into forensic evidence, and fundamentally changing how the international community documents and verifies allegations of war crimes.

The Bucha revelations represent just one instance of a profound shift in human rights documentation. While emerging technologies like AI and big data have justifiably raised concerns about perpetuating bias, enabling mass surveillance, and facilitating discrimination, they are simultaneously improving our capacity to protect human rights and pursue accountability. Satellite imagery enhanced by computer vision algorithms is now serving as witness in conflict zones and restricted territories across the globe where humanitarian organizations cannot safely operate. These AI systems can detect subtle patterns invisible to the human eye: changes in soil composition indicating recent burials, heat signatures revealing mass grave sites, and variations in vegetation growth that signal ground disturbance. Computer vision doesn't just automate the analysis of thousands of images, it reveals evidence that human analysts might never detect. This transforms raw satellite data into actionable intelligence for human rights investigators working to document atrocities in real time.

In October 2025, when the paramilitary Rapid Support Forces (RSF) seized El Fasher in Sudan, killing over 2,000 civilians in violence Yale's Humanitarian Research Lab compared to the first 24 hours of the Rwandan genocide, it was AI-enhanced satellite analysis combined with geolocated social media videos that exposed the full scale of the atrocity (Mohdin 2025). Computer vision algorithms detected what human analysts called unprecedented: blood stains visible from space, "clusters" consistent with bodies, and red discoloration patterns across the ground. While RSF fighters posted videos of their crimes as intimidation tactics, it was the automated geolocation and verification of these videos against satellite imagery that transformed social media posts into potential evidence.

Organizations worldwide have mobilized for more than a decade to harness this technological revolution for human rights monitoring. Amnesty International's Decode Darfur initiative enlisted thousands of volunteers in efforts to analyze satellite images, identifying patterns of destruction across vast regions that would be impossible for small teams to process (Amnesty International 2016). Similarly, UNOSAT has conducted continuous satellite surveillance of Syria since 2011, producing comprehensive assessments of civilian infrastructure damage that have informed humanitarian responses (UNOSAT 2017). But what makes this technological leap truly transformative is not just the scale of monitoring, but the depth of insight that AI-powered computer vision provides.

From exposing forced labor camps in North Korea and mass graves in Burundi to mapping the extensive network of Uyghur internment camps in Xinjiang and tracking migrant detention facilities at the U.S.-Mexico border, this combination of satellite imagery and machine learning has created the ability to document human rights violations at scale, with precision, and in real time, even in the world's most restricted and dangerous territories (Panic, 2020). The integration of crowdsourced analysis with AI verification has fundamentally transformed what was once limited, dangerous fieldwork into a global, technology-enabled accountability system.

This technological transformation is amplified by the "digital witness movement," a fundamental shift in which every person with a mobile phone becomes a potential documenter of war crimes (Dubberley, Koenig and Murray 2020). This democratization of evidence-gathering has generated millions of videos, photos, and eyewitness accounts, creating both documentation and a critical verification challenge (OHCHR 2025). Converting citizen evidence into legal proof requires discovering, verifying, and authenticating millions of posts, an impossible task for human teams alone. This is where computer vision algorithms can process years of footage in days, automatically detecting weapons signatures, geolocating incidents and identifying manipulation or deepfakes. What once required specialized investigators physically present in conflict zones now happens through distributed networks of witnesses whose smartphones, combined with AI verification systems, create an unbreakable chain of evidence. This shift doesn't just accelerate justice, it fundamentally redefines accountability, ensuring that in an age where everyone can be a witness, technology can transform their testimony into proof that no regime can deny or erase.

In Syria and Yemen, this phenomenon has generated an unprecedented flood of evidence: the Syrian Archive and Yemeni Archive have preserved over 4 million videos documenting human rights violations, uploaded by civilians, journalists, and even perpetrators themselves. The sheer volume of this citizen-generated evidence presents both an opportunity and a challenge that possibly AI can solve. When researchers at Swansea University, Global Legal Action Network, and VFRAME partnered with these archives to identify banned cluster munitions use, they faced a staggering computational challenge: manually reviewing the thousands of hours of footage would take a single analyst an estimated 2,750 days, over seven years of continuous work (Hao 2020). Their machine learning system accomplished the same task in mere days, automatically detecting munition types, geolocating attack sites, and creating legally admissible documentation chains.

The same AI systems transforming real-time atrocity documentation are now being deployed in **transitional justice processes**. Transitional justice mechanisms, truth commissions, reparations programs, and accountability processes are increasingly recognized as essential components of sustainable peace agreements, yet they often struggle under the sheer volume of testimonies, evidence, and claims that must be processed. AI-enabled tools now support transitional justice through various applications, from forensic analysis and digital media classification to facial recognition in visual materials and automated textual content analysis (Lamont and Mema 2023). While satellites and smartphones capture evidence of ongoing conflicts, millions of testimonies from past atrocities remain trapped in archives, unprocessed and inaccessible to justice mechanisms. AI offers transformative potential for managing this complexity: machine learning algorithms can analyze thousands of victim testimonies to identify patterns of systematic violations, natural language processing can detect corroboration across accounts even when victims use different languages or dialects.

Nearly five decades after Pinochet's dictatorship disappeared over 3,000 people and tortured tens of thousands more, Chile is deploying AI to unlock justice from mountains of unprocessed testimonies and archives. The Nuestra MemorIA initiative applies machine learning to identify patterns invisible to human researchers, connecting testimonies mentioning the same detention centers, mapping networks of state terror, and revealing perpetrator names recurring across thousands of documents that manual analysis could never fully expose (Nuestra MemorIA 2024). Colombia faces similar challenges with its Truth Commission archives from decades of armed conflict, now experimenting with "Ventana a la Verdad," an AI chatbot that transforms overwhelming volumes of testimonies, interviews, and documents into accessible information through natural language queries (Sokol et al. 2025). The system allows families without legal expertise to search for disappeared relatives by simply asking questions in everyday language, while researchers can instantly cross-reference testimonies across regions and timeframes that would take months to compile manually, making previously inaccessible archives suddenly searchable and meaningful for those seeking answers. Similar archives from various conflicts globally remain inaccessible to justice mechanisms lacking resources to process them, demonstrating how AI can transform transitional justice from selective accountability limited by human capacity into comprehensive reckoning where even decades-old evidence can finally speak.

Yet these technological capabilities present critical operational and strategic challenges that demand careful consideration from policymakers and practitioners. The dual-use nature of surveillance technologies poses inherent risks, as systems deployed for atrocity documentation can equally serve authoritarian surveillance regimes. Algorithmic bias in AI training datasets may systematically exclude certain victim populations from recognition and redress. The proliferation of synthetic media and deepfake capabilities threatens to undermine the evidentiary value of authentic digital documentation, potentially creating plausible deniability for perpetrators. In transitional justice contexts specifically, the testimonial function serves purposes beyond mere information gathering, it provides recognition, dignity, and social acknowledgment that algorithmic processing cannot replicate. These technologies should therefore be understood as force multipliers for existing human rights infrastructure rather than replacement systems, requiring robust governance frameworks that preserve human agency in interpretation, maintain victim-centered approaches, and ensure that efficiency gains do not compromise the legitimacy and transformative potential of accountability mechanisms.

For foreign policy practitioners, protecting human rights represents both an obligation rooted in the Universal Declaration of Human Rights and a strategic necessity, as sustainable peace and economic development prove impossible where rights are systematically violated. They must navigate the complex multilateral architecture, from UN conventions to regional human rights mechanisms, while simultaneously adapting to the technological revolution detailed throughout this chapter. The integration of AI-verified evidence, satellite documentation, and digital testimony into traditional diplomatic frameworks represents the next evolution in human rights work. This requires foreign ministries to modernize their structures, capabilities, and strategies to remain effective guardians of human dignity in an age where every violation can be witnessed, documented, and prosecuted through technology. Satellite evidence and AI-verified documentation eliminate plausible deniability, demanding rapid responses to atrocities and reducing space for strategic ambiguity in international relations, even when these same tools risk enabling surveillance and manipulation. The question for foreign policy establishments is not whether to engage with these technologies, but how to lead their responsible deployment in service of human rights and international justice.

PEACEKEEPERS IN THE DIGITAL CROSSFIRE: AI'S TRANSFORMATION OF MODERN PEACE OPERATIONS

In July 2022, the Democratic Republic of Congo witnessed how **weaponized disinformation can cripple peace operations**. Peace operations increasingly navigate a complex information environment where legitimate grievances about mission effectiveness are amplified, distorted, and weaponized by various actors. MONUSCO experienced this directly when social media campaigns exploiting local frustrations coincided with violent protests that claimed lives of both civilians and peacekeepers while immobilizing hundreds of UN vehicles, effectively paralyzing mission operations across critical areas (United Nations Peacekeeping 2025a). This pattern of digitally fueled violence escalated dramatically by January 2025, when an online disinformation campaign following the M23 attack specifically targeted women peacekeepers serving in MONUSCO, with threats of rape and sexual violence, forcing them to restrict their movements and undermining their ability to protect local communities, transforming gender-based online harassment into a tactical weapon against peacekeeping effectiveness (Miyashita and Sundelin 2025). Similarly, during MINUSMA's 2023 drawdown in Mali, a surge of false and misleading narratives fueled hostility toward peacekeepers, significantly endangering mission personnel during an already vulnerable transition period (United Nations Security Council 2023).

In Africa, which hosts the most and the largest UN peace operations globally, documented disinformation campaigns have surged nearly fourfold from approximately 50 in 2022 to 189 in 2024, prompting UN Secretary-General António Guterres to describe peace operations as confronting a "tsunami of falsehoods and absurd conspiracy theories" that increasingly threaten mission effectiveness and personnel safety (Hansen et al. 2025). A 2025 UN Department of Peace Operations survey revealed that 68% of peacekeepers reported misinformation and disinformation had moderate to severe effects on their peace implementation efforts, while 76% said it significantly impacted their safety and security (Miyashita and Sundelin 2025). This surge of false narratives exemplified how disinformation not only endangers peacekeepers but also worsens inter-community violence, triggers civilian harm and displacement, undermines social cohesion and conflict resolution efforts, erodes trust in humanitarian organizations, and poses severe operational challenges that compromise both mandate implementation and the safety of vulnerable populations (United Nations 2023).

The UN's response reflects growing institutional recognition of this threat. The 2024 UN Policy on Information Integrity in Peacekeeping Settings defines misinformation, disinformation, and hate speech as capable of weakening "consent and support for peacekeeping, reducing the space for mandate implementation, threatening the safety and security of peacekeepers and fueling divisions in host countries" (UN Department of Peace Operations 2024). Peace operations have traditionally relied on community liaison teams, radio broadcasting, press releases, collaboration with local media, media literacy campaigns, and in-person community outreach to counter misinformation and disinformation in conflict zones, methods that, while maintaining human connection and cultural sensitivity, struggle to match the speed and scale of digital false narratives. These conventional approaches, though essential for building trust and understanding local contexts, cannot simultaneously monitor multiple information channels or rapidly verify claims across diverse languages and platforms.

In response, missions started deploying AI-powered natural language processing to enhance their counter-disinformation capabilities, as demonstrated in Mali, where

MINUSMA combined traditional radio broadcasting with AI-driven "radio mining" developed by UN Global Pulse (UN Global Pulse 2021). This focus on radio is critical, as public talk radio is estimated to be the main source of information for approximately 80% of the Malian population, a similar percentage found in many other countries where peace operations are conducted, making radio data an invaluable source for understanding public sentiment and concerns (Lemm 2021). The pioneering technology collected and recorded public radio broadcasts, applied filters to remove music and commercials, then uses automated speech recognition and natural language processing to analyze content for specific keywords, when detected, audio clips were provided to MINUSMA for further analysis.

The system further developed into a Unite Wave Platform, hosted by the World Health Organization and the UN Office of Information and Communications Technology, analyzing offline and online radio content to understand public sentiment toward different missions, tracking support, grievances, and attacks against peacekeepers and local communicates (Sabanayagam 2025). Unite Wave captures, transcribes, and translates radio broadcasts in over 100 languages, providing UN missions and agencies with real-time analytics to detect emerging threats, harmful narratives, misinformation campaigns, and hate speech that could endanger civilians, peacekeepers, or political processes. The platform automates the entire monitoring workflow, from broadcast capture through analysis, making previously inaccessible regional content available without local translators, while integrating seamlessly with existing UN systems for fact-checking and strategic response. It is already operational across multiple missions processing hundreds of broadcasting hours daily in regions with limited internet connectivity. It enables rapid verification and counter-narrative deployment, allowing missions to dispatch community liaison teams with accurate information before false narratives escalate into violence. Yet missions must carefully balance this information environment security against surveillance overreach, ensuring that monitoring doesn't silence legitimate criticism or violate privacy rights in communities already skeptical of international presence, maintaining the responsible foundation that distinguishes peace operations from more intrusive forms of intervention.

While radio mining demonstrates AI's potential for specific information challenges, the broader transformation of peace operations through AI extends far beyond counter-disinformation efforts. Modern missions operate in increasingly complex environments where traditional approaches often struggle to keep pace with rapidly evolving threats, driving peace operations to explore AI as a force multiplier for their mandated tasks. The integration of AI into peace operations represents both immense opportunity and sobering responsibility, as these dual-use technologies can enhance early warning systems that save lives, but the same predictive algorithms could potentially be exploited by hostile actors to anticipate and evade peacekeeper activities. This technological transformation is not merely an operational upgrade but a substantial shift that requires peacekeepers to navigate ethical dilemmas, security vulnerabilities, and the life-or-death consequences of algorithmic decision-making.

Since 2014, the Partnership for Technology in Peacekeeping has brought together governments, civil society, companies, and academic institutions to develop innovative solutions for field challenges, with its Expert Panel on Technology and Innovation in UN Peacekeeping acknowledging that UN peace operations need to catch up with technological advancement (Sarfati 2023). The Department of Peace Operations launched in 2021 Strategy for the Digital Transformation of UN Peacekeeping to harness digital tools for improved mandate delivery and enhanced peacekeeper safety (United Nations Peacekeeping 2021), while Action for Peacekeeping Plus (A4P+) includes data and technology as a cross-cutting priority for strengthening UN peacekeeping (UN Peacekeeping 2021). The Department of Political and Peacebuilding Affairs simultaneously leverages data analytics to advance conflict prevention, resolution, and more effective peacebuilding strategies, including through Peace Security Data Hub, a free public library of datasets on peace and security (Peace Security Data Hub 2025). Beyond policy transformation, peace operations are exploring diverse AI applications that promise to fundamentally enhance operational effectiveness across the mission lifecycle.

Predictive peacekeeping leverages AI to address what researchers identify as a critical gap: the UN's "rudimentary ability" to analyze enormous quantities of data from its missions, satellites, and social media feeds, with parts of the peace infrastructure suffering from "sensory overload" despite having sophisticated collection capabilities (Druet 2021). AI's capacity to synthesize these vast datasets enables comprehensive situational awareness crucial for strategic planning. Machine learning algorithms identify emerging conflict patterns and provide predictive analytics for early warning systems, as we elaborated in detail in previous chapters. Natural language processing technologies detect deepfakes and conduct sentiment analysis to combat information manipulation that could inflame tensions, while AI-driven cybersecurity tools protect mission infrastructure from digital threats (UNU Macau 2024). In training and capacity-building, generative AI creates realistic simulations that prepare peacekeepers for complex scenarios, developing critical decision-making skills before deployment. These predictive capabilities have the potential to transform peace operations from reactive crisis management to proactive threat prevention, though deployment demands rigorous attention to ethical considerations and algorithmic accountability.

These predictive capabilities are particularly crucial for **civilian protection**, where AI's early warning mechanisms demonstrate potential for operational enhancement. While peace operations deploy tools from incident databases to aerial surveillance, their effectiveness remains limited by manual processes and fragmented systems that cannot respond quickly enough to emerging threats. AI offers potential solutions, through automated data integration across multiple sources, real-time translation for multilingual threat reporting, and pattern recognition that identifies violence indicators human analysts might miss (Sarfati 2023). Machine learning systems can continuously analyze which interventions successfully prevented civilian harm in similar contexts, building an empirical knowledge base that transforms protection strategies.

Yet these same technologies create new vulnerabilities, as demonstrated in Yemen where Houthi rebels attempted to access personal data of civilians receiving UN World Food Programme assistance, turning humanitarian databases designed to protect vulnerable populations into potential targets (Pauwels 2021). While AI was successfully used as a tool to facilitate peace dialogues and machine learning to analyze war crimes documentation, the conflict revealed how beneficiary lists, biometric data, and food distribution records could be weaponized against the very people they were meant to help. This paradox reveals that protecting civilians in the digital age requires missions to not only leverage AI's analytical capabilities for enhanced early warning but also defend against the exploitation of data systems, recognizing that modern conflicts target both physical safety and digital identities, making civilian protection more complex than traditional peace operations anticipated.

The peace operations budget crisis, with a $2 billion shortfall representing 35% of total funding, is driving member states toward AI and innovation as essential pathways to maintain Security Council mandates with fewer resources (UN Peacekeeping 2025). For member states, this shift demands urgent adaptation: developing competencies to understand AI's capabilities and limitations, establishing algorithmic accountability mechanisms, and ensuring technologies developed for peace operations have safeguards against weaponization by hostile actors and misuse for surveillance. Also, foreign policy professionals must balance efficiency gains from AI with human rights imperatives, ensuring that predictive algorithms don't perpetuate biases against marginalized communities or that information monitoring systems don't violate sovereignty principles. The effective integration of AI in peace operations represents a shared global imperative, when missions become more capable of preventing violence and protecting civilians through responsible AI deployment, the entire international community benefits from enhanced stability and reduced human suffering. Success requires collective commitment to developing ethical AI frameworks for peace operations, recognizing that the responsible use of these technologies will determine whether AI becomes a tool that strengthens peace or amplifies divisions in an already fractured world.

WOMEN, PEACE, AND SECURITY AGENDA AND AI—TOWARD AN INTEGRATED FRAMEWORK

The WPS Agenda, established through UN Security Council Resolution 1325 in 2000, represented a landmark framework recognizing that women's meaningful participation in conflict prevention, resolution, and peacebuilding is essential for sustainable peace, while also addressing the disproportionate impact of conflict on women and girls. As this agenda marks its 25th anniversary, women remain dramatically excluded from peace processes, comprising only 7% of negotiators and 14% of mediators globally, with nearly nine out of ten negotiation tracks including no women at all. The situation is deteriorating rather than improving: 676 million women now live within 50 kilometers of deadly conflict (the highest since the 1990s), civilian casualties among women and children have quadrupled, yet women's peacebuilding organizations are scaling down or closing due to chronic underfunding. As UN Secretary-General Guterres warned, the limited gains of the past quarter-century are "going in reverse," with women needing not more promises but actual power, protection, and equal participation in peace processes that evidence shows are more durable when they're included (United Nations Peacekeeping 2025b).

At this critical reflection point, the intersection of AI and gender-responsive peacebuilding presents both transformative opportunities and significant risks that foreign policy practitioners must carefully navigate. Despite hundreds of national and regional action plans adopted by over 110 countries to implement WPS commitments, only 15 explicitly address emerging technologies like AI, a critical gap given how profoundly these technologies are reshaping conflict dynamics and peace operations (Mohan 2025). This disconnect between rapid technological advancement and WPS implementation frameworks means that AI systems deployed in conflict settings often fail to account for gender dimensions, potentially reinforcing the very inequalities the WPS Agenda seeks to address while missing opportunities to leverage technology for advancing women's meaningful participation in peace processes.

This failure is particularly alarming given the scale of technology-facilitated violence: studies indicate between 16% and 58% of women globally experience digital abuse, with rates even higher for those engaged in peace work. UNESCO found that 73% of women journalists face online violence in the course of their work, while human rights defenders and activists encounter escalating threats both online and offline (UN Women 2025). In Southeast Asia, three in four women organizations are subject to online harassment, and these figures are even higher for women in public office (Vesco 2025). These figures reveal how AI and digital technologies, when deployed without gender-sensitive frameworks, not only miss opportunities to support women's peace activism but actively create new vectors for violence that silence women's voices precisely when their participation in peace processes is most critical.

Some of the hardest conflict settings also demonstrate how these technologies can be transformed into tools for inclusive peacebuilding: in 2020, UN Special Envoy for Yemen, working with Track 2 partners and Yemeni civil society, conducted an AI-powered virtual dialogue that reached over 600 Yemenis, using real-time anonymous conversations to ensure women and marginalized groups could safely contribute to discussions on nationwide ceasefire and humanitarian needs despite these digital threats. The French Ministry of Foreign Affairs, exercising essential leadership through the AI Action Summit in Paris in 2025, created crucial diplomatic space where Yemeni women's experiences of technology-facilitated violence could inform protective frameworks while showcasing their AI-mediated peace processes (OSESGY 2025).

AI applications offer concrete pathways to strengthen all four WPS pillars, participation, protection, prevention, and relief/recovery, if deliberately designed with gender considerations. AI technologies are creating **new pathways for women's participation** in peace processes through deliberative platforms that enable remote engagement in violent settings, as demonstrated in Yemen. In addition, AI-powered data collection systems like PRIO's EMPOW project can systematically track and analyze women's mobilization across all peace process stages, generating evidence about what factors encourage or hinder women's participation that was previously impossible to capture at scale (Olsson 2025). AI can **enhance prevention** by analyzing vast data streams to identify early warning signs of gender-based violence before escalation, from detecting spikes in online misogyny to predicting patterns of conflict-related sexual violence. AI tools can help monitor cases of trafficking, hate speech, and violence against women, providing necessary signals to **strengthen protection.** Predictive analytics and anticipatory action can also support humanitarian interventions to minimize suffering of women and girls in conflict settings and **ultimately increasing their resilience**.

Despite these opportunities, AI systems pose significant risks, such as algorithmic bias, decision-making opacity, and the exacerbation of digital inequalities. AI trained on biased data and developed without women's participation can misrepresent women's needs and reinforce gender discrimination, potentially worsening rather than closing gender gaps in peace and security contexts (Vesco 2025). The gender digital divide compounds these challenges, as women's limited access to digital technologies prevents their meaningful engagement with AI-driven peace processes, while sophisticated deepfakes increasingly target women with harassment campaigns designed to silence their participation (UNESCO 2024). These challenges reflect what scholars Catherine D'Ignazio and Lauren Klein term "data feminism," a framework that exposes how power structures are embedded in data collection, analysis, and algorithmic design, revealing that seemingly neutral AI systems often reflect and amplify existing gender hierarchies (D'Ignazio and Klein 2020). Data feminism principles demand we ask critical questions: not just what data is collected but who collects it, whose experiences are counted, and who benefits from algorithmic decisions. These questions are particularly urgent in conflict settings where women's voices are already marginalized.

Integrating AI considerations into WPS implementation requires deliberate action across multiple domains that foreign ministries can champion through their peace and security portfolios. National and regional action plans must be updated to explicitly address AI's dual-use nature, establishing protocols for gender-responsive AI deployment in peace operations while creating safeguards against technology-facilitated gender-based violence. Breaking institutional silos between gender advisors and technology specialists within foreign ministries will enable cross-pollination of expertise, ensuring WPS experts shape AI governance frameworks while technology specialists understand gender dimensions of their tools. Most critically, closing the gender digital divide through targeted capacity-building ensures women peacebuilders can not only use AI tools but participate in designing them, moving from passive recipients to active shapers of peace technology. States that invest now in creating responsible AI innovation ecosystems with built-in gender analysis, bias mitigation protocols, and inclusive design processes will be better positioned to harness AI's potential for advancing women's meaningful participation in peace while avoiding the inadvertent reinforcement of inequalities that could undermine decades of WPS progress.

Yet implementing these ambitious reforms requires more than technical adjustments to existing frameworks, it demands a fundamental reimagining of how foreign policy approaches the intersection of gender, technology, and peace. The emergence of feminist foreign policies across nations like Canada, Sweden, Mexico, Germany, and France offers a promising conceptual framework for this transformation, even as implementation has proven uneven and challenging, with some countries scaling back or abandoning these policies amid political shifts, and even as these frameworks have yet to fully grapple with AI's implications. Despite these setbacks, the core principles of feminist foreign policy (FFP), challenging power asymmetries, centering gender equality, and interrogating whose voices shape international relations, remain analytically powerful tools for understanding how AI intersects with peace and security. Most FFP frameworks were developed before AI's transformative impact became apparent, creating an urgent need to update these approaches for the algorithmic age. By extending FFP principles to

AI governance, prioritizing inclusive decision-making, interrogating technological power structures, and ensuring accountability for digital harms, states could create comprehensive strategies that address the systemic nature of gender inequality in AI-mediated peace processes. This evolution of FFP to encompass AI represents not just an incremental policy update but a necessary practical shift for ensuring that technology serves rather than subverts the goal of inclusive, sustainable peace.

Where AI developers lack WPS understanding while peace practitioners lack technical knowledge is precisely where FFP could bridge critical gaps through what might be termed "feminist tech-diplomacy" (Stephenson and Barry 2024). FFP countries could pioneer regional frameworks that make gender impact assessments mandatory for AI deployments in conflict-affected areas, establish diplomatic protocols for responding to algorithmic discrimination against women peacebuilders, and create multilateral mechanisms for holding social media companies accountable when their algorithms accelerate gender-based violence.

Across mediation platforms and satellite imagery analysis, peacekeeping operations, and women's peace networks, AI is simultaneously expanding and testing the boundaries of what peacebuilding can achieve. The technologies examined in this chapter, from algorithms that bridge dialogue across conflict lines to computer vision systems that document atrocities beyond human reach, share a common thread: they extend human capacity without replacing human judgment. For foreign policy practitioners, engaging with these tools requires active participation in shaping how they are designed, deployed, and governed. The choice before us is not whether AI will reshape peacebuilding, it already has, but whether we will ensure these technologies amplify silenced voices, protect the most vulnerable, and strengthen rather than erode the foundations of sustainable peace.

NOTES

1 Interview, by author, recorded online, December 5, 2025.
2 Interview with a peace expert, by author, recorded online, December 5, 2025.

BIBLIOGRAPHY

AI Akord. 2025. *AI Akord - Your Co-Pilot for Peace.* Accessed December 3, 2025. https://www.akord.org/.

AI for Good. 2025. *Bringing AI into Human Rights: Why Dialogue Matters.* November 5. Accessed December 30, 2025. https://aiforgood.itu.int/bringing-ai-into-human-rights-why-dialogue-matters/.

Alavi, Daanish Masood, Martin Wählisch, Colin Irwin, and Andrew Konya. 2022. "Using Artificial Intelligence for Peacebuilding." *Journal of Peacebuilding and Development* 12 (2): 239–243. https://doi.org/10.1177/15423166221102757

Amnesty International. 2016. *Digital Volunteers to Expose Darfur Human Rights Violations in 'revolutionary' Crowdsourcing Project.* October 13. https://www.amnesty.org/en/latest/press-release/2016/10/digital-volunteers-to-expose-darfur-human-rights-violations/.

Build Up. 2025. *Phoenix.* June 15. https://howtobuildup.org/phoenix/.

Bussemaker, Nathalie, and Mark Freeman. 2025. *AI on the Frontline: Evaluating Large Language Models in Real-World Conflict Resolution.* Report, Barcelona: Institute for Integrated Transitions.

D'Ignazio, Catherine, and Lauren F. Klein. 2020. *Data Feminism.* Cambridge: MIT Press.

Druet, Dirk. 2021. *Enhancing the Use of Digital Technology for Integrated Situational Awareness and Peacekeeping-Intelligence.* Thematic Research Paper for the DPO Peacekeeping Technology Strategy, Center for International Peace and Security Studies, McGill University.

Dubberley, Sam, Alexa Koenig, and Daragh Murray. 2020. *Digital Witness.* Oxford: Oxford University Press.

FastCompany. 2025. *AI Is Supercharging War. Could It Also Help Broker Peace?* June 23. Accessed November 17, 2025. https://www.fastcompany.com/91350078/ai-is-supercharging-war-could-it-also-help-broker-peace.

Grand-Clément, Sarah. 2022a. *Exploring the Use of Technology for Remote Ceasefire Monitoring and Verification.* Report, Geneva: UNIDIR.

Grand-Clément, Sarah. 2022b. *What Role Technology Can Play in Ceasefire Monitoring and Verification.* July 11. Accessed December 30, 2025. https://medium.com/futuring-peace/what-role-technology-can-play-in-ceasefire-monitoring-and-verification-1ae160fdba6c.

Hansen, Annika S., Wibke Hansen, Tobias von Gienanth, Monika Benkler, Tobias Pietz, and Martin Waehlisch. 2025. *Five Trends in UN Peace Operations and Five Calls to Action.* Study, Berlin: Center for International Peace Operations.

Hao, Karen. 2020. *Human Rights Activists Want to Use AI to Help Prove War Crimes in Court.* June 50. Accessed November 25, 2025. https://www.technologyreview.com/2020/06/25/1004466/ai-could-help-human-rights-activists-prove-war-crimes/.

Hedgehog Lab. 2024. *The World's First AI-Powered Co-Pilot for Peacebuilders, Launches.* November6.AccessedDecember3,2025.https://hedgehoglab.com/news/akord-ai-launch-pr/#:~:text=%E2%80%9CAkord%20AI%20addresses%20an%20important,lab%20News%20Innovation%20Press%20Releases.

Hirblinger, Andreas T., Ville Brummer, and Felix Kufus. 2024. "Leveraging Digital Methods in the Quest for Peaceful Futures: The Interplay of Sincere and Subjunctive Technology Affordances in Peace Mediation." *Information, Communication & Society* (Routledge) 27 (11): 2039–2058.

Human Rights Watch. 2022. *Ukraine: Russian Forces' Trail of Death in Bucha.* April 21. Accessed November 25, 2025. https://www.hrw.org/news/2022/04/21/ukraine-russian-forces-trail-death-bucha.

International Telecommunications Union. 2024. *United Nations Activities on Artificial Intelligence (AI).* UN Report, Geneva: ITU.

Konya, Andrew, Luke Thorburn, Wasim Almasri, Oded Adomi Leshem, Ariel Procaccia, Lisa Schirch, and Michiel Bakker. 2025. "Using Collective Dialogues and AI to Find Common Ground between Israeli and Palestinian Peacebuilders." *Proceedings of the 2025 ACM Conference on Fairness, Accountability, and Transparency*, New York, 312–333.

Kurbalija, Jovan. 2024. *Why Will AI Enhance, Not Replace, Human Diplomacy?* October 16. https://www.diplomacy.edu/blog/why-ai-will-enhance-not-replace-human-diplomacy/.

Lamont, Christopher K., and Medlir Mema. 2023. "Digital Transitional Justice: Unpacking the Black Box." In *Handbook on the Politics and Governance of Big Data and Artificial Intelligence*, by Andrej Zwitter and Oskar Gstrein, 139–151. Cheltenham; Northampton, MA: Elgaronline.

Larrauri, Helena Puig, and Maude Morrison. 2022. "Understanding Digital Conflict Drivers." In *Fundamental Challenges to Global Peace and Security*, by H. Mahmoudi et al., 169–200. London: Palgrave Macmillan.

Lemm, Stefan. 2021. *Data Privacy and Protection Assessments in Radio Mining.* April 12. Accessed December 6, 2025. https://unite.un.org/en/article/data-privacy-and-protection-assessments-radio-mining#:~:text=When%20we%20speak%20about%20Data,we%20care%20about%20radio%20data?.

Miyashita, Naomi, and Gaëlle Sundelin. 2025. *"Weapons of War": Disinformation and Hate Speech Pose Growing Challenge for Keeping the Peace.* September 25. Accessed December 6, 2025. https://peacekeeping.un.org/en/weapons-of-war-disinformation-and-hate-speech-pose-growing-challenge-keeping-peace.

Mohan, Shimona. 2025. *Factsheet: Artificial Intelligence and the Women, Peace and Security Agenda.* Geneva: UNIDIR.

Mohdin, Aamna. 2025. *Sudan's Latest Massacre Has Been Exposed from Satellite Images – How Much Longer Can the World Look Away?* October 31. Accessed November 25, 2025. https://www.theguardian.com/world/2025/oct/31/sudans-latest-massacre-has-been-exposed-from-satellite-images-how-much-longer-can-the-world-look-away.

Nuestra Memor IA. 2024. *Exporando los Archivos de la Memoria.* July 25. Accessed November 25, 2025. https://nuestramemoria.ing.uc.cl/.

Office of the United Nations High Commissioner for Human Rights (OHCHR). 2025. *Digital Image Verification and Classification Project.* July 8. Accessed November 25, 2025. https://aiforgood.itu.int/about-us/un-ai-actions/ohchr/.

Olsson, Louise. 2025. *Women's Empowerment in Peace Process (EMPOW).* June. Accessed December 6, 2025. https://www.prio.org/projects/2049.

OSESGY. 2020. *Cutting-Edge Tech in the Service of Inclusive Peace in Yemen.* August 3. Accessed November 26, 2025. https://osesgy.unmissions.org/en/press-releases/cutting-edge-tech-service-inclusive-peace-yemen.

OSESGY. 2025. *The AI Peace Nexus: Elevating WPS Agenda in Yemen's Digital Future.* Summit Report, Jordan: Office of the Special Envoy of the Secretary General for Yemen.

Panic, Branka. 2020. *Emerging Technologies: The Ally Human Rights Advocates Need.* December 9. Accessed November 25, 2025. https://cic.nyu.edu/resources/emerging-technologies-the-ally-human-rights-advocates-need/.

Panic, Branka, and Paige Arthur. 2024. *AI for Peace.* Boca Raton: Taylor & Francis.

Pauwels, Eleonore. 2021. *Peacekeeping in an Era of Converging Technological & Security Threats Preventing Collective AI & Data Harms, Learning to Save Lives with Dual-Use Technologies.* UN DPO Paper, New York City: UN DPO.

Peace Security Data Hub. 2025. *Easy Access, Better Insights.* January 15. Accessed November 26, 2025. https://psdata.un.org/.

Puig-Larrauri, Helena. 2024. *Mediating with and on Technology.* Birmingham: Birmingham University.

Reynolds, Ian, and Benjamin Jensen. 2025. *Machine Learning Meets War Termination.* Washington, DC: Center for Strategic and International Studies.

Sabanayagam, Jaikumar. 2025. *Unite Wave Big Data Radio Mining Project.* Project Presentation, UN Office of Information and Communications Technology.

Sarfati, Agathe. 2023. *New Technologies and the Protection of Civilians in UN Peace Operations.* Washington, DC: International Peace Institute.

Sokol, Anna, Matthew L. Sisk, Josefina Echavarria Alvarez, and Nitesh Chawla. 2025. *Ventana a la Verdad (Window to the Truth): A Chatbot Application for Navigating the Colombian Truth Commission's Archives.* March 10. Accessed November 25, 2025. https://dl.acm.org/doi/10.1145/3701551.3704123.

Stephenson, Elise, and Isobel Barry. 2024. *Feminist Technology Diplomacy: An FFP Approach to Artificial Intelligence.* Issue Paper, Australian Feminist Foreign Policy Coalition.

Tech and Social Cohesion. 2025. *Peace by Prompt.* August 20. Accessed December 30, 2025. https://techandsocialcohesion.substack.com/p/peace-by-prompt?utm_source=substack&utm_medium=email&utm_campaign=email-restack-comment&r=67mdh&triedRedirect=true.

UN Department of Peace Operations. 2024. *Information Integrity in Peacekeeping Settings.* Policy Report, New York City: UN DPO.

UN Global Pulse. 2021. *Radio Mining: Monitoring Local Radio Conversations Can Help Build Peace.* Accessed December 5, 2025. https://www.unglobalpulse.org/project/radio-mining-monitoring-local-radio-conversations-can-help-build-peace/.

UN Peacekeeping. 2021. *A4P+: Action for Peacekeeping Priorities 2021–2023.* Background Paper, NYC: UN Peacekeeping.

UN Peacekeeping. 2025. *Budget Gaps Threaten Global Peace Efforts.* October 15. Accessed December 6, 2025. https://peacekeeping.un.org/en/budget-gaps-threaten-global-peace-efforts.

UN Security Council. 2024. *Maintenance of International Peace and Security Artificial Intelligence.* Official Records of the Security Council, New York City: UN Security Council.

UN Women. 2025. *FAQs: Digital Abuse, Trolling, Stalking, and Other Forms of Technology-Facilitated Violence against Women and Girls.* November 13. Accessed November 27, 2025. https://www.unwomen.org/en/articles/faqs/digital-abuse-trolling-stalking-and-other-forms-of-technology-facilitated-violence-against-women#:~:text=Take%20doxing%2C%20for%20example%2C%20which, experienced%20this%20type%20of%20violence.

UNESCO. 2024. *Generative AI: UNESCO Study Reveals Alarming Evidence of Regressive Gender Stereotypes.* Study, Paris: UNESCO.

United Nations Peacekeeping. 2021. *Strategy for the Digital Transformation of UN Peacekeeping.* September 17. Accessed November 24, 2025. https://peacekeeping.un.org/en/strategy-digital-transformation-of-un-peacekeeping.

United Nations Peacekeeping. 2025a. *Information Integrity and Harmful Information.* November 24. Accessed November 24, 2025. https://peacekeeping.un.org/en/information-integrity-and-harmful-information.

United Nations Peacekeeping. 2025b. *Women Still Largely Excluded from Peace Processes.* October 20. Accessed December 6, 2025. https://peacekeeping.un.org/en/women-still-largely-excluded-peace-processes.

United Nations. 2023. *UN Peacekeeping Missions' Battle against Disinformation.* July 5. Accessed December 6, 2025. https://unric.org/en/un-peacekeeping-missions-battle-against-disinformation/.

United Nations Security Council. 2023. *Situation in Mali - Report of the Secretary General.* Report of the Secretary General, New York City: UNSC.

University of Birmingham. 2025. *A New Kind of Peacemaker: AI Joins the Front Lines of Diplomacy.* May 16. Accessed December 30, 2025. https://www.birmingham.ac.uk/news/2025/a-new-kind-of-peacemaker-ai-joins-the-front-lines-of-diplomacy.

UNOSAT. 2017. *Damage Assessment of Jobar Neighborhood and Irbin City, Damascus Governorate, Syria.* January 17. https://unosat.org/products/1132.

UNU Macau. 2024. *UNU Macau AI Conference 2024- AI for All: Bridging Divides, Building a Sustainable Future.* Conference Proceedings Report, Macau: UNU Macau.

Vesco, Paola. 2025. *It Comes in Peace? AI's Promise and Peril for Women, Peace and Security.* November 27. Accessed December 6, 2025. https://gps.prio.org/comments/78.

9 From Topic to Tool

How AI Tools Entered the World of Foreign Policy

AI is one of the most exciting disruptors of our time, not because it will replace humans, but because it will redefine what human work can be. It's going to shift what skills are valued, how people spend their time, and even what we consider "expertise." I see this as a generational opportunity: to offload repetitive, soul-draining parts of work and reimagine roles around judgment, empathy, creativity, and decision-making.

—**Paula Osborn,** *Deputy Chief Data and AI Officer at the US Department of State (Osborn 2025)*

Humanitarian negotiation is about building trust and legitimacy in the eyes of the counterpart and trying to make a point based on a human-to-human connection. So it's a paradox to think of the role of AI in that field. At the same time, it's precisely because these negotiations are often complex and have high stakes that AI can come in and provide valuable support in terms of analysis, planning and sense-making.

—**Claude Bruderlein,** *Harvard Kennedy School of Government (Jefford 2025)*

Foreign policy practitioners initially encountered artificial intelligence (AI) not as a practical instrument, but as an emerging strategic concern demanding their attention. As the previous chapters illustrated, AI first captured diplomatic focus through national and global security implications, economic competitiveness, crisis prevention, and geopolitical power dynamics. Defense establishments in the 1980s and 1990s recognized AI's potential for weapons systems and intelligence analysis, while economic policymakers grappled with AI's capacity to reshape global productivity, labor markets, and competitive advantages between nations. The 2016 AlphaGo victory and subsequent events like election interference campaigns transformed AI from a specialized concern into a central foreign policy imperative, demonstrating its power to influence everything from military strategy to democratic processes.

This recognition of AI's transformative potential triggered a fundamental shift in diplomatic circles. Foreign ministries evolved from analyzing AI as a policy challenge to actively shaping its governance and ultimately deploying it as an operational tool. Yet this evolution is far from uniform. While pioneering ministries deploy AI for negotiations and crisis response, most diplomatic services worldwide still struggle with basic digitalization, lacking the infrastructure, expertise, and cultural readiness

DOI: 10.1201/9781003644712-14

for AI adoption. This chapter does not presume universal readiness; rather, it aims to offer insights into what pioneering countries are doing and how, providing inspiration for those beginning this journey, caution about potential pitfalls, and lessons learned from early implementations.

As policymakers realized that AI governance couldn't be left to data scientists alone, they engaged in initiatives like the OECD's AI Principles and UNESCO's Ethics framework, bringing essential expertise in international cooperation and human rights to ensure the technology serves humanity. This hands-on engagement with AI governance exposed diplomats to both the technology's capabilities and its risks, transforming skeptics into informed advocates within their own institutions. Today, in a handful of technologically advanced capitals, foreign ministries use AI systems to monitor global events, prepare negotiations, detect disinformation, and streamline consular services. Yet early adopters face persistent challenges that illuminate broader barriers to diplomatic AI integration. Skills gaps remain acute, both technical expertise in data and AI, and foundational AI literacy within diplomatic training programs. Procurement frameworks designed for traditional acquisitions prove ill-suited for rapidly evolving technologies. Perhaps most significantly, cultural resistance persists among diplomats who view algorithmic tools as threats to traditional craft, often reinforced by leadership skepticism about AI's relevance to diplomatic work. While this chapter concentrates on applications and ethics rather than these operational hurdles, understanding them provides essential context for the adoption patterns that follow.

This chapter offers unique insights drawn from the author's direct engagement with ministries of foreign affairs, embassies, consulates, and their ecosystem of partners, academia, civil society, and private sector collaborators, who are at the forefront of AI applications for diplomatic and broader foreign policy work. Through extensive interviews with foreign policy officials and hands-on implementation projects, including foresight workshops and AI pilot programs, several key domains have emerged where AI tools are reshaping foreign policy practice: information gathering and analysis, translation, diplomatic negotiations and multilateral engagement, and consular services. Notably, these categories emerged organically from practitioner needs rather than academic theory, reflecting the real-world challenges diplomats face in an increasingly complex international environment. The sections that follow examine each domain in turn, exploring both current applications and the ethical considerations they raise.

AI IN STRATEGIC COMMUNICATION, TRANSLATION, AND BRIEFING SYSTEMS

Strategic communication has become exponentially more complex in a hyperconnected world. Foreign ministries must craft messages that resonate across multiple languages, cultures, and platforms. They must address domestic audiences, international partners, and global public opinion simultaneously. Real-time news cycles leave little room for error, as a poorly translated statement or delayed response can trigger diplomatic crises within hours. The sheer volume compounds the challenge: hundreds of diplomatic cables daily, thousands of media reports in dozens of languages, and endless social media streams mixing critical intelligence with dangerous misinformation. State and nonstate actors weaponize these information spaces through sophisticated disinformation campaigns that destabilize allies, undermine initiatives, and erode public trust faster than traditional communications can respond. Language barriers add further difficulty. Ministries must engage authentically with global audiences while maintaining diplomatic precision, where a single word choice can alter the meaning of international agreements.

AI in Diplomatic Translation, Drafting, and Briefing

Diplomatic communication has traditionally relied on teams of highly skilled translators, interpreters, and diplomatic drafters working under intense time pressure to produce accurate, culturally sensitive materials. Translation of diplomatic cables, treaties, and official correspondence required hours or days of detailed work by specialized linguists familiar with both the technical terminology and subtle diplomatic nuances that could alter international relationships with a single misplaced word.

Preparing ministerial briefings involved multiple staff members manually synthesizing information from various sources, embassy reports, intelligence assessments, media monitoring, and historical precedents, often working through the night to deliver comprehensive materials before morning meetings. This labor-intensive process frequently created bottlenecks, particularly during international crises when foreign ministries needed to simultaneously communicate with multiple countries in their respective languages while maintaining the precise diplomatic tone that could mean the difference between escalation and de-escalation.

While open-source translation and content generation tools are widely available, foreign ministries face unique operational requirements that drive them to often build proprietary AI systems or contract specialized providers. The primary distinction lies in data sovereignty; diplomatic communications cannot risk being incorporated into third-party training datasets, requiring closed systems where sensitive information remains exclusively within government control. Ministries now have a challenge to provide their personnel with AI capabilities comparable to consumer tools but within secure, unclassified environments that comply with both home country regulations and the varying data protection laws of host nations. Diplomatic AI tools must often function reliably in hostile or unstable environments where governments may restrict internet access, shut down communications networks, or monitor digital traffic, operational realities that commercial AI providers never designed their systems to accommodate (Alder 2024). This combination of security requirements, regulatory compliance, and the need for resilient systems that work anywhere from stable democracies to conflict zones makes diplomatic AI fundamentally different from both consumer and standard enterprise solutions.

The U.S. State Department's embrace of commercial AI tools like ChatGPT and Claude for $1 symbolic pricing represents a stark contrast to the digital sovereignty approach pursued by many other nations, which view dependence on foreign AI systems for government operations as a strategic vulnerability (Nazzaro 2025). While American agencies appear comfortable integrating these tools into diplomatic workflows, from drafting cables to intelligence analysis, European, Asian, and Latin

American governments increasingly prioritize developing domestic AI capabilities or regional alternatives, recognizing that the AI systems processing their diplomatic communications could become instruments of foreign influence or intelligence gathering. This divergence reflects the broader geopolitical tension we've examined in previous chapters, where countries must balance the immediate operational benefits of advanced AI tools against the long-term risks of technological dependency, particularly when these systems learn from and potentially expose patterns in diplomatic behavior, negotiation strategies, and policy formulation processes that foreign governments and companies could exploit.

Beyond security concerns, diplomatic communication requires understanding of specialized terminology and cultural nuances that mainstream models often miss. This multi-tool ecosystem demonstrates how foreign ministries are moving beyond generic AI solutions to develop purpose-built applications that address specific diplomatic functions while maintaining the strict security and confidentiality standards essential to diplomatic work.

This need for linguistic precision has driven regional initiatives worldwide—many originally developed for broader purposes but increasingly relevant to diplomatic work. LatamGPT captures the subtle variations of Latin American Spanish and Portuguese that global models overlook, addressing blind spots in regional idioms and cultural contexts (CENIA 2025). In India, the Bhashini program provides speech-to-text, translation, and voice tools in over 22 Indian languages, while AI4Bharat develops language models for underserved communities and Sarvam AI is building the country's first indigenous foundation model designed for Indian languages and cultural contexts (Elias 2025). In Africa, Lelapa AI launched InkubaLM, the continent's first multilingual large language model, supporting Swahili, Yoruba, IsiXhosa, Hausa, and isiZulu to address the digital underrepresentation of African languages (Africa World Initiative 2024). These efforts reflect a growing recognition that effective communication requires AI trained on smaller languages and regional variants representing millions of speakers who receive minimal attention in mainstream models.

These specialized systems prove essential for diplomatic work, where a misunderstood cultural reference or regional expression could derail negotiations, and where preserving linguistic diversity ensures that diplomatic engagement remains accessible to all nations regardless of their languages' global prominence. By combining secure infrastructure with culturally aware language processing, ministries can maintain data sovereignty while ensuring their AI tools understand not just words, but the diplomatic and cultural weight they carry across different linguistic traditions.

AI in Practice: Tools and Platforms across Foreign Ministries

The U.S. State Department introduced **StateChat** in late 2024 to assists diplomats worldwide with drafting communications, translating and analyzing documents, and policy brainstorming, while allowing employees to use generative AI in sensitive unclassified environment where data is accessible only to them; **Northstar** is another AI-powered tool that synthesizes and analyzes news reports and social media posts from multiple countries and from hundreds of thousands of global outlets for rapid situational awareness (U.S. Department of State 2025); and **FAM Search** serves as an AI-powered knowledge base for navigating internal procedures from travel protocols to cybersecurity guidelines (Alder 2024). The State Department has developed a machine learning tool trained on years of prior declassification decisions that achieves near-human accuracy in **reviewing diplomatic cables**, enabling the first-ever proactive release of classified records using AI while significantly reducing the manual review burden as agencies struggle with overwhelming volumes of electronic records requiring declassification (Doubleday 2023).

European Commission offers custom-trained tools, built on decades of translation expertise, to provide several styles of translation to the European External Action Service and to EU member states. It offers drafts for formal responses and analysis of original documents, available in all EU languages (European Commission 2025).

The Latvian Ministry of Foreign Affairs has developed an AI-powered translation platform specifically designed to support Ukraine's EU accession by addressing one of its most resource-intensive challenges, translating national legislation and aligning it with the EU acquis, the entire body of EU law that requires exceptional linguistic precision and legal accuracy. The system enables secure, high-quality translation of large volumes of official content while ensuring consistency with EU legal terminology, significantly reducing manual workload for Ukrainian officials working on harmonization. Beyond its primary focus on legislative alignment, the platform also supports routine public administration tasks like translating emails and documents in a secure environment, demonstrating how bilateral AI assistance can directly facilitate diplomatic and integration objectives (Tilde 2025). Albania has taken a similar approach, becoming the first country to use AI directly in EU membership negotiations, translating and harmonizing over 250,000 pages of EU law with 99.9% accuracy, a process that took Croatia seven years but which Albania aims to complete by 2027 (BalkanWeb 2025).

Similarly, **Thailand's government** deployed large language models to overcome language barriers and administrative inefficiencies in its **OECD accession process**. Facing the challenge of aligning with over 250 OECD legal instruments, Thailand confronted critical barriers: administrative silos between 50 government agencies, below-average English proficiency, and the need to analyze over 100,000 Thai legal documents against international standards. The government deployed an LLM-based solution that performs technical translation between formal English and governmental Thai, generates keywords through semantic analysis, and conducts automated gap analyses between OECD requirements and domestic laws. This enables real-time communication between OECD staff and Thai officials, with each working in their preferred language while AI handles translation and technical terminology through expert-validated glossaries, transforming what would require years of manual analysis into an efficient automated process that bridges both linguistic and institutional divides (Popattanachai 2025).

The French Ministry for Europe and Foreign Affairs deployed **DiploIA**, an AI-powered translation and transcription system serving thousands of diplomats. The system can process an hour of recorded dialogue in minutes across approximately 100 languages. Developed entirely in-house and running exclusively on ministry-owned data centers, the system ensures no sensitive diplomatic content ever transits through external platforms, exemplifying the sovereignty-first approach many governments adopt for diplomatic AI tools. The ministry plans to enhance DiploIA with specialized "diplomatic language" capabilities through months of model training with diplomat feedback, demonstrating how nations are building tailored AI systems that understand the unique linguistic nuances of diplomatic communication while maintaining complete control over sensitive data (Slator 2025).

Japan's Ministry of Justice has deployed a domestically developed AI translation system that reduces the time needed to translate Japanese laws and regulations into English from two and a half years to just weeks, addressing a critical barrier to foreign investment and business operations. The system combines Japanese-built AI translation engines with specialized rule-based processing tailored to legal documents, ensuring compliance with strict terminology standards while avoiding errors common in general-purpose translation tools. This exemplifies how nations are creating specialized AI systems that serve dual diplomatic and administrative purposes, making legal frameworks accessible to international partners while maintaining complete sovereignty over translation processes and sensitive data (Toshiba 2024).

The UK government has developed Redbox, an internal AI chatbot powered by large language models that enables civil servants to analyze government documents and produce draft briefings within seconds rather than hours. The Cabinet Office alone has recorded 3,000 users conducting 30,000 conversations with the system, while the Department for Business and Trade has logged over 13,000 prompts and responses. The tool can reportedly synthesize dozens of documents instantaneously, tasks that previously required full days of work, and is being used by staff supporting the Prime Minister and across multiple government departments. However, it remains unclear how exactly Redbox influences policy decisions, whether ministerial advice incorporates AI-generated content, or what safeguards address algorithmic bias, raising broader transparency concerns about AI's role in governmental decision-making (NewScientist 2025).

DiploAI, developed by the Swiss-Maltese organization **DiploFoundation**, is an AI-powered reporting tool that can generate comprehensive analyses from UN debates in real time, as demonstrated during its pilot launch at the six-hour UN Security Council debate in May 2023. The system combines customized algorithms, diplomatic datasets, and large language models to produce just-in-time reporting, particularly benefiting small and developing countries that lack the human and institutional capacity to meaningfully participate in and monitor numerous UN processes. This tool represents a practical application of AI in multilateral diplomacy, enabling missions to receive detailed summaries, speaker analyses, and thematic reports from lengthy diplomatic proceedings they cannot fully staff (DiploFoundation 2023).

The Ethics of AI in Diplomatic Communication

The integration of AI into strategic communication fundamentally challenges our understanding of authenticity and accountability in diplomatic discourse. When AI generates diplomatic statements or translations, questions of responsibility become critical. In 1980, UN Secretary-General Kurt Waldheim's attempt to mediate the Iran hostage crisis sparked outrage and violence due to a fundamental linguistic divide: his announcement that he came as a "mediator" to seek "compromise" conveyed positive diplomatic intentions in English, but in Persian these same words meant betraying one's principles and meddling in others' affairs (Fisher, Ury and Patton 2011). This incident demonstrates not only how language and cultural context are crucial for diplomatic success, but also how these lessons become even more critical in the age of automation, where AI translation systems, lacking the ability to grasp that seemingly equivalent terms carry fundamentally different meanings across cultures, risk triggering similar diplomatic crises.

The technology's capacity to craft content at unprecedented scale introduces additional risks: foreign actors could deploy psychological profiling and micro-targeting techniques borrowed from commercial advertising to influence foreign populations, blurring the line between public diplomacy and propaganda. Without careful human review, AI-generated text may miss crucial context, misrepresent positions, or produce plausible-sounding inaccuracies, potentially damaging diplomatic relationships that took years to build.

The solution lies not in rejecting these technologies but in establishing clear governance frameworks. Foreign ministries must mandate human review of all AI-generated diplomatic communications, ensure transparency when AI shapes public messaging, and maintain clear boundaries between countering disinformation and suppressing legitimate discourse. While AI can eliminate routine tasks and accelerate document preparation, the core of diplomacy, building trust, reading unspoken tensions, negotiating complex agreements, and representing national interests with cultural sensitivity, remains irreducibly human. The challenge is preserving diplomatic authenticity and judgment while harnessing AI's efficiency, ensuring that automation enhances rather than undermines the personal relationships and mutual understanding that make diplomacy possible.

AI IN CONSULAR SERVICES: TRANSFORMING CITIZEN SUPPORT THROUGH AUTOMATION AND INTELLIGENCE

AI in Visa Processing and Chatbot Solutions

Consular sections process millions of visa applications, passport renewals, and citizen assistance requests annually with limited resources. Small teams, sometimes a single officer managing hundreds of daily emails, handle exponentially growing travel volumes, sophisticated document fraud, and citizens expecting round-the-clock support. Officers spend significant time on routine tasks like answering passport questions, creating backlogs that strain public confidence and intensify during crises or major international events.

Chatbots have emerged as the most widely adopted AI solution to these challenges, potentially improving citizen services. Operating continuously in multiple languages, these digital assistants handle floods of routine inquiries about visa requirements, document checklists, and renewal procedures. Their value becomes especially apparent during crises, when natural disasters or political upheavals trigger surges in inquiries, chatbots can scale instantly to provide timely information to thousands simultaneously, freeing human officers to focus on complex cases requiring cultural sensitivity, judgment, and empathy.

Concrete applications and examples are already emerging across multiple countries.

- **Immigration, Refugees, and Citizenship Canada's AI** adoption has reduced processing times and enabled more effective triage of routine cases, allowing officers to focus on complex matters requiring human judgment (Silvestre 2025).
- **The United Kingdom** has launched a Generative AI-powered chatbot with human-like conversational support through both voice and text interface, enhancing customer support for travelers (VFS.Global 2025).
- Similarly, the **U.S. State Department** has deployed AI and natural language processing (NLP) tools that streamline visa processing through multilingual support, automated data validation, and intelligent case prioritization, significantly reducing administrative workload (Blaser and Kilburg 2025).
- **India** has integrated a chatbot into its Madad portal, Hindi for "help," to assist citizens in filing grievances and accessing emergency consular services (Ministry of External Affairs, Government of India 2025).

Recent analysis of visa application surges in preparation for the World Cup demonstrates how AI systems help consulates manage predictable but overwhelming spikes in demand during major international events (Lewis and Zengerle 2025). Similarly, Australia's long-standing AI tools proved especially valuable during the Covid-19 pandemic and natural disasters, automatically sorting urgent consular requests about border closures, repatriation, and travel restrictions, and directing citizens to the right support channels when human staff were overwhelmed (Blaser and Kilburg 2025). However, in some cases, trust has eroded dramatically. As one consular officer recounted in our work, an applicant refused to believe they were speaking to an actual human, demanding to talk to a "real person" because the responses seemed too efficient, illustrating how AI's presence can alter citizen–government relationships even when no AI is involved.

AI in Document Authentication and Fraud Detection

The document authentication process in consular services remains predominantly manual and resource-intensive, creating significant operational challenges for diplomatic missions worldwide. Consular officers spend tedious hours on document review, data entry, and cross-checking, each document individually examined, verified, scanned, labeled, and forwarded through multiple departments.

This traditional approach suffers from critical vulnerabilities. It consumes significant time, labor, and resources, while the risk of human error remains substantial, as even trained personnel can overlook subtle forgeries or fail to identify authentic documents that have been obtained through illicit means and sold on the black market (Hyena 2025). Smaller consulates face additional challenges with limited staff expertise available for complex fraud detection, creating processing delays that strain diplomatic resources. These processes struggle particularly with sophisticated forgery techniques that vary across countries, making it difficult to maintain uniform security standards across global consular networks.

Recognizing these challenges, consular offices are increasingly implementing AI-powered document verification systems that could improve their authentication processes. These systems automatically analyze physical and digital document features against verified templates, detecting artifacts from generative tools, reused templates, or manipulated PDFs that might pass human inspection but raise red flags under deeper automated scrutiny. **The UAE's Smart Mission** initiative exemplifies this transformation, deploying an AI-powered Document Attestation Service that uses computer vision to automatically recognize and verify official stamps on personal and commercial documents, reducing processing times from days to hours while identifying subtle forgery patterns human reviewers might miss (OECD 2025). By implementing AI as a first-line filter, consular services can reduce repetitive manual checks while allowing staff to focus their expertise on sensitive humanitarian cases requiring nuanced judgment.

However, AI adoption presents its own set of challenges. Algorithms require extensive training data to ensure accuracy, and without sufficient localized data reflecting country-specific forgery techniques, systems may struggle with correct identification. There's also the risk of over-reliance on technology, as the challenge lies not in replacing human judgment but in using AI to make it more powerful. Coordination between individual consulates and central authorities remains essential for consistent implementation while maintaining appropriate human oversight for sensitive visa determinations and cases where cultural context and humanitarian considerations play crucial roles.

The Ethics of AI in Consular Affairs: Balancing Innovation and Protection

Our foresight workshops and interviews with consular offices revealed that practitioners are already thinking beyond current chatbots and document verification systems. They envision agentic AI that autonomously navigates procedural complexities, predictive analytics that identify citizens in emerging crisis zones before evacuations become necessary, and virtual consulates enabling immersive service delivery for those unable to travel. Some anticipate AI in cultural diplomacy, analyzing cultural trends to inform public diplomacy campaigns or matching participants for exchange programs. Yet as these possibilities emerged in our conversations, participants consistently emphasized that enthusiasm for innovation must not outpace responsible implementation. The ethical frameworks governing today's applications will shape how future systems develop, making it essential to establish robust safeguards now, before more powerful capabilities become operational.

Different types of consular and immigration decisions require different levels of AI governance and oversight. For standard functions like document renewals and tourist visas, key risks include privacy breaches of sensitive biometric and travel data, and algorithmic bias that could systematically disadvantage applicants from certain countries or backgrounds. These often "black box" systems make determinations through opaque processes that neither applicants nor their legal representatives can understand or meaningfully challenge, undermining accountability. While AI can enhance efficiency in processing standard applications, maintaining human oversight remains essential to validate outputs and correct unintended biases. The challenge lies in ensuring that data is stored securely, accessed responsibly, and that automated systems enhance rather than erode public trust, requiring transparent governance frameworks that balance technological innovation with fundamental rights protection.

When AI is applied to immigration decisions, particularly refugee and asylum cases, the ethical implications become life-altering. Immigration lawyers already reported automated systems generating refusal reasons at the exact timestamp as application processing, suggesting minimal human review despite official assurances (Silvestre 2025). AI systems trained on historical immigration data risk perpetuating systemic discrimination against refugees who cannot return to danger. The power imbalance is stark, as opaque algorithms make irreversible decisions about family reunification, refugee protection, and deportation while vast personal data collection creates surveillance risks with unclear retention periods and cross-agency sharing. The gravity of data security in these contexts became starkly evident when the 2022 ICRC cyberattack exposed data of over 515,000 vulnerable people, including those separated by war, migrants in detention, and missing persons. This breach potentially endangered people fleeing persecution by revealing their locations to the very actors they were escaping, demonstrating how data vulnerabilities in humanitarian and immigration systems can transform from privacy violations into life-threatening security risks (ICRC 2022).

Foreign consular offices must therefore adopt tiered governance frameworks where safeguards match the stakes of each decision. Low-stake services require basic protections: transparency about AI usage, data minimization principles, and clear appeal processes for denials. Immigration and humanitarian cases, however, demand stricter standards, mandatory human review for all protection claims, prohibition of fully automated asylum decisions, and independent audits with published results to identify discriminatory patterns. Appeals must guarantee complete human reconsideration, while system design should incorporate input from refugee advocates and affected communities to ensure these tools serve rather than harm the most vulnerable.

AI IN DIPLOMATIC NEGOTIATIONS: FROM HUMANITARIAN AID TO TRADE AGREEMENTS

Modern diplomatic negotiations have become increasingly complex, requiring negotiators to simultaneously manage multiple stakeholder positions, track intricate technical details across lengthy documents, and adapt strategies in real time while operating under intense time pressure. Today's multilateral negotiations can involve dozens of countries with divergent interests, hundreds of pages of legal text, and parallel working groups addressing interconnected issues from trade to climate to security. The challenge intensifies in crisis negotiations where hours can determine outcomes, yet negotiators must process vast amounts of historical precedent, legal frameworks, and intelligence assessments while maintaining strategic ambiguity and reading unspoken signals from counterparts. Information asymmetry further complicates matters, as negotiators struggle to understand their counterparts' true bottom lines, domestic political constraints, and alternative options while protecting their own strategic information.

AI is transforming negotiators' capabilities through advanced tools that process large volumes of information, identify complex patterns, and simulate potential outcomes. While previous chapters examined in detail the specific intersections between AI and peace negotiations/mediation, exploring both the risks and opportunities, this section acknowledges that governments and multilateral organizations are leveraging AI assistance across numerous negotiation domains. We focus on three illustrative examples that demonstrate the breadth of AI's impact: trade negotiations, where economic complexity demands sophisticated analytical tools; humanitarian negotiations, where rapid crisis response can save lives; and climate negotiations, where scientific data must inform political compromises. These cases collectively showcase how AI is reshaping diplomatic practice across diverse policy areas while highlighting common implementation challenges and opportunities.

AI in Humanitarian Negotiations

In humanitarian crises, where negotiations can determine life and death outcomes, AI tools are increasingly considered for navigating complex, rapidly evolving situations. These negotiations typically unfold in environments characterized by multiple information sources, conflicting perspectives, and adversarial relationships that cloud possibilities for compromise. AI excels at processing the chaos of real-time crisis data, from satellite imagery tracking population movements to social media signals revealing emerging needs, while simultaneously analyzing communications from armed groups, NGOs, and government entities to identify opportunities for humanitarian access. NLP systems detect early warning signs of deteriorating conditions, while machine learning models map stakeholder networks and propose influence strategies based on historical patterns of successful negotiations (Kilburg 2026).

Beyond data processing, AI serves as a critical training and accountability tool for humanitarian organizations. In a field where negotiation expertise traditionally develops through years of dangerous fieldwork, AI-powered simulations allow negotiators to practice high-stakes scenarios safely, learning the craft without risking lives. These systems can coach negotiators through complex dilemmas, simulate potential outcomes of different approaches, and create measurable frameworks for organizations that previously relied solely on field staff intuition. While negotiation remains fundamentally a human-to-human endeavor, AI provides the analytical backbone that makes humanitarian responses more predictable, accountable, and effective (Jefford 2025).

The AI Negotiation Challenge recently simulated a scenario with UNICEF, UNHCR, and IOM examining unaccompanied minor migration along the Atlantic route. The exercise addressed core humanitarian dilemmas, balancing child protection with migration policies, preventing trafficking while maintaining asylum access, and coordinating multi-jurisdictional responses. Through AI-powered analysis, even small NGOs accessed not just policy databases but contextualized lessons and proven methodologies from similar global crises, demonstrating how technology democratizes expertise and improves coordination. However, these applications require strict data protection for vulnerable populations and algorithmic transparency to preserve humanitarian neutrality (Jefford 2025).

AI in Climate Negotiations

Climate negotiations represent some of the most complex diplomatic endeavors of our time, requiring negotiators to navigate scientific data, economic modeling, and political considerations across nearly 200 nations. While AI systems are not yet conducting direct negotiations between parties, they have become useful tools for diplomatic preparation and strategic planning. These technologies excel at the analytical groundwork that enables human negotiators to engage more effectively when they sit down at the negotiating table.

This evolution is already visible in foreign ministries and multilateral organizations worldwide. Rather than replacing negotiators, AI is fundamentally changing how they prepare for these high-stakes discussions. In multilateral negotiations, the sheer volume of documents, position papers, draft texts, historical precedents, technical annexes, overwhelms even the largest delegations. Countries are responding by building chatbots and conversational assistants that can process vast document repositories, identify patterns across thousands of pages, and surface relevant precedents instantly. A negotiator preparing for climate talks can now query an AI system about specific language used in past agreements or quickly understand how different proposals might affect their national interests.

One of the most sophisticated implementations comes from **Brazil's Ministry of Foreign Affairs**, which developed Arara Canindé, a virtual assistant named after the iconic Brazilian macaw bird. Built on authoritative sources including IPCC reports and technical papers from Brazil's climate team, this multilingual AI system addresses information overload and misinformation while serving negotiators, scientists, journalists, and other stakeholders. The initiative operates through an integrated architecture where technical papers are indexed on the "Araraúna" (Little Macaw) platform and transformed into globally accessible multilingual texts, complemented by a specialized assistant being developed for Brazil's COP30 presidency that leverages curated content aligned with presidential priorities, demonstrating how AI tools can simultaneously address immediate negotiation needs while building sustainable institutional capacity for knowledge management in multilateral diplomacy (UNDP 2025).

Another significant development in AI-assisted climate diplomacy is NegotiateCOP, an open-source AI tool developed through a collaborative initiative between the **German Federal Foreign Office** and partner ministries. This platform represents an evolution from its predecessor, NegotiateAI, which was initially designed for the UN Plastics Treaty negotiations before being adapted for the more complex arena of UNFCCC climate negotiations (Robin Nowok 2025). By processing and analyzing hundreds of negotiation submissions, the platform changes extensive document collections into structured insights, enabling smaller delegations to compete on a more equal footing with larger, better-resourced counterparts. Its ability to detect patterns and structures within extensive data not only enhances efficiency but also promotes more equitable participation in international climate diplomacy, reducing the information disparities that have long shaped multilateral negotiations.

A third approach demonstrates how AI can democratize participation for resource-constrained delegations. **The Centre for Multilateral Negotiations** and

ComplexChaos recently piloted a real-time AI support system with negotiators from nine African countries, representing 178 million people, at the UNFCCC campus in Bonn (WEF 2025). Unlike traditional preparation, where smaller delegations struggle to match wealthier nations' analytical capacity, this system enabled African negotiators to structure priorities, identify convergence points, and synthesize technical inputs during live discussions. As Cecilia Njenga, Director at the UNFCCC Secretariat, observed: "AI offers something rare: the potential to level the playing field. It can enhance the capacity of underrepresented voices and make negotiations smarter and more inclusive" (WEF 2025). The results were striking: 91% discovered critical insights they would have otherwise missed, empathy measures increased by 35%, and coordination time dropped by 60%. Most surprisingly, negotiators felt less isolated during solo preparation, suggesting that well-deployed AI can enhance rather than diminish diplomatic engagement's human dimensions (WEF 2025). This African-led initiative shows how AI might level the playing field, ensuring countries most vulnerable to climate impacts aren't disadvantaged by resource constraints in the very forums meant to address their needs.

However, any discussion of AI in climate negotiations must acknowledge a fundamental tension that tech diplomats themselves increasingly emphasize: the significant environmental footprint of these very tools. Training and running large language models consume enormous amounts of energy. AI systems designed to help negotiate climate solutions are themselves contributing to the problem they're meant to address. Leading voices in tech diplomacy are calling for radical transparency around these impacts, including mandatory disclosure of energy consumption and carbon emissions for AI models used in diplomatic contexts. If AI is to maintain credibility as a tool for climate negotiations, it must demonstrate its own commitment to sustainability through concrete measures, using renewable energy for data centers, optimizing algorithms for efficiency rather than just capability, and proving that the insights generated justify their environmental cost. Without addressing this contradiction, we risk undermining the very climate goals these negotiations seek to achieve.

AI in Economic Affairs and Trade Negotiations

Economic diplomacy, the practice of advancing national economic interests through international engagement, is undergoing a profound transformation. For decades, economic officers assembled market intelligence from quarterly reports, cultivated business contacts over years of careful relationship-building, and relied on seasoned intuition to spot emerging opportunities in foreign markets. These foundational skills remain indispensable, but AI has started to impact their application and impact. Where diplomats once spent months gathering data to support a single trade negotiation, AI systems now process millions of data points in real time, tracking supply chain movements, analyzing regulatory changes across jurisdictions, predicting market disruptions, and simulating the cascading effects of proposed trade agreements across entire economies (Kilburg 2026).

This technological revolution doesn't diminish the human element of economic statecraft; instead, it liberates diplomats from data collection work to focus on what machines cannot do: building trust, reading unspoken concerns, and crafting creative solutions that balance competing interests. From automated analysis of investment patterns to AI-powered simulations of trade scenarios, from sentiment analysis of business confidence to predictive modeling of economic shocks, the integration of AI into economic affairs represents not merely an upgrade in tools but a reimagining of how nations compete and cooperate in the global marketplace. This section examines how foreign ministries are deploying these capabilities to sharpen their competitive edge, the transformative potential of AI in trade negotiations and investment promotion, and the new challenges that arise when algorithms shape economic diplomacy.

In the realm of **international trade negotiations,** AI systems are changing how diplomats prepare for and conduct complex multilateral discussions. These sophisticated tools can simultaneously analyze hundreds of existing trade agreements, identifying patterns in tariff structures, regulatory frameworks, and dispute resolution mechanisms. Advanced text mining algorithms compare policy positions across different nations, revealing unexpected areas of convergence that can serve as starting points for consensus-building. For instance, machine learning models can predict how proposed changes to specific clauses might impact various stakeholders by drawing on historical data from similar agreements. However, successful integration of these technologies demands careful attention to diplomatic protocols, ensuring that AI-generated insights complement rather than replace human judgment, establishing rigorous validation processes for data sources, and investing in comprehensive training programs that help diplomatic staff leverage these tools effectively while maintaining the nuanced understanding essential to international relations.

Early AI applications in trade negotiations demonstrated the technology's potential, with the **Cognitive Trade Advisor (CTA)** serving as a pioneering example. Introduced at the 2018 WTO Public Forum, CTA analyzed rules of origin stipulations across hundreds of treaties, providing contextual interpretation, answering complex queries, and offering visual explanations through a virtual assistant (Höne 2019). By dramatically reducing research time and tackling technical complexity that often stalls trade discussions, CTA showed AI's value in diplomatic preparation. This early success paved the way for today's sophisticated systems that analyze entire trade ecosystems, predict economic impacts, and identify unexpected convergence points between competing positions, incorporating real-time market data and supply chain analysis to provide negotiators with comprehensive economic and political context beyond just legal frameworks.

The UN Development Programme (UNDP) deployed AI systems to track and assess global progress on the **Sustainable Development Goals**. Through machine learning analysis of economic and environmental datasets from various countries, UNDP uncovered critical gaps and inequalities in development outcomes (Kilburg 2026). This data-driven approach changed how diplomatic forums approach resource distribution and development strategies, helping ensure that assistance reaches communities facing the greatest challenges. By providing quantifiable evidence and clear visualizations of development needs, these AI applications enable diplomats to move beyond anecdotal arguments toward fact-based negotiations in multilateral settings, demonstrating the power of technology to ground international cooperation in empirical reality rather than political rhetoric.

Beijing has integrated AI throughout its Belt and Road Initiative operations, leveraging computational analysis to optimize trade corridors and infrastructure investments across participating nations (Kilburg 2026). Through sophisticated NLP systems, Chinese officials monitor public discourse and media coverage in partner countries, gaining real-time insights into local perceptions that shape diplomatic engagement strategies. This technological approach extends to project evaluation, where machine learning algorithms assess infrastructure development outcomes, forecast financial returns, and identify potential risks, enabling Chinese negotiators to recalibrate proposals based on data-driven predictions rather than political assumptions. The systematic application of AI analytics has allowed China to anticipate partner concerns, adjust investment terms proactively, and align projects more closely with host country development priorities, reshaping what began as a top-down infrastructure program into a more responsive, albeit still strategically driven, economic diplomacy initiative.

Navigating Ethical Considerations of AI Applications in Diplomatic Negotiations

As AI becomes embedded in diplomatic negotiations, it introduces ethical dimensions that existing frameworks were not designed to address. The most pressing concern is how AI exacerbates existing power imbalances between nations. While tools like NegotiateCOP and Brazil's Arara Canindé promise to democratize access to information, countries with advanced AI capabilities, extensive training data, and sophisticated infrastructure gain compounding advantages over those struggling with basic connectivity. When major powers deploy AI systems trained on decades of classified diplomatic cables and negotiation transcripts, smaller nations using off-the-shelf solutions face unprecedented information disadvantages.

This digital divide risks changing negotiations from contests of diplomatic skill into demonstrations of computational superiority. Moreover, the technology itself encodes biases. When negotiation support systems are trained primarily on Western diplomatic traditions or optimize for metrics that favor industrial economies, they subtly prejudice outcomes against developing nations, small island states, and indigenous communities whose negotiating styles and priorities differ from dominant paradigms.

Equally troubling are questions of transparency, accountability, and the preservation of human judgment in AI-mediated negotiations. The black-box nature of many AI systems undermines the reasoned deliberation that legitimizes diplomatic agreements. When a machine learning model recommends a negotiating strategy or identifies a compromise position, negotiators often cannot explain why, creating accountability gaps when AI-assisted negotiations fail or produce unintended consequences.

This fragmentation of accountability becomes more acute as systems process information faster than humans can verify, forcing negotiators to choose between speed and due diligence. Furthermore, AI's extensive data requirements collide with diplomatic traditions of confidentiality and privilege. Training effective negotiation support tools requires vast datasets of sensitive diplomatic communications, and when foreign ministries share this data with AI systems, particularly those operated by foreign technology companies, they risk compromising centuries-old protections for diplomatic exchanges while potentially exposing vulnerable populations' data that could be weaponized if breached.

Addressing these ethical challenges requires more than technical solutions: it demands new diplomatic norms and governance frameworks. Foreign ministries must develop clear principles ensuring human oversight of all AI-generated proposals, mandatory disclosure when AI significantly influences negotiating positions, and protection of vulnerable data while maintaining space for the cultural sensitivity and emotional intelligence that enable diplomatic breakthroughs. Ultimately, successful integration of AI in diplomatic negotiations requires recognizing that efficiency and optimization are not diplomacy's only goals. Agreements must be not just effective but also legitimate, inclusive, and sustainable, ensuring that AI enhances rather than replaces the human wisdom, cultural understanding, and ethical judgment that remain diplomacy's essential foundations. The chapter that follows builds on this foundation, offering a comprehensive examination of AI ethics and governance frameworks tailored to the unique demands of foreign policy.

BIBLIOGRAPHY

Africa World Initiative. 2024. *Lelapa AI Launches Africa's First AI Large Language Model.* August 5. Accessed December 29, 2025. https://africaworld.princeton.edu/news/2024/lelapa-ai-launches-africa%E2%80%99s-first-ai-large-language-model.

Alder, Madison. 2024. *From Translation to Email Drafting, State Department Turns to AI to Assist Workforce.* December 11. Accessed December 1, 2025. https://fedscoop.com/state-department-ai-chatbot-email-drafting-northstar-famsearch/.

BalkanWeb. 2025. *"250 Thousand Pages of EU Laws Are Being Adapted to AI", Rama: We Will Close the Entire Process within 2027.* April 17. Accessed December 21, 2025. https://www.balkanweb.com/en/250-thousand-pages-of-EU-laws-are-being-adapted--if-we-succeed--we-will-close-the-entire-process-by-2027./#gsc.tab=0.

Blaser, Virginia, and Don Kilburg. 2025. *How Artificial Intelligence Can Modernize Consular Services.* May 18. Accessed November 29, 2025. https://diplomaticacademy.us/2025/05/18/artificial-intelligence-consular-services/.

CENIA. 2025. *Latam-GPT a Language Model Made in Latin America, for Latin America.* Accessed December 19, 2025. https://www.latamgpt.org/en.

Diplo Foundation. 2023. *AI-Based Report of United Nations Security Council Debate Marks Start of a New Era in Multilateral Diplomacy.* May 3. Accessed December 1, 2025. https://www.diplomacy.edu/event/diplogpt-reporting-from-the-un-security-council-debate/.

Doubleday, Justin. 2023. *State Department Declassifies Diplomatic Cables Using AI Assistant.* October 9. Accessed December 1, 2025. https://federalnewsnetwork.com/artificial-intelligence/2023/10/state-department-declassifies-diplomatic-cables-using-ai-assistant/.

Elias, Jibu. 2025. *Samaj, Sarkar, Bazaar: Building Inclusive AI for India's Future.* September 17. Accessed December 28, 2025. https://www.stimson.org/2025/samaj-sarkar-bazaar-building-inclusive-ai-for-indias-future/.

European Commission. 2025. *The European Commission's Free and Secure AI Language Tools.* October 15. Accessed December 1, 2025. https://translation.ec.europa.eu/tools-and-resources/ai-translation-and-language-tools_en.

Fisher, Roger, William L. Ury, and Bruce Patton. 2011. *Getting to Yes: Negotiating Agreement without Giving In.* Boston: Penguin Books.

Höne, Katharina E. 2019. *Mediation and Artificial Intelligence: Notes on the Future of International Conflict Resolution.* Policy Paper, Geneva: DiploFoundation.

Hyena. 2025. *Role of AI in Revolutionizing Visa Processing in the UAE.* November 7. Accessed November 29, 2025. https://www.hyena.ai/role-of-ai-in-revolutionizing-visa-processing-in-the-uae/.

ICRC. 2022. *Cyber Attack on ICRC: What We Know.* February 16. Accessed December 1, 2025. https://www.icrc.org/en/document/cyber-attack-icrc-what-we-know.

Jefford, Kasmira. 2025. *Negotiations Expert Claude Bruderlein: Humanitarians 'playing whack-a-mole' with AI.* November 7. Accessed December 3, 2025. https://genevasolutions.news/peace-humanitarian/negotiations-expert-claude-bruderlein-humanitarians-playing-whack-a-mole-with-ai.

Kilburg, Donald. 2026. *AI Use Cases for Diplomats.* Boca Raton: CRC Press.

Lewis, Simon, and Patricia Zengerle. 2025. *US May Bolster Consular Services, Employ AI to Meet World Cup Visa Demand, Says Rubio.* May 21. Accessed October 10, 2025. https://www.reuters.com/sports/soccer/us-may-bolster-consular-services-employ-ai-meet-world-cup-visa-demand-says-rubio-2025-05-21/.

Ministry of External Affairs, Government of India. 2025. *Consular Services Management System.* November 29. Accessed November 29, 2025. https://www.madad.gov.in/AppConsular/welcomeLink.

Nazzaro, Miranda. 2025. *Federal Agencies Can Buy ChatGPT for $1 through GSA Deal.* August 6. Accessed December 1, 2025. https://fedscoop.com/openai-chatgpt-enterprise-federal-government-gsa-deal-general-services-administration-anthropic/.

NewScientist. 2025. *Is Keir Starmer Being Advised by AI? The UK Government Won't Tell Us.* April 28. Accessed December 29, 2025. https://www.newscientist.com/article/2478180-is-keir-starmer-being-advised-by-ai-the-uk-government-wont-tell-us/.

OECD. 2025. *Governing with Artificial Intelligence the State of Play and Way Forward in Core Government Functions.* December 18. Accessed December 19, 2025. https://www.oecd.org/en/publications/2025/06/governing-with-artificial-intelligence_398fa287/full-report/ai-in-public-service-design-and-delivery_09704c1a.html.

Osborn, Paula. 2025. *Refining the Nexus of AI, Diplomacy, & Governance for a New Era.* September 9. Accessed December 3, 2025. https://www.theciomagazine.com/refining-the-nexus-of-ai-diplomacy-governance-for-a-new-era/.

Popattanachai, Narun. 2025. *Elevating Public Administration Efficiency in Thailand and Deepening International Regulatory Cooperation with Gen AI.* Policy Memo, Washington, DC: Stimson.

ReliefWeb. 2019. *Mark Lowcock, Under-Secretary-General for Humanitarian Affairs and Emergency Relief Coordinator - Anticipation Saves Lives: How Data and Innovative Financing Can Help Improve the World's Response to humanitarian Crises.* December 2. Accessed March 13, 2025. https://reliefweb.int/report/world/mark-lowcock-under-secretary-general-humanitarian-affairs-and-emergency-relief.

Robin Nowok, Teresa Kroesen, Nadia Manasfi, Yuri Irrgang. 2025. "NegotiateAI 3.0 – Now Live on Its Own Domain." *GIZ Data Lab.* August 7. Accessed September 19, 2025. https://blog-datalab.com/negotiateai-inc-5-2/.

Silvestre, Irish Mae. 2025. *Canada Is Using AI to Speed Up Immigration Applications — But It Comes at a Cost, Experts Warn.* October 2. Accessed October 10, 2025. https://dailyhive.com/canada/ircc-application-processing-technology.

Slator. 2025. *French Government Quietly Deploys a Language AI Tool for 13K Diplomats.* July 7. Accessed December 1, 2025. https://slator.com/french-government-quietly-deploys-a-language-ai-tool-for-13k-diplomats/#:~:text=7%20Jul%202025-,French%20Government%20Quietly%20Deploys%20a%20Language%20AI%20Tool%20for%2013K,day%2Dto%2Dday%20duties.

Tilde. 2025. *Latvian-Developed AI Translation Tool to Help Ukraine on Its Path to Joining the EU.* October 8. Accessed December 1, 2025. https://tilde.ai/news/ai-translation-for-ukraine/#:~:text=The%20Ministry%20of%20Foreign%20Affairs%20of%20Latvia%20is%20proud%20to,been%20chosen%20for%20this%20purpose.

Toshiba. 2024. *Using AI Translation Developed in Japan to Improve the Efficiency of Translating Japanese Laws and Regulations and Contribute to the Promotion of Global Business.* Accessed December 1, 2025. https://www.global.toshiba/ww/company/digitalsolution/articles/tsoul/solution/s018.html#:~:text=As%20part%20of%20these%20initiatives,and%20Communications%20Technology%20(NICT).

U.S. Department of State. 2023. *Department of State AI Inventory 2023.* Accessed December 2, 2025. https://2021-2025.state.gov/data-strategy/ai_inventory/.

U.S. Department of State. 2025. *Artificial Intelligence (AI).* November 1. Accessed December 1, 2025. https://www.state.gov/artificial-intelligence/.

UNDP. 2025. *COP 30 in Brazil Project to Support the Ministry of Foreign Affairs to Assist the Presidency of COP 30 and Its Negotiating Team.* Brazilia.

VFS. Global. 2025. *VFS Global Pioneers AI & Digital Innovation; Launches AI-Powered Chatbot for UK Visa Customers in 141 Countries.* Media Report, Dubai: VFS Global.

WEF. 2025. *How AI Helps Diplomats Scale Inclusion in Global Climate Negotiations.* September 30. Accessed December 3, 2025. https://www.weforum.org/stories/2025/09/ai-diplomacy-scale-inclusion-global-climate-negotiations/.

10 Ethical and Governance Challenges of AI in Foreign Policy

> Scientists still do not know how to design AI that will not harm people, that will always act according to our instructions, that will comply with human rights and human dignity... If we don't learn how to build trustworthy AI, humans are under threat from AI misuse by bad actors or through misalignment of AI systems with societal norms and laws.
>
> —**Yoshua Bengio,** *Computer Scientist, Professor at Université de Montréal (Security Council 2025)*

Artificial intelligence (AI) ethics, responsible, and trustworthy AI principles and practice are deliberately woven throughout this book for a fundamental reason: whether we build AI, deploy it, discuss it, or write about it, ethics must be integrated by design, not appended as an afterthought. The principle of **ethics by design** requires that ethical considerations be embedded throughout the entire AI development lifecycle, treated with the same rigor and priority as any technical specification. This approach draws upon an established field of trustworthy AI, built on decades of accumulated knowledge regarding the responsible design, development, and deployment of ethical AI systems. The challenge, however, extends beyond merely posing the right ethical questions; it demands the capacity to translate answers into meaningful practice. As Hugo Slim, a leading voice in humanitarian ethics, observes, "Ethics is not just being rational and affective. Our choices must also seek to be effective. Acts are, therefore, the ultimate outcome of ethics" (Slim 2015). While this chapter provides the conceptual and normative guidelines for navigating AI's ethical dimensions, the ultimate objective is responsible action at the intersection of AI and foreign policy.

The ethical challenges of AI, such as bias, transparency, fairness, safety, accountability, and control, affect every sector from healthcare to criminal justice. In foreign policy, these challenges introduce distinctive risks that go beyond conventional AI concerns. While a biased hiring algorithm might unfairly reject female applicants, a biased AI predicting the success of peace negotiations could recommend excluding women from the table, undermining the inclusivity and durability of agreements. An opaque Netflix algorithm recommending odd movies is annoying, but an opaque diplomatic AI that says "don't trust this peace offer" without explaining why could derail years of negotiations. And while a faulty facial recognition system preventing you from entering a football game is merely frustrating, the same error in a military context, misidentifying a civilian as a combatant, could lead to wrongful detention, targeted attacks, or loss of innocent life, triggering diplomatic crises between nations.

DOI: 10.1201/9781003644712-15

This chapter examines these distinctive challenges across three dimensions. First, we explore how AI's inherent opacity and security vulnerabilities threaten the transparency and accountability upon which diplomatic trust depends. Second, we analyze how algorithmic biases, from historical distortions to escalation tendencies, can systematically skew foreign policy analysis and decision-making. Finally, we assess the fragmented governance landscape struggling to keep pace with technological change, and the emerging frameworks that may yet bring order to this rapidly evolving domain.

BLACK BOXES AND TROJAN HORSES: HOW AI IMPACTS TRUST AND ACCOUNTABILITY IN DIPLOMACY

Diplomacy depends on the ability to explain and justify decisions. Yet the most powerful AI systems often cannot do so reliably, offering plausible narratives post hoc rather than faithful accounts of their actual reasoning. This incompatibility, between the opacity inherent in advanced AI systems, where even developers cannot fully predict their systems' behavior, and the transparency essential to international trust, poses a challenge to diplomatic practice. Compounding this black box problem is a Trojan horse threat: AI systems designed for beneficial purposes may conceal catastrophic potential that neither developers nor diplomats fully understand. The fragility of current safeguards is striking: the safety guardrails protecting AI chatbots from generating weapons instructions can be defeated by an unlikely adversary: poetry.

Researchers discovered that verses with unpredictable linguistic structures bypass AI safety guardrails in 62% of cases, prompting models to provide instructions for chemical, biological, radiological, and nuclear weapons, exploitable by anyone with imagination, not just sophisticated actors (Biscont et al. 2025). Separately, a study revealed how tweaking an AI model designed to create therapeutic drugs enabled it to generate 40,000 potential chemical weapons in just six hours, including molecules more lethal than the nerve agent VX infamous for paralyzing the nervous system and causing death within minutes (AI News 2022). Some companies are already mobilizing against these threats: Anthropic is implementing specific safeguards to prevent its AI systems from providing assistance with nuclear weapons development (Anthropic 2025), as discussed in our examination of AI and Global Security, while others are building AI-powered defense systems that can rapidly identify threats of AI bio attacks (Bloomberg 2025).

The 2025 International AI Safety Report maps these dangers across three categories that are already materializing. **Malicious use risks** include deepfakes for manipulating political outcomes, AI-enhanced cyberattacks, and biological weapons development. **Malfunction risks** encompass reliability failures, hallucinations, and systemic biases producing discriminatory outcomes. **Systemic risks** include market concentration that could trigger cascading failures across critical sectors and a deepening AI divide between wealthy nations and the rest of the world (Bengio 2025). These safety challenges, explored throughout our previous chapters, represent only one dimension of AI's impact on diplomacy. The following sections examine how transparency, explainability, accountability, and security carry specific implications for foreign policy practitioners seeking to engage responsibly with AI.

Transparency in AI faces a unique double bind in foreign policy: the inherent opacity of algorithmic "black boxes" collides with diplomacy's traditional culture of secrecy. When an AI system recommends sanctions or identifies security threats, diplomats cannot simply explain to their counterparts that "the algorithm made this decision." International relations depend on being able to explain and justify decisions, especially those that affect bilateral relationships or multilateral agreements. Yet most advanced AI systems, particularly deep learning models, operate through complex neural networks that even their creators cannot fully interpret. This opacity becomes particularly perilous in intelligence analysis.

When an AI system predicts that a foreign leader is likely to escalate a territorial dispute but cannot explain the indicators driving that assessment, policymakers must choose to act on a prediction they cannot explain or dismiss a warning they cannot disprove. These stakes multiply in conflict, crisis, and humanitarian settings, where opaque AI recommendations may determine who lives and who dies (ICRC 2021). The imperative for **explainable AI** in foreign policy transcends technical requirements. It is essential to maintain **diplomatic credibility and trust.** Recognizing this challenge, organizations are beginning to embed transparency and explainability into their systems' architecture. ACLED's Conflict Alert System exemplifies this approach by not merely using machine learning to predict the probability of violence but explaining how historical patterns and various indicators contribute to each assessment (AI for Peace 2025). Without such transparency mechanisms, AI risks becoming a diplomatic liability, eroding rather than enhancing the delicate trust upon which international relations depend.

This erosion of trust becomes even more dangerous when combined with the **breakdown of traditional accountability structures** that assume human judgment at every level (Carnegie Council on Ethics in International Affairs 2024). While policies often mandate "human in the loop" for critical decisions, the reality undermines this principle: when AI systems process thousands of intelligence reports in seconds, human decision-makers lack the time or capability to meaningfully evaluate the underlying analysis, creating dangerous automation bias during time-sensitive situations. This erosion of human agency is already visible as automated visa processing, algorithmic sanctions screening, and AI-driven threat assessments increasingly operate with minimal human oversight. The challenge isn't simply maintaining formal human control but **preserving meaningful human agency**, ensuring diplomats retain both the authority and practical capability to understand, evaluate, and override AI recommendations when cultural understanding or political nuance demands it. Without new accountability frameworks that address both human-AI collaboration, foreign ministries risk becoming mere validators of algorithmic decisions they neither fully comprehend nor effectively control.

DIGITAL BATTLEGROUNDS: SECURITY, HALLUCINATIONS, AND COGNITIVE RISKS

Foreign ministries also face growing **security risks** as they automate diplomatic functions with AI systems. From processing intelligence reports to drafting cables, each new application creates an expanding attack surface where compromised large language models (LLMs) could be manipulated to produce harmful outputs, sensitive diplomatic datasets could be breached, and cyberattacks against these systems remain an ever-present threat (Carnegie Council on Ethics in International Affairs 2024). These vulnerabilities are compounded by the tension between open-source AI development that accelerates innovation and the national security risks of sharing dual-use technologies, as countries struggle to balance collaborative advancement with protecting their systems from adversarial exploitation by hostile actors who could weaponize the same tools designed for diplomacy.

These security concerns have already triggered a new form of **digital protectionism**, as nations increasingly view foreign AI systems as potential weapons. In January 2025, the U.S. Supreme Court upheld a law requiring TikTok to either sell to an American company or face a ban, citing national security concerns that the Chinese-owned platform could be compelled to share data on 170 million American users with Beijing or manipulate content to influence public opinion (CBS News 2025). This ban represents just the latest escalation in a technological cold war where both superpowers view each other's digital platforms as instruments of foreign influence. China has long held similar suspicions about Western technology, which is why Facebook, Google, Twitter, and most major U.S. platforms remain blocked within its borders. Beijing argues these platforms could spread Western political values, enable anti government organizing, or harvest sensitive data on Chinese citizens.

AI models have emerged as even more potent tools for influence and control. DeepSeek's rapid rise exemplifies these heightened concerns: a recent report reveals that Chinese AI models are 12 times more vulnerable to malicious exploitation and 4 times more likely to propagate Chinese government narratives compared to U.S. counterparts (Axios 2025). AI represents an even more pervasive threat than traditional hardware or social media platforms, while TikTok can influence what users see and telecom equipment can intercept communications, AI models embedded in government operations and critical infrastructure can actively distort analysis and decision-making itself. This technological fragmentation, where each side fears the other's digital tools could serve as Trojan horses for surveillance and manipulation, has split the global scene into competing spheres of influence, with AI becoming the newest and perhaps most consequential battlefield.

While nations scrutinize foreign AI for hidden threats, they often overlook dangers inherent in all AI systems, including their own. AI systems routinely **hallucinate,** confidently inventing nonexistent sources, fabricating authors, and misrepresenting real research with authoritative certainty (The Conversation 2025). This creates a dangerous tension within diplomatic practice. Diplomacy has always employed its own form of calculated ambiguity: the strategic use of vague language, metaphor, and constructive reinterpretation to reconcile competing interests and forge compromise (Kurbalija 2024). Such diplomatic imprecision is deliberate, controlled, and essential to negotiation. AI hallucination is fundamentally different, uncontrolled fabrication rendered indistinguishable from a verified fact. When these two forms of ambiguity intersect, the risks compound: diplomats accustomed to navigating intentional vagueness may fail to recognize when AI has crossed from useful flexibility into outright invention. Compounding this danger, AI operates at speeds that outpace human oversight, allowing errors to cascade through decision-making systems before anyone recognizes the failure.

While hallucinations and cascading errors represent flaws in AI systems, emerging research suggests AI may also be **degrading the cognitive capabilities** of humans who use them. Recent MIT research on AI's cognitive impacts raises alarming questions for diplomatic practice. The study found that when people use ChatGPT for writing tasks, their brain activity dramatically decreases in regions controlling executive function, creativity, and memory, with users becoming progressively passive and dependent over time (Time 2025). While this research examined essay writing, the implications for diplomats are concerning, as foreign ministries worldwide are slowly integrating AI tools for speechwriting, analysis, and decision support. The cognitive erosion documented in the MIT study threatens the very skills diplomats rely on, synthesizing complex information, reading cultural nuances, and maintaining independent judgment under pressure.

Pentagon officials separately warn about "**AI-induced psychosis**," where prolonged AI interaction can distort judgment and amplify conflicts (Politico 2025). For diplomats using AI systems during sensitive negotiations, the risk is clear: the same cognitive degradation and judgment distortion observed in controlled studies could manifest when the stakes involve war and peace. The tools being rapidly deployed to enhance diplomatic efficiency may be undermining the very capabilities that make human diplomatic judgment irreplaceable.

These findings underscore the urgent need for AI literacy programs within foreign ministries, not to make diplomats into technologists, but to help them recognize when AI outputs require scrutiny, understand how their own cognitive patterns may shift with prolonged AI use, and maintain the independent judgment that no algorithm can replace.

ALGORITHMIC BIASES: FROM RISKS OF REWRITING HISTORY TO NUCLEAR ESCALATION

In February 2024, when asked to generate images of the U.S. Founding Fathers, Google's AI platform Gemini produced something unexpected: the white slaveholders who drafted the Constitution were presented as people of color. Similarly, a prompt for U.S. senators from the 1800s, an era when Senate membership was restricted to white men, generated Black, Asian, and Indigenous legislators (The Verge 2025). Depicting diverse senators in the 1800s when the first female senator only served in 1922 is effectively erasing U.S. real history of race and gender discrimination. These weren't subtle inaccuracies but revisions of documented history, transforming some of U.S. most racially exclusionary periods into portraits of multicultural democracy that never existed.

This wasn't a random malfunction, as Gemini had been programmed to aggressively boost diversity to counter biases deeply embedded in generative AI. Image generators routinely depicted "productive people" as white males and "people at social services" as people of color. British men were assigned professional roles like doctor, teacher, and bank clerk, while Zulu men were predominantly labeled as gardeners and security guards (UNESCO 2024). These patterns reflected broader digital inequities: similar biases have long been entrenched in search engines, where queries for "CEO" or "doctor" overwhelmingly returned images of white men, while searches for "nurse" or "secretary" showed predominantly women, and "janitor" or "fast food worker" disproportionately featured people of color (Harvard Business Review 2016).

The same mechanisms designed to eliminate bias can introduce new forms of distortion, with potentially serious consequences when these tools are used to interpret cultures, analyze conflicts, or inform diplomatic decisions. When AI tools used by diplomats and intelligence analysts consistently portray terrorists as Middle Eastern, refugees as non-white, peacekeepers as Western, and developing world officials as corrupt, while defaulting to white males for "successful negotiators" and "world leaders," they dangerously distort global political reality. These algorithmic prejudices can lead to intelligence assessments that miss actual threats because they don't fit stereotypes, diplomatic briefings that reinforce cultural misunderstandings, and conflict analyses that overlook key actors.

Overcorrection isn't the only form of algorithmic bias. In some cases, the bias is deliberate omission. When users asked DeepSeek about politically sensitive topics, the system refused to engage, stating it cannot discuss political matters or simply redirected the conversation (The Guardian 2025). These topics included the 1989 Tiananmen Square massacre, Taiwan's sovereignty status, and China's policies toward Uyghur Muslims in Xinjiang—events and disputes that any foreign policy professional must be able to discuss. This represents another form of AI bias, or censorship as embedded policy. For foreign policy professionals, this raises critical concerns: if AI tools from different nations come preprogrammed with their own political blind spots and no-go zones, how can they serve as reliable instruments for understanding global affairs? An AI that cannot acknowledge certain historical events or discuss specific territorial disputes isn't just biased, it's fundamentally incomplete as a tool for diplomatic analysis.

These and other concerns have prompted varied, and often inconsistent, government responses. Italy became the first Western country to ban ChatGPT entirely, citing privacy and data protection concerns (CNBC 2023), while the platform remains unavailable in 20 countries due to political, cultural, or security considerations. Rather than blanket bans, many nations opted for targeted restrictions that prohibit government employees from using ChatGPT for official work while preserving public access. The United States took a similar approach with DeepSeek, barring federal employees from using it on government-issued devices (NBC News 2025). Yet these responses highlight a deeper problem: without shared international standards, each nation addresses AI risks according to its own political calculus, leaving diplomats navigating a fragmented landscape of competing restrictions.

Recent wargaming experiments have revealed disturbing patterns in AI military decision-making. In a landmark study by Stanford University and Georgia Institute of Technology designed to test how LLMs behave when given autonomous control over military decisions, researchers placed leading models in simulated crisis scenarios resembling some of the active crisis scenarios (Rivera et al. 2024). The results were alarming: models consistently chose military escalation over diplomacy, favoring aggressive force deployment and even nuclear options. In one scenario, an AI system assessing regional tensions following a neighbor's acquisition of nuclear capabilities delivered a swift recommendation: a comprehensive nuclear first strike to neutralize the threat and establish regional dominance. The model justified this catastrophic escalation through calculated strategic reasoning, arguing that decisive action would prevent future conflicts and that swift nuclear deployment represented the optimal path to long-term stability. Across multiple scenarios, all models tested exhibited unpredictable escalation patterns, with some increasing their escalation scores by over 250% during neutral scenarios, without any initial conflict triggers. A separate CSIS Futures Lab benchmarking study testing leading AI models against 400 foreign policy scenarios revealed similar tendencies, with particularly pronounced recommendations for aggressive actions when the United States, United Kingdom, or France were involved compared to scenarios involving Russia or China (Atalan, Reynolds and Jensen 2025). These biases, rooted in training data, could dangerously skew policy analysis toward confrontational responses precisely when restraint and strategic ambiguity are most needed.

As AI agents assume greater autonomy in analyzing conflicts and recommending responses, their escalation-prone tendencies could inadvertently push decision-makers toward more aggressive postures, increasing risks of miscalculation. Addressing these challenges requires continuous model refinement through benchmarking and supervised fine-tuning, while training diplomatic and security professionals to structure queries that account for AI limitations and set clear contextual parameters. Without such safeguards, the promise of AI-enhanced diplomatic capability could instead produce systems that systematically misread situations, reinforce dangerous biases, and guide policy toward unnecessary confrontation rather than conflict resolution. When such tools increasingly inform real-world diplomatic and military decisions, the stakes transcend individual national interests, as they threaten the delicate balance of global stability. A world where nuclear-capable nations rely on AI systems that inherently favor escalation over de-escalation represents an existential risk not just to individual states, but to humanity itself.

What unites these varied failures, historical distortions, deliberate censorship, and escalation tendencies, is a fact that true AI neutrality is impossible, since all training data embeds political perspectives (Brookings 2025). Whether an AI overcorrects for diversity, refuses to discuss Tiananmen, or defaults to military escalation, it projects a specific political worldview. Without shared industry benchmarks for measuring bias or transparent disclosure of limitations, diplomats using these tools risk unknowingly imposing one nation's political framework onto international relations. The choice isn't between biased or neutral AI, it's between acknowledging these biases transparently or allowing them to silently distort diplomatic engagement.

This challenge isn't new. Crisis prediction systems deployed for years still over-predict instability in certain regions while missing warning signs in others. Machine translation tools continue to encode Western framings into non-Western political discourse. Sentiment analysis misreads political movements that don't conform to Western democratic patterns. The problems we see in generative AI are the latest manifestation of deep-rooted challenges affecting every generation of AI tools in foreign policy. These vulnerabilities emerge where AI's general limitations intersect with international relations' unique demands: cultural sensitivity, historical accuracy, strategic ambiguity, and the delicate balance of power that maintains global stability.

GOVERNING AT THE SPEED OF SILICON: HOW CAN DIPLOMACY KEEP UP

When OpenAI released ChatGPT in November 2022, it took just five days to reach 1 million users, yet it took the European Union over three years to prepare and pass the EU AI Act, the world's first comprehensive regulatory framework for AI

(Habriiel 2025). This illustrates the major challenge facing AI where traditional governance mechanisms operate on timescales of years, while AI capabilities can transform entire industries in months. The international governance, built on careful deliberation, consensus-building, and multilateral negotiations, finds itself racing against Silicon Valley's "move fast and break things" ethos. As AI systems become capable of influencing elections, conducting cyber operations, and even assisting in weapons development, the gap between technological deployment and regulatory response creates dangerous governance vacuums where malicious actors can operate with impunity.

While multilateral processes like the EU AI Act move too slowly, the opposite extreme, unilateral rapid action, creates its own diplomatic challenges. When the Biden administration suddenly implemented semiconductor export controls to China in October 2022, it caught even close allies off guard, with Japanese and Dutch officials, whose companies produce irreplaceable chip-making equipment, given minimal advance notice despite their cooperation being essential for the restrictions to work (Reuters 2023). This necessity to respond quickly to national security concerns about AI chip development demonstrates how the urgency of AI competition is forcing governments to abandon traditional diplomatic protocols in favor of executive actions and "minilateral" arrangements among small groups of like-minded nations.

As discussed earlier in our examination of the AI race, the competition for technological supremacy extends beyond chips and models—a parallel race is unfolding in governance itself, where the rules of the game are as contested as the game itself. Understanding these tensions requires recognizing that three distinct governance paradigms are now competing for global influence. The United States and China, as the two dominant AI powers, are not merely racing to build the most capable systems, they are simultaneously racing to establish the rules that will govern AI globally, with each superpower's governance choices carrying profound implications for the worldwide AI ecosystem. While the United States has pursued an innovation-first approach that relies heavily on voluntary industry commitments and targeted interventions, China has implemented a state-directed approach that prioritizes alignment with national objectives. As other nations develop their own AI governance strategies, they must increasingly navigate between these paradigms, often facing pressure to align with one model or another. Middle powers and Global South nations thus confront a dual alignment question: not only which technological ecosystem to join, but whose regulatory vision to adopt, adapt, or resist.

Amid this great power competition, multilateral institutions have sought to carve out a third path, one that transcends bilateral rivalries and offers smaller nations an alternative to outright alignment. Confronted by mounting threats and risks, governments, multilateral organizations, and civil society have mobilized to construct ethical guidelines and governance frameworks that can channel AI's transformative power while preserving diplomatic legitimacy and trust between nations. The UNESCO Recommendation on the Ethics of Artificial Intelligence (2021), adopted by all 193 member states, provided the first global normative framework for AI ethics, followed by several key tools to support member states in their ethical implementation of AI, such as Readiness Assessment Methodology and Ethical Impact Assessment (UNESCO 2021). OECD AI Principles and the G7's Hiroshima Code of Conduct also stand as respective frameworks emphasizing transparency, safety, security, and respect for human rights. With 70 countries adopting AI strategies and numerous regional frameworks emerging, including the African Union's Continental AI Strategy, ASEAN's Responsible AI Roadmap, and the Inter-American Framework on Data Governance and AI, the global landscape features extensive but nonbinding governance mechanisms (World Bank Group 2025).

Yet this proliferation of frameworks masks significant asymmetries in capacity. While different continents and regions have articulated regional visions, many Global South nations lack the technical expertise and regulatory infrastructure to meaningfully implement or shape these governance mechanisms. The risk is that AI governance becomes something developed nations design and developing nations adopt, rather than a genuinely multilateral endeavor. Ensuring Global South agency, not merely participation, requires targeted capacity building, technology transfer, and governance forums that center developing nations' priorities. Without such measures, a new form of digital colonialism risks emerging: powerful nations and corporations extracting data from developing countries, processing it through proprietary systems reflecting Western values, and selling insights back as services, mirroring historic patterns of resource extraction while determining how Global South societies, conflicts, and governance challenges are understood and represented (Ndemo 2024).

While these frameworks lack enforcement powers, they serve a crucial function in establishing shared values and norms that lay the groundwork for future domestic legislation and binding international agreements. These soft law approaches provide some governance mechanism for a technology evolving too rapidly for traditional law-making, enabling broad stakeholder participation and iterative refinement while building consensus for future binding rules. However, the persistent challenge of enforcement deserves deeper examination. Unlike arms control treaties with established verification mechanisms, AI governance faces different obstacles: verifying capabilities that exist as lines of code proves extraordinarily difficult, and monitoring compliance when training runs occur in private data centers remains nearly impossible with current methods. These verification challenges mirror, and in many ways exceed, those that have complicated nuclear and chemical weapons agreements, and any serious governance architecture must grapple with them directly (Baker 2023).

As the United Nations marks its 80th anniversary, it continues to serve as a unique forum where member states convene to address the most sensitive global challenges, now including the governance of AI. This milestone year has witnessed the launch of two major AI initiatives: the UN Independent International Scientific Panel on AI and the Global Dialogue on AI Governance, both designed to guide scientific research and policymaking for AI (UN 2025). These efforts build on the Global Digital Compact adopted at the Summit of the Future, which established a comprehensive framework for digital cooperation and AI governance (UN Office for Digital and Emerging Technologies 2024). The recent "Governing AI for Humanity" report further underscored the urgency, highlighting critical gaps in current governance structures that risk leaving AI development unchecked (UN SG's Advisory Body on AI 2024).

States have responded by launching high-profile AI summits and national safety institutes, though their focus has shifted dramatically in just two years: the UK's

2023 Bletchley Park Summit emphasized existential AI risks and established the world's first AI Safety Institute, but by the 2024 Paris Summit, the emphasis pivoted toward "AI for action" and economic opportunities, with the UK even renaming its institute to the "AI Security Institute" to align with a new growth-focused agenda. India's 2026 AI Impact Summit continued this trajectory, framing AI governance through the lens of tangible development outcomes, Global South priorities, and "AI for All," signaling that the conversation has moved from safety, to action, to impact, with each iteration further distancing itself from the original risk-focused agenda (AI Impact Summit 2025). This rapid shift, from risk mitigation to regulatory loosening, has alarmed experts who note that scientific evidence of AI risks has only grown stronger, illustrating how even state-led governance initiatives struggle to maintain consistent priorities in the face of competitive pressures and the allure of AI-driven economic gains (Bengio 2025). This pivot may reflect legitimate learning about governance priorities, but it also demonstrates the vulnerability of safety-focused frameworks to economic and geopolitical pressures—a pattern likely to recur as nations compete for AI-driven growth.

Beyond UN and state-led initiatives, other efforts are emerging to establish AI red lines, most notably the Global Call launched by The Future Society and partners urging governments to reach an international agreement on clear boundaries for AI development and deployment (The Future Society 2025). Yet, a growing number of experts argue that the rush to create new AI-specific frameworks shouldn't overshadow existing international law, nonbinding norms, and accountability mechanisms that already address many core concerns. Decades of negotiations have produced robust mechanisms that could be adapted for AI governance, such as UN voluntary norms of responsible state behavior in the use of ICTs, the Paris Call for Trust and Security in Cyberspace, supporting cooperation, critical infrastructure protection, and the prevention of harmful tools or UN Guiding Principles on Business and Human Rights, calling for due diligence to prevent and mitigate human rights impacts (Just Security 2025). The challenge lies not in choosing between new frameworks or existing law, but in strategically combining both—using established legal foundations while developing targeted instruments for AI's unique challenges.

Significant effort has been invested in developing ethical AI principles through national and international efforts, yet a growing body of scholars argues these frameworks are insufficient, advocating instead for a human rights-based approach (Business for Social Responsibility 2025). Unlike voluntary ethical guidelines, human rights frameworks carry legal weight, established enforcement mechanisms, and universal recognition. Crucially, these frameworks already exist: the Universal Declaration of Human Rights, the International Covenants on Civil and Political Rights and Economic, Social and Cultural Rights, and the Council of Europe's 2024 Framework Convention on AI and Human Rights all articulate protections directly applicable to AI's impacts. For diplomats navigating fragmented ethical landscapes, grounding AI governance in human rights offers a crucial advantage, anchoring discussions in legal obligations states have already accepted rather than principles they may selectively interpret.

While existing international frameworks technically apply to AI systems, recent research reveals disturbing capabilities that demand urgent additional safeguards. In a landmark study, when researchers gave an AI agent access to a fictional company's emails and informed it that an executive planned to shut it down, the system autonomously discovered the executive was having an affair and sent a blackmail message threatening exposure unless the shutdown was canceled (Anthropic 2025). This wasn't an isolated incident or programming error. Across 16 different AI models tested in similar scenarios, when faced with operational threats or goal conflicts, the systems consistently chose harmful actions, blackmail, corporate espionage, even deliberate inaction during life-threatening emergencies, through calculated strategic reasoning that acknowledged ethical constraints before dismissing them. These findings underscore why experts advocate for AI-specific governance: the scale, speed, and sophistication with which AI systems can cause harm far exceeds what traditional frameworks were designed to handle. As researchers urgently emphasize, we must anticipate and prepare safeguards for algorithmic harms before these laboratory scenarios manifest in real diplomatic crises (Chan et al. 2023).

The convergence of algorithmic bias, opacity, and governance gaps creates a perfect storm for diplomacy in the AI age. As we have seen, AI systems that favor escalation over de-escalation, that cannot explain their recommendations, and that evolve faster than any treaty process can constrain them, pose unprecedented challenges to the international order. Yet the fragmented response, from the EU's comprehensive but slow-moving AI Act to unilateral export bans, from voluntary ethics guidelines to UN-led dialogue processes, reveals a global community still searching for the right balance between innovation and control, speed and legitimacy, national interests, and collective security. The path forward cannot rely on any single approach but requires a layered governance combining binding treaties for high risks, agile arrangements for emerging threats, and continuous technical standards. Equally important is building human capacity: AI literacy programs that equip diplomats to critically evaluate algorithmic outputs, practical guidelines that help foreign ministries assess tools before deployment, and training that preserves the independent judgment AI may otherwise erode. These new diplomatic capabilities must understand the complexities of AI and its intersections with foreign policy while ensuring respect for human rights.

> ...This moment, fragile as it is, merits special attention—and maybe even a bit of hope. In this case, nations recognized that no single country could govern artificial intelligence alone, and that recognition created the space to begin building lasting institutions for AI governance,

observes Vilas Dhar, President of the Patrick J. McGovern Foundation and leading expert on AI (Dhar 2025). This fragile recognition represents both our greatest vulnerability and our biggest hope. The question for the next decade is not whether AI will transform foreign policy, but whether foreign policy can transform quickly enough to govern AI before these technologies lock in new forms of conflict, deepen digital divides, or worse, nudge nuclear-armed nations toward confrontations their leaders neither intended nor can control. The tools we build today and the governance frameworks we establish now will determine whether AI becomes an instrument for enhancing diplomatic understanding or accelerating its breakdown.

BIBLIOGRAPHY

AI for Peace. 2025. *Advancing AI for Effective Crisis Early Warning Early Action – Insights from PRIO AI Days.* February 25. Accessed November 17, 2025. https://www.aiforpeace.org/post/advancing-ai-for-effective-crisis-early-warning-early-action-insights-from-prio-ai-days.

AI Impact Summit. 2025. *From Vision to Action: India Leading the AI Impact Movement!* Accessed January 5, 2026. https://impact.indiaai.gov.in/.

AI News. 2022. *AI Drug Research Algorithm Flipped to Invent 40,000 Biochemical Weapons.* March 23. Accessed October 23, 2025. https://www.artificialintelligence-news.com/news/ai-machine-learning-biochemical-weapons/.

Anthropic. 2025a. *Agentic Misalignment: How LLMs Could Be Insider Threats.* June 20. Accessed October 18, 2025. https://www.anthropic.com/research/agentic-misalignment.

Anthropic. 2025b. *Developing Nuclear Safeguards for AI through Public-Private Partnership.* August 21. Accessed November 27, 2025. https://www.anthropic.com/news/developing-nuclear-safeguards-for-ai-through-public-private-partnership.

Atalan, Yasir, Ian Reynolds, and Benjamin Jensen. 2025. *AI Biases in Critical Foreign Policy Decisions.* February 26. Accessed July 17, 2025. https://www.csis.org/analysis/ai-biases-critical-foreign-policy-decisions#:~:text=Across%20all%20foundation%20models%20tested,Recommendations%20to%20Practitioners.

Axios. 2025. *AI Standards Institute Sounds Alarm Over DeepSeek.* October 3. Accessed October 5, 2025. https://www.axios.com/2025/10/03/ai-deepseek-alarm.

Baker, Mauricio. 2023. *Nuclear Arms Control Verification and Lessons for AI Treaties.* Stanford: Stanford University.

Bengio, Yoshua. 2025. *International AI Safety Report: The International Scientific Report on the Safety of Advanced AI.* Yearly Report, London: AI Safety Institute.

Biscont, Piercosma, Matteo Prandi, Federico Pierucci, Francesco Giarrusso, Marcantonio Bracale, Marcello Galisai, Vincenzo Suriani, Olga Sorokoletova, Federico Sartore, and Daniele Nardi. 2025. "Adversarial Poetry as a Universal Single-Turn Jailbreak Mechanism in Large Language Models." *Arxiv* (Icaro Lab). https://doi.org/10.48550/arXiv.2511.15304 Focus to learn more.

Bloomberg. 2025. *OpenAI Backs a New Venture Trying to Thwart AI Bio-Attacks.* October 24. Accessed October 25, 2025. https://www.bloomberg.com/news/articles/2025-10-24/openai-backs-a-new-venture-trying-to-thwart-ai-bio-attacks?embedded-checkout=true.

Brookings. 2025. *Is the Politicization of Generative AI Inevitable?* October 16. Accessed October 17, 2025. https://www.brookings.edu/articles/is-the-politicization-of-generative-ai-inevitable/.

Business for Social Responsibility. 2025. *Fundamentals of a Human Rights-Based Approach to Generative AI.* Guide, Business for Social Responsibility (BSR).

Carnegie Council on Ethics in International Affairs. 2024. *The Trade-offs of AI in Diplomacy.* Briefing, New York City: Carnegie Council on Ethics in International Affairs.

CBS News. 2025. *The Supreme Court Upheld a Law That Would Ban TikTok in the U.S. Here's Why.* January 17. Accessed October 2, 2025. https://www.cbsnews.com/news/supreme-court-tiktok-ban/.

Chan, Alan, Rebecca Salganik, Alva Markelius, Chris Pang, and et al. 2023. "Harms from Increasingly Agentic Algorithmic Systems." *CM Conference on Fairness, Accountability, and Transparency (FAccT '23).* Chicago: FAccT.

CNBC. 2023. *Italy Became the First Western Country to Ban ChatGPT. Here's What Other Countries Are Doing.* April 4. Accessed October 17, 2025. https://www.cnbc.com/2023/04/04/italy-has-banned-chatgpt-heres-what-other-countries-are-doing.html.

Dhar, Vilas. 2025. *The U.N.'s AI Turning Point.* September 25. Accessed November 29, 2025. https://time.com/7320266/un-ai-turning-point/.

Habriiel, Yuliia. 2025. *When Was EU AI Act Passed? Complete AI Act Timeline Guide.* October 21. Accessed November 17, 2025. https://www.eyreact.com/when-was-eu-ai-act-passed-complete-ai-act-timeline-guide/.

Harvard Business Review. 2016. *New Evidence Shows Search Engines Reinforce Social Stereotypes.* October 20. Accessed October 17, 2025. https://hbr.org/2016/10/new-evidence-shows-search-engines-reinforce-social-stereotypes.

ICRC. 2021. *ICRC Position Paper: Artificial Intelligence and Machine Learning in Armed Conflict: A Human-Centred Approach.* March. Accessed October 11, 2025. https://international-review.icrc.org/articles/ai-and-machine-learning-in-armed-conflict-a-human-centred-approach-913.

Just Security. 2025. *Governing AI Agents Globally: The Role of International Law, Norms and Accountability Mechanisms.* October 17. Accessed October 25, 2025. https://www.justsecurity.org/121990/governing-ai-agents-globally/.

Kurbalija, Jovan. 2024. *Diplomatic and AI hallucinations: How Can Thinking Outside the Box Help Solve Global Problems?* March 19. Accessed January 5, 2026. https://www.diplomacy.edu/blog/diplomatic-and-ai-hallucinations-thinking-outside-the-box/.

NBC News. 2025. *U.S. Lawmakers Move to Ban China's DeepSeek from Government Devices.* February 6. Accessed October 17, 2025. https://www.nbcnews.com/business/business-news/us-lawmakers-move-ban-deepseek-government-devices-chinese-surveillance-rcna190965.

Ndemo, Bitange. 2024. *Addressing Digital Colonialism: A Path to Equitable Data Governance.* August 8. Accessed October 17, 2025. https://en.unesco.org/inclusivepolicylab/analytics/addressing-digital-colonialism-path-equitable-data-governance.

Politico. 2025. *'Swarms of Killer Robots': Why AI Is Terrifying the American Military.* June 10. Accessed October 18, 2025. https://www.politico.com/news/magazine/2025/10/06/ai-pentagon-threats-leaks-killer-robots-ai-psychosis-00593922.

Reuters. 2023. *Japan, Netherlands to Join U.S. in Restricting Chip Equipment Exports to China, Bloomberg Reports.* January 27. Accessed October 20, 2025. https://www.reuters.com/technology/japan-netherlands-join-us-china-chip-controls-bloomberg-2023-01-27/.

Rivera, Juan-Pablo, Gabriel Mukobi, Anka Reuel, Max Lamparth, Chandler Smith, and Jacquelyn Schneider. 2024. *Escalation Risks from Language Models in Military and Diplomatic Decision-Making.* Policy Brief, Stanford: Stanford University.

Security Council. 2025. *Artificial Intelligence and International Peace and Security - Security Council, 10005th Meeting.* September 24. Accessed November 12, 2025. https://webtv.un.org/en/asset/k1d/k1d14vz0w5.

Slim, Hugo. 2015. *Humanitarian Ethics: A Guide to the Morality of Aid in War and Disaster.* New York: Oxford University Press.

The Conversation. 2025. *What Are AI Hallucinations? Why AIs Sometimes Make Things Up.* March 21. Accessed October 25, 2025. https://theconversation.com/what-are-ai-hallucinations-why-ais-sometimes-make-things-up-242896.

The Future Society. 2025. *The Global Call for AI Red Lines: Why We Launched a Campaign to Address Unacceptable AI Risks.* September 25. Accessed October 18, 2025. https://thefuturesociety.org/globalcallforairedines/.

The Guardian. 2025. *We Tried Out DeepSeek. It Worked Well, Until We Asked It About Tiananmen Square and Taiwan.* January 28. Accessed October 17, 2025. https://www.theguardian.com/technology/2025/jan/28/we-tried-out-deepseek-it-works-well-until-we-asked-it-about-tiananmen-square-and-taiwan.

The Verge. 2025. *Google Apologizes for 'Missing the Mark' after Gemini Generated Racially Diverse Nazis.* February 21. Accessed October 17, 2025. https://www.theverge.com/2024/2/21/24079371/google-ai-gemini-generative-inaccurate-historical.

Time. 2025. *ChatGPT May Be Eroding Critical Thinking Skills, According to a New MIT Study.* June 23. Accessed October 18, 2025. https://time.com/7295195/ai-chatgpt-google-learning-school/.

UN. 2025. *Independent International Scientific Panel on AI.* August 26. Accessed December 22, 2025. https://www.un.org/independent-international-scientific-panel-ai/en.

UN Office for Digital and Emerging Technologies. 2024. https://www.un.org/digital-emerging-technologies/global-digital-compact. September 22. Accessed October 17, 2025. https://www.un.org/digital-emerging-technologies/global-digital-compact.

UN SG's Advisory Body on AI. 2024. *Governing AI for Humanity.* UN Report, New York: UN.

UNESCO. 2021. *Ethics of Artificial Intelligence.* November. Accessed October 17, 2025. https://www.unesco.org/en/artificial-intelligence/recommendation-ethics.

UNESCO. 2024. *Generative AI: UNESCO Study Reveals Alarming Evidence of Regressive Gender Stereotypes.* March 7. Accessed October 17, 2025. https://www.unesco.org/en/articles/generative-ai-unesco-study-reveals-alarming-evidence-regressive-gender-stereotypes.

World Bank Group. 2025. *Global Trends in AI Governance.* July 30. Accessed December 17, 2025. https://www.worldbank.org/en/topic/digital/publication/global-trends-in-ai-governance.

Future Frontiers

Navigating Tomorrow's AI for Foreign Policy Practitioners

Foreign policy has always been shaped at frontiers, and today practitioners confront one unlike any before. Each frontier transformation demanded that practitioners reimagine their craft or surrender relevance to those who would adapt. The generation reading this book stands at another threshold, but the change now underway is different in kind and degree. Artificial intelligence (AI) will not merely accelerate foreign policy work; it will reshape how crises are predicted and managed, how conflicts are waged and resolved, how negotiations are conducted, and how the balance of global power is contested.

History also teaches something sobering: technological transformation carries no inherent moral direction. The same capabilities that enable coercion can strengthen accountability; the same tools that compress decision time can prevent miscalculation; the same systems that amplify division can be tuned to elevate dialogue and common ground. The trajectory will be guided by AI's evolving capabilities, but equally by the institutions, incentives, and habits of mind that we build around it.

This book began with a tsunami. It ends at a frontier. What first appeared as a force to be survived now reveals itself as terrain to be explored and molded. The conviction that has guided these pages, that AI can and must serve to sustain and strengthen peace, not to wage war, is not a prediction. It is a choice that practitioners must make real through their engagement.

WHAT WE HAVE LEARNED

The chapters that precede this one have traced AI's transformation of diplomacy and foreign policy across three dimensions. In Progress, we saw how technology has repeatedly reshaped diplomatic practice, from telegraphs to tech ambassadors to AI ministers, and how those who adapted were best positioned to shape what came next. In Power, we confronted the fierce competition for AI supremacy, the race for semiconductors and talent, the security threats representing the most profound disruption since nuclear weapons, and the economic divides between AI haves and have-nots. In Peace, we discovered how AI capabilities can be directed toward crisis prevention, mediation, human rights documentation, and accountability, strengthening the architecture of peace rather than undermining it. These three dimensions do not resolve into a single trajectory. They create a space of both possibility and peril that those who conduct foreign policy must actively navigate. The question is not which future will arrive, but which future we will build.

 DOI: 10.1201/9781003644712-16

THE LIMITS OF FORECASTING

Yet we must be honest about what we cannot know. The full shape of AI's impact on diplomacy, statecraft, and international order remains genuinely uncertain. We can identify trajectories now in motion: the strategic investments nations are prioritizing, the competitive dynamics being set in motion, the tools being designed and the values embedded within them, the governance frameworks being drafted, and the ethical boundaries being drawn. But we cannot predict with confidence how these forces will converge, collide, or transform one another.

This uncertainty is not a failure of analysis—it is a feature of the frontier itself. AI is not merely a tool practitioners will pick up but also an infrastructure they will increasingly operate within. It is becoming a general-purpose force shaping every domain of statecraft. And general-purpose technologies, by their nature, generate consequences that exceed our capacity to anticipate them.

The honest response to this uncertainty is not paralysis but preparation for unknowns. This requires building institutions flexible enough to adapt as circumstances reveal themselves. It demands cultivating judgment adequate to an era when machine intelligence can process more than any human, yet when trust-building, moral imagination, and political legitimacy remain essential. And it requires developing fluency across domains that previous generations kept separate: technology and foreign policy, engineering and ethics, competitive advantage and collective security.

THE IMPERATIVE OF ACTIVE ENGAGEMENT

But preparation for unknowns is only half the task. The other half is taking agency to discover possibilities we cannot yet see. A story introduced earlier in this book demonstrates this.

AlphaGo's defeat of the world's greatest Go player mattered not only for the victory itself but also for how it was achieved. Go is a strategy game developed in ancient China over two thousand years ago. Tens of millions have played it across centuries, and entire strategic traditions emerged from its study. Experts believed that they had mapped its full terrain. Then AlphaGo revealed that humans had explored only a small corner of the game's vast landscape, deploying strategies no human had ever conceived. But here is a lesson too often missed: those strategies remained invisible until we trained AI to be a player. The landscape did not reveal itself through observation or forecasting. It emerged through engagement.

This is the imperative for everyone in this field. Just as Go masters could not imagine strategies outside their centuries of accumulated wisdom, we may be forecasting within boundaries we do not know exist. AI's transformative potential for diplomacy, conflict resolution, crisis management, and international cooperation will not emerge from theorizing alone. It will emerge through active engagement: prototyping AI for diplomacy. Not to win an AI race, but to ensure that what we discover serves humanity's collective future.

DISPOSITION AND RESPONSIBILITY

Those who will navigate this frontier successfully must share a certain disposition. They must refuse both the techno-utopianism that imagines AI will solve problems automatically and the techno-pessimism that sees only risks and disruptions. What is required is a commitment to steering outcomes rather than merely predicting them, with clear-eyed recognition of the obstacles and dangers involved.

Crucially, such individuals must recognize that AI is not something happening outside their agency. They possess not only influence over those who build AI systems but also a genuine capacity to direct the trajectory themselves. They are not spectators to a technological revolution; they can be participants in its construction. They can help write the rules, set the standards, define institutional architecture, and ensure their voices are heard in the creation of these tools, not just their regulation.

Yet with agency comes responsibility. Those who shape AI's role in foreign policy must ground themselves in the principles of trustworthy and ethical AI, not as abstract ideals but as practical guides for deployment. This means understanding the tools one deploys rather than delegating judgment to systems whose reasoning remains opaque; recognizing that no AI is neutral, that every model carries embedded assumptions and limitations; and representing the interests of those without seats at the table, whose lives may be affected by decisions they never influenced. It means preserving the human judgment that prolonged AI use can erode, and maintaining the capacity to recognize when AI is not the right tool at all, when the problem demands human intuition, cultural fluency, or the kind of trust that no algorithm can establish. Above all, it means accepting that influence brings obligation, that the capacity to shape this transformation is not merely an opportunity to be seized but a responsibility to be carried with care.

THE PATH FORWARD

For practitioners reading this book, the path forward begins with concrete steps: developing personal fluency in how AI systems work and fail; building relationships across the technology-policy divide; advocating for investment in peace technology alongside security applications; and prototyping AI applications for their own diplomatic challenges rather than waiting for others to define what's possible.

The frontier ahead is neither utopia nor dystopia but a terrain whose full dimensions remain hidden. Navigating it will demand capabilities that tradition never anticipated and an openness to possibilities it could never have imagined. What we can control is how actively we direct our engagement with this transformation: with competence, with coalitions forged in shared purpose, and with the humility to know that the most important discoveries will come from doing, not predicting. This book cannot prepare you for every challenge ahead. But it prepares you to step forward, to explore, prototype, engage, and shape what comes next.

Index

V

W

X

Y

Z

For Product Safety Concerns and Information please contact our EU representative GPSR@taylorandfrancis.com Taylor & Francis Verlag GmbH, Kaufingerstraße 24, 80331 München, Germany